FOURTH EDITION

CLOUD COMPUTING

Architecting Next-Gen Transformation Paradigms

Dr. Kumar Saurabh

WILEY

CLOUD COMPUTING

Architecting Next-Gen Transformation Paradigms

FOURTH EDITION

Author: Dr. Kumar Saurabh

Published by Wiley India Pvt. Ltd.,
Plot No. 382, 383 Shahabad Daulatpur, New Delhi-110042

Printed at: Parksons Graphics, Mumbai.

Reprint: 2026

First Edition : 2011
Second Edition: 2012
Third Edition: 2014
Fourth Edition: 2018

ISBN: 978-81-265-7096-6
ISBN: 978-81-265-8541-0 (ebk)

Cover Image: VLADGRIN/Getty Images

Other Wiley Editorial Offices:
John Wiley & Sons, Inc. 111 River Street, Hoboken, NJ 07030, USA
Wiley-VCH Verlag GmbH, Boschstr. 12, 69469 Weinheim, Germany
John Wiley & Sons Australia, Ltd (ACN:009 673 081) at Level 4,600 Bourke St, Melbourne Victoria 3000
John Wiley & Sons Singapore Pte. Ltd, 134 Jurong Gateway Road, #04-307H, Singapore 600134
John Wiley & Sons Canada Ltd, 22 Worcester Road, Etobicoke, Ontario, Canada, M9W ILI
John Wiley & Sons, Ltd, New Era House, 8 Oldlands Way, Bognor Regis, West Sussex, PO22 9NQ, UK

www.wileyindia.com

Dedicated to my loving wife Anju
and adorable daughters Shivika and Ashna
Dr. Kumar Saurabh

Foreword

I feel happy writing the foreword of this book.

Tech Mahindra has placed Connectedness at the core of its ambition. The emergence of new technologies has resulted in possibilities with customers and participants across the value chain, co-innovating and sharing real-time feedback using collaborative means and methods. Connectedness, localization, usability, and sophistication of solutions are the pillars of the new age Digital Enterprise.

Cloud computing is the new method of delivering Information Technology. This is where application, data, and computing resources are provisioned in a shortest time possible and provided as reliable offerings. It is the next-generation technological disruption to the conventional on-premise computing model and method to transform organization IT delivery and services model. The business is viewing a paradigm shift in the way computing is achieved across the globe.

I have read this new revised fourth edition book and must admit that it comes with the essence-based revisions and transformation across the content in many of its chapters. It has taken a pragmatic approach to carve cloud solutions to the real-world problems, catering to audience of any level of expertise – sales, consulting, technical architecture, and students. A new chapter on cloud governance, newly added cloud solutions, platform approach, standards, paradigms, use cases, and business perspective makes the book extremely relevant in the times we live in.

I applaud the incredible work done by Dr. Kumar Saurabh and wish him all the best.

C P Gurnani
Managing Director and Chief Executive Officer
Tech Mahindra

Prologue

I am very happy to witness (from close quarters) the growth of the disrupting technologies like cloud computing, mobility, SOA, Virtualization, etc. I have been writing the prologues for this book, right from its first edition. It gives me immense pleasure to write prologue for my dear colleague Dr. Kumar Saurabh once again for the revised (4th) edition.

Today, cloud computing is all pervasive because it promises to reduce the IT complexities and costs. We consider this as a disruptive technology. It is the methodology where the scalable resources such as computing resources, storage, and network are offered in a service-based model over the network. The entire self-service experience is highly automated and it usually takes just a few minutes to provision the services. It is based on self-service scalable delivery to use various offerings based on bundles of computing resources, middleware, operating systems, and applications.

In this edition, Dr. Saurabh has depicted his experience and knowledge with the help of real-world examples and his articulation on the topics has given the new dimension to cloud computing arena. The portrayed perspective of 'service-based computing' in the current scenario of consumer and service provider is very helpful to understand the gamut of new era computing solutions, models, infrastructure, platforms, applications, processes, governance and processes for virtualization, mobility, cloud computing and SOA technologies.

The text is fully revised with the addition of one new chapter on Cloud governance. It talks about the never-ending concerns about security, compliances, risk, governance, legal issues, interoperability, and information management.

Cloud is inevitable and it will be staying as a robust technology. Most of the organizations are moving their IT Operations and Services to the cloud. Mobility, collaboration, and data sharing are the new platforms that demand new governance models. The text visualizes the cloud concepts with the sign for real-time business environment across the value chain by encompassing the frontiers of the transformed enterprise datacenter to handheld devices.

The revised edition is a paragon of knowledge to understand the need of Cloud computing that is based on infrastructure management coupled with platform development and is achieved by maintaining massive number of servers in a virtualized fashion from the same pool to deliver the services enabling self-service provisioning of IT resources, service accounting, multi-tenancy, and dynamic workload management.

I congratulate Dr. Kumar Saurabh for his marvelous work and wish him all the best for his future endeavors!!

A S Murty
Chief Technology Officer
Tech Mahindra

Preface

WHY THIS BOOK?

Cloud computing is a term that describes the means of delivering any and all Information Technology – from computing power to computing infrastructure, applications, business processes, and personal collaboration – to an end-user as a service wherever and whenever they require it.

When technology succeeds – when it meets the wishes of the people who use it, when it performs impeccably over a long interlude of time, when it is easy to adapt and even easier to employ – it can and does revolutionize things for the superior reasons. But when technology fails – when its users are disgruntled, when it is error prone, when it is complicated to transform, and even difficult to use – dreadful things can and do happen. We all want to build technology that makes things healthier, avoiding the bad things that creep around in the shadow of disastrous hard work. To succeed, we need regulation when technology is architected, designed, and built.

In the last 8 years since the first edition of this book was written, Cloud computing has evolved from an incomprehensible idea practiced by a fairly low number of aficionado to a legitimate business computing discipline. Today, it is acknowledged as a subject commendable of serious research, reliable study, and turbulent debate. Although managers and practitioners identically identify the need for a more disciplined approach to Cloud computing, they prolong to deliberate the manner in which it is to be applied to the business domain. Many individuals and companies are still adopting cloud technologies without proper cloud ROI and readiness assessments, even as they build systems to service today's most advanced technologies. Many professionals and students are unaware of modern methods of new-era infrastructure. And as a result, the quality of the architectures that we architect suffers and terrible things happen.

This fully revised fourth edition book would be useful for developers, modelers, thinkers, analysts, architects, research executives, managers, or any other IT professionals already having experience of computing facts; or for those interested in virtualization, cloud offerings, and different types of real-world cloud implementation case studies. A developer making the transition from a conventional computing or traditional infrastructure to a cloud technology world; somebody already familiar with the general principles of cloud computing, but needs to know the drivers of cloud computing, its components, and its future for enterprise solutions; or someone who wants to make sure how cloud solution fits naturally into the real-world system and behaves as users expect them to all would find this new edition an apt resource.

A computing enthusiast should find in this book enough food for thought to start playing with the cloud solutions and concept implementations, and should be able to join the group of technocrats continually working on new capabilities and performance enhancements. This book makes for a good introduction to cloud concepts and to cloud implementation in general.

Cloud computing is still a work in progress, and there's always place for new technocrats to jump into the game. This book is not intended to be a comprehensive guide or a reference to all aspects of cloud computing. Instead, we will be reviewing services, introducing the most important concepts and techniques, and giving examples of how to use them.

APPROACH

This book addresses the core issues of cloud computing, infrastructure, and virtualization. It presents everything one needs to know to be a successful system architect, technical manager, and infrastructure specialist for cloud computing. The book focuses on the real-world goals for services provided by cloud computing; the constraints on cloud computing infrastructure; the precise specification of cloud system structure and the implementation of specifications; the activities required in order to develop an assurance that the specifications and real-world goals have been met; and the evolution of cloud computing over time and across computing arena. It is also concerned with the processes, methods, and tools for the development of cloud infrastructure in an economic and timely manner.

Cloud computing, dynamic infrastructure, and virtualization have been deployed within every corporate function and within a broad section of businesses and markets. It involves changing paradigms about the way the world works, the way corporations function, and the human role in each case. The book reflects the core insights of cloud models, service offerings, and other benefits.

The widespread acceptance and deployment of cloud computing means virtualized cloud environments are now more critical than ever before. In the financial community as well as other market segments, even a relatively small system failure or outage can result in significant financial impact or have other far-reaching implications.

I have made essence-based revisions and transformed the organization in many of the chapters. Most importantly, I have added one new chapter on cloud governance and reorganized the virtualization and cloud paradigms, model, standard, and related concepts.

This new edition will give you the knowledge of important sections from the scratch, step-by-step procedures and the skills necessary to effectively understand the cloud computing concepts and implementation. It is meant to be very practical in nature and focuses only on the more important elements of cloud computing, not impenetrable subjects that have little relevance to the important issues faced by today's technocrats.

AUDIENCE

This fourth edition is intended to serve as a text to a maturing business era of cloud computing. Like the previous editions, this edition, too, is intended for both students and practitioners.

This book should be an interesting source of information both for people who want to experiment with cloud computing case studies and those who face the need to deal with the inner levels of cloud infrastructure. I hope this book would be useful as a starting point for people who want to experiment in the area of cloud computing, and review what cloud vendors are offering.

On the technical side, this book should offer a hands-on approach to understand the cloud computing infrastructure, different types of real-world case studies, and a techno-socioeconomic view of cloud infrastructure and some of the design choices made by the frontiers of cloud computing.

ORGANIZATION OF THE BOOK

In addition to many new and appreciably revised chapters, the chapters are ready with the new cloud computing paradigms, use cases and case studies for the ease of reading. All chapters are conceptualized with the relative success story based on standards, policies, compliances, and benchmarks.

As I wrote this fourth edition, I was guided by the many observations and suggestions received from readers of the previous editions, as well as by my own interpretation about the rapidly changing fields of cloud computing. All the chapters are rewritten and the material in most of the chapters is well-run by bringing older fabric up to date and removing bits and pieces that are no longer of interest.

This revised book deals with the essentials of cloud computing. It visualizes the cloud benefits and services and gives insights for cloud as a virtualization strategy. It discusses the set of hardware, software, networks, storage, services, and interfaces that combine to deliver aspects of computing as a service with shared resources, software, and information. This book works with concepts of cloud computing for enabling available, convenient, on-demand network access to a shared pool of configurable computing resources (e.g., networks, servers, storage, software, and services) that can be rapidly provisioned and released with minimal management effort or service provider interaction. It will take care of different cloud models, layers, and different types of cloud offerings.

The new text focuses on cloud system management. It provides best practices to optimize the available resources and illustrates these practices by using practical examples. It also details how to secure and maintain virtual environments. It gives insights on the role of the virtualization technology in implementing the cloud infrastructure. It will aid in helping a client achieve the three *Cloud* delivery economic drivers: virtualization, standardization, and automation. The book also emphasizes on the future of cloud computing, the different cloud vendors, and cloud offering reviews. It discusses the business issues that provide compelling reasons regarding when to adopt the cloud offerings. It also gives the SOA-view of the enterprise cloud solution, its roadmap and driving forces. It describes how to monitor a virtualization infrastructure. Rather than presenting a list of tools, it addresses practical situations to help and use the monitoring tool that best shows the resources one is interested in. It also talks about the sizing aspects of the cloud infrastructure. The new edition is significantly more than a simple update. The book has been revised comprehensively and rationalized to emphasize new and important cloud computing processes and practices. In addition, a new chapter *"Cloud Governance"* is added as enterprise must reach a cloud service provider as an agent of change. The cloud service provider should also help the enterprise to understand the cloud features, its Portability and Interoperability with respect to the governance, policies, regulations, risk management, and compliance maturity and requirement.

Two new chapters entitled "Data Center Transformation and Workload Migration" and "Cloud Readiness and Migration Assessment" have been added in this fourth edition. This era is focused towards economies of scale. Both the chapters are very apt to understand the migration assessment fundamentals and then how to transform the holistic journey of IT.

Dr. Kumar Saurabh

Acknowledgements

I take this opportunity to express my deep sense of gratitude to my research guide Dr V. B. Gupta, Devi Ahilya University, Indore, India, for his enormous help, dynamic guidance, and enthusiastic encouragement.

I am very much thankful to Mr. Vineet Nayyar, Honourable Executive Vice Chairman, Tech Mahindra, for evincing keen interest in my work and continuous encouragement. I would like to thank Tech Mahindra, especially Mr. C P Gurnani, Managing Director and Chief Executive Officer, Tech Mahindra; Mr. Rakesh Soni, Chief Operating Officer, Tech Mahindra; and Mr. A S Murty, Chief Technology officer, Tech Mahindra, for motivating and encouraging me to work. I take immense pleasure in offering my acknowledgements to Mr. Sudhir Nair, Sr. Vice President, Infrastructure Management Services, Tech Mahindra; Mr. Pravin Bolar, Sr. Vice President, Infrastructure Management Services; Mr. Rishi Ranjan, Vice President - Global Practice Head, End User Computing; and Mr. Kapil Uniyal, Global Practice Head, Datacenter Transformation, Infrastructure Management Services, Tech Mahindra for their valuable guidance that not only acted as a source of inspiration, but also encouraged me to discuss the problems critically and provided concrete suggestions without which it would have been impossible to bring this work in the present form.

I wish to place on records my sincere thanks to my wife Ms. Anju Varshney for her unconditional support and constant encouragement throughout while preparing this book. No form of acknowledgement can encompass the multitude of contribution that my family members have made. Their support, motivation, affection, and patience made me to work hard and complete this book successfully. Special thanks to my mother and father for their continued love and patience. I cannot forget the continuous support, affection, and love provided by my younger brother Mr. Anuj Saxena.

I am very much grateful to my lovely daughters Shivika Saxena and Ashna Saxena who in their own ways provided me support and comfort. Thanks are also due to all the colleagues at Tech Mahindra and many others who directly or indirectly helped me in completing my book

Finally, I thank Wiley-India for the continuing support, especially Meenakshi Sehrawat (Associate Publisher) and Rupnarayan Das (Developmental Editor).

Dr. Kumar Saurabh
Bangalore
December 2017

Special recognition towards the subject matter expertise brought in the book by

Mr. Rishi Ranjan

Vice President and Global Head, End User Computing

Infrastructure Management Services, Tech Mahindra

for authoring

Desktop Service: A VDI Perspective

Special thanks to
Ms. Anju Varshney
for authoring
Cloud Performance Monitoring Commands
and
Understanding Sizing Lifecycle

About the Author

Dr. Kumar Saurabh has several years of industry experience with companies like Tech Mahindra and IBM. Currently, he is Principal Technical Architect – Cloud Computing and Virtualization at Tech Mahindra. He was Technical Consultant with IBM and worked on Sizing for IBM hardware platform and servers.

Saurabh is M.Tech and Ph.D. with specialization in System Dynamics Simulation and Modeling from Devi Ahilya University, Indore, India. He is also M.Sc. in Computer Science and has a PMP® certification. He is the author of more than 20+ research papers that have been published in various national and international journals and proceedings, presented in various international forums. He has also authored the book "*Unix Programming – The First Drive*" published by Wiley-India. Saurabh's research interests include virtualization, cloud computing, and project management. His main area of research is System Dynamics and Simulation, Process Synchronization and Optimizations of UNIX Kernel and Device Drivers. Dr. Saurabh has also handled several large-scale systems performance and planning projects in a wide range of professional environments, such as science and research, software companies and R&D products.

Dr. Saurabh has been Panelist, Keynote Speaker, Editorial Member for cloud computing forums like Cloud Connect, INTEROP, Cloud Developer Conference Silicon India, TÜV SÜD, RES, etc.

Contents

CHAPTER

1 First Drive

CONTENTS

1.1 Introduction

One of the latest drift in small and medium businesses and enterprise-sized IT is the need for a significant transformation of the IT environment. Cloud computing provides a major shift in the way companies see the IT infrastructure. This technology is primarily driven by the Internet and requires rapid provisioning, high scalability, and virtualized environments. It provides abstraction for the business and is handled by the actual owners of the infrastructure experts. In this demanding world, the raison d'être to adopt cloud computing over standard IT deployments is flexibility, stability, rapid provisioning, reliability, scalability, and green solutions. Cloud computing can trace its intellectual roots back to grid computing, but it is often confused as the outcome of grid computing advancements and research during the recent period which is not totally true. Grid computing paves the way for the evolution of cloud computing concept. While these may be examples of applications of cloud computing for IT infrastructure, they are not the only ingredients of it. So, before going into the details of cloud computing, let us have a cursory glance at grid computing that gives you an immense computing grid to tap into as you need it, and scale up and down as per the requirement.

Grid computing approach starts with the breaking of the silos by inserting an additional layer on each server included in the grid. The main function of this additional layer is to create logical servers that distribute over different physical servers the computational needs (job, tasks) required by the different applications they are virtually executing. In this way, it is possible to decouple the applications from the physical systems on which they were running; at the same time, it is also possible to dynamically increase or decrease the computational power of logical servers as per application needs.

1.1.1 Grid Computing

A grid is made up of a number of resources and layers with different levels of implementation (Fig. 1.1). As said, there are different types of grids that are usually organized according to this taxonomy. Starting from the layer at the bottom – **virtualization**, which involves only physical resources – we may have then

1. **Information grids:** These are aimed to provide an efficient and simple access to data without worries about platforms, location, and performance.
2. **Compute grids:** These exploit the processing power from a distributed collection of systems.
3. **Services grids:** They provide scalability and reliability across different servers with the establishment of simulated instance of grid services.
4. **A mix of them:** Each of these has specific sets of characteristics that are peculiar of the hybrid characteristics of compute and service grids.

Conceptually, we can imagine the following three layers:

1. **Lower layer:** This is a physical layer where we have servers, storage devices, and interconnecting network.
2. **Middle layer:** This layer represents different operating systems mapped one-to-one with servers.
3. **Upper layer:** This is an application layer in which we map different applications supporting enterprise business processes.

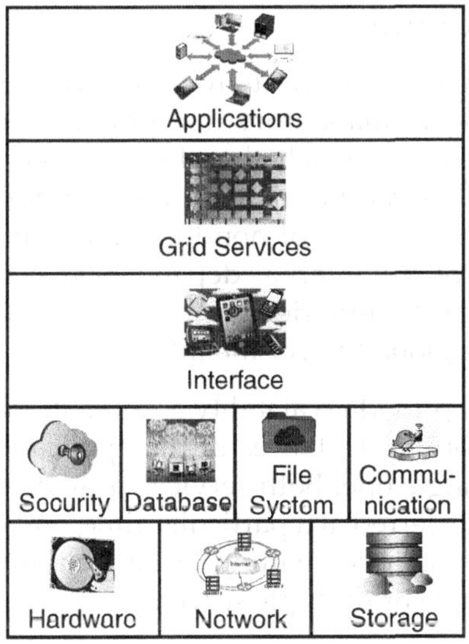

FIGURE 1.1 Simple grid architecture.

The concept of grid computing evolved from distributed computing that utilizes open standards to allow you to see independent and physically scattered computing resources as though they were a unique large virtual computer.

With these concepts in mind, we can consider a 'compute grid', where the grid's goal is to exploit the processing power from a distributed collection of systems. Main functionalities of a compute grid are to manage resources' workload, apply utilization policies and security rules, schedule and execute parallel tasks across distributed resources, and provision (reserving, adding, removing) resources according to the scheduling needs. It is a special kind of compute grid where resources – typically distributed all over the world, but could also be within an enterprise – are used by the grid only when these resources are idle, which means provisioning and scheduling policies are very 'relaxed'.

Information grid provides transparent and efficient access to data independent of their location, type, and platform, and allows end-users a secure and transparent access to any information source regardless of where it exists. It supports sharing of data for processing and large-scale collaboration, and provides logical views of data without having to understand where the data is located or whether it is replicated. It manages data cache or data replication automatically to get the most efficient and secure access.

Information is usually defined as 'meaningful data' from the perspective of the end-user. An information grid provides an abstraction over disparate and distributed information sources, such as a Database Management System (DBMS), flat files (for example, comma-separated files), structured files (for example, XML documents), or a Content Management System (CMS).

An information grid also has the ability to federate or integrate data and information from heterogeneous resources into a unified virtual repository. The whole idea is to present a single view of the information.

1.1.2 Grid – The Way to Cloud

The concept of cloud computing can trace its roots to grid computing that provides rapid provisioning of resources. It is not mandatory that grid computing should be in the cloud; actually it depends on the type of users, whether they are consumers or administrators. Grid computing requires software that can be divided and computed or serviced on a single or multiple systems. This creates a problem of non-functioning of the overall solution if one of the components fails because of the internal dependency. With the advent of the Internet, computing crossed geographical boundaries and networks and has given us the chance to exploit services and computing globally over the Internet.

Both cloud and grid services provide scalability as a functionality. This is achieved through load balancing and high availability instances of the applications running either on variety of operating systems or on a single one. Both services provide on-demand services for users, storage, networks, and data transferred at a particular time, and can be de-allocated when they are not required. These computing involve multi-tasking environments available on single or multiple instances based on single or multiple servers.

Optimization is a grid type where the primary focus is optimization of underutilized IT resources in an organization. Grids require a different way of thinking about how to deliver IT datacenter services, and resistance to changing behavior is always the toughest hurdle to overcome in technology adoption. Lack of industry standards is a barrier to widespread adoption, as clients perceive the risk of not-protected technology investment. Security will have to be proven over time to potential customers at a number of levels for grids to be considered for adoption in shared workload environments. The cost of computational power (both CPU and storage) continues to decline, which may erode part of the financial benefits of grids. To fully exploit the grid advantages, physical resources across heterogeneous systems can be virtualized building a single resource image.

The following list will help us understand the benefits of grid computing when deployed for infrastructure management and extended to cloud computing arena (Fig. 1.2). These benefits are also discussed in detail later in the chapter.

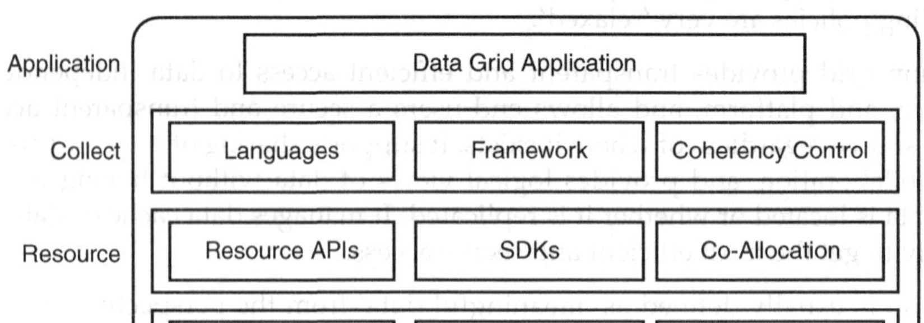

FIGURE 1.2 Standard grid architecture.

1. **Storage/data/information:** It provides logical views of data without having to understand where the data is located or whether it is replicated.
2. **System management:** It defines, controls, configures, and removes components and/or services (could be physical) on a grid using automated or physical methods.
3. **Metering, billing, and software (SW) licensing:** It provides tools to monitor and distribute the number of licenses while using licensed software. It also provides metering and billing techniques, such as utility-like services, so that the owners of the resources made available are accurately compensated for providing the resources.
4. **Security**
   - *Authentication:* The grid has to 'be aware' of the identity of the users who interact with it.
   - *Authorization:* The grid has to restrict access to its resources to the users who are eligible to access it.
   - *Integrity:* Data exchanged among grid nodes should not be subject to tampering.

Differing grid solutions may hit differing stages, but majority of the grid marketplace is transitioning from the 'early adoption' to the 'early majority' phase. Over the past few years, the market has evolved from specialist customers – predominantly in the academic and research sectors – using grid to accelerate internal simulations to a stage where corporate users are starting to apply grid and virtualization in a meaningful way that delivers clear business benefits (risk and portfolio analysis, seismic applications, clash analysis, etc.).

Organizations are now starting to use grid and virtualization technologies to unleash idle computing capacity to accelerate critical business processes and to optimize and improve resiliency of their IT infrastructure.

1.2 Essentials

Cloud computing is a term that describes the means of delivering any and all IT – from computer applications, software, business processes, messaging, and collaboration – to end-users as a service wherever and whenever they need it.

The cloud refers to a group of hardware computing devices, software, storage devices, and application programming interfaces (APIs) that integrate and interface with each other to deliver the characteristics of cloud computing in a service model. Shared resources, software, and information are provided to computers and other devices on demand. It allows people to do things they want to do on a computer without the need to buy and build an IT infrastructure or to understand the underlying technology.

1.2.1 Emerging Through Cloud

Cloud computing is a new paradigm for delivering IT where rapid provisioning is an important characteristic for computing resources, data, applications, and IT. This is offered as the highly standardized offering to the consumers over the Web portal via the Internet.

Cloud computing provides a way of managing large pools of servers that are virtualized. However, from the consumer point of view, it is regarded as a single, large resource pool.

Today it is the need of the business. This disrupting technology gives us the offerings to face the challenges in multiple ways by

1. Decreasing the capex and opex cost.
2. Enhancing the service quality and offer the next generation services.
3. Maintaining the desired and right level of security, compliances, regulations, and policies across the different functions of enterprise.
4. Rapid provisioning, agility, and business transparency for consistent self-service delivery.

Thus, cloud computing is the service and deployment model using large resource pool based provisioning of virtual or physical resources in a service model using the Internet (public cloud) or intranet (private cloud).

1.3 Benefits

Today cloud computing is emerging because it promises to reduce the IT complexities and costs. It is a new user experience especially over the Web traffic where the consumer is mostly related to social media, networking, and Web 2.0. This provides the mechanism to request and use the services with the abstraction of the technology. Today we are using the cloud in many ways without understanding the technology; for example, it can be experienced when we are sharing photos, streaming any video, using smart phones, transacting in banks, or even attending a meeting with Web-based Internet bridges.

When we see this concept as a disrupting technology, it is the methodology where the scalable resources such as computing resources, storage, and network are offered in a service-based model over the network. The entire self-service experience is highly automated and usually takes minutes to provision the services. It is based on self-service scalable delivery to use various offerings based on bundles of computing resources, middleware, operating systems, and applications. Organizations are adopting these disrupting technology models for faster services to their consumer to increase staff productivity, to decrease time to market, for economies of scale, and for effective workload management. These cases can be test and development, virtual desktop infrastructures, messaging and collaboration, and business analytics.

1.4 Why Cloud?

The cloud typically contains a significant pool of resources, which could be reallocated to different purposes within short time frames, and allows the cloud owner to benefit significantly from economies of scale as well as from statistical multiplexing (Fig. 1.3). The entire process of requesting and receiving resources is typically automated and is completed in minutes.

Cloud services today are delivered in a user-friendly manner and offered on an unprecedented scale. The payment model is pay-as-you-go and pay-for-what-you-use, eliminating the need for an up-front investment or a long-term contract. This presents a less disruptive business opportunity for businesses with spiky or unpredictable IT demands, as they are able

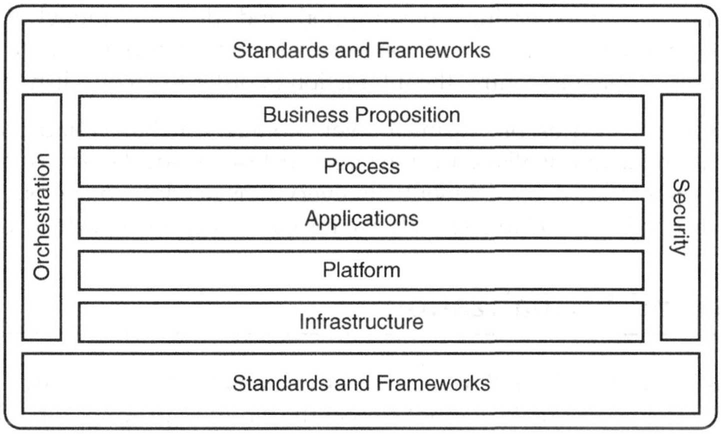

FIGURE 1.3 Basic cloud computing model.

to easily provision massive amounts of resources on a moment's notice and release them back into the cloud just as quickly.

The different reasons for adopting the cloud are as follows:

1. Very big, Web-scale infrastructure that is abstracted.
2. Dynamic allocation, scaling, movement of applications.
3. Pay-per-use.
4. No long-term commitments.
5. Operating system (OS), application architecture independent.
6. No hardware or software to install.

This results in the following business- and IT-aligned benefits:

1. More emphasis on innovation to launch new offerings.
2. IT as an enabler for innovation and rapid deployment.
3. Use of self-service based consistent delivery model.
4. Higher service quality and increased agility, ubiquitous computing.
5. Uniqueness via service models and competitive in the ecosystem.
6. Anytime anywhere computing for consumers over the Internet to deliver next generation technologies.
7. Reduced IT obstacles enabling launch of new offerings.
8. Building and integration of modular services – in record time – by leveraging 'rentable' IT services capabilities, pay only for what you use.

1.5 Business and IT Perspective

Businesses are now looking internally and saying to themselves that we need to deliver this same level of end-user experience with our own IT for our end-users – employees, partners, and customers. So 'cloud computing' refers to delivering IT-enabled services via the Internet that are built for the end-user to be in control.

Cloud computing is an emerging consumption and delivery model that enables the provisioning of standardized business and computing services through a shared infrastructure, where the end-user is enabled to control the interaction in order to accomplish the business task.

Computing resources such as processing power, storage, databases, and messaging are no longer confined within the four walls of an enterprise. Instead, abstract – or virtual – resources are tapped into whenever they are needed. Essentially, everything needed from a computing resources standpoint is provisioned by the cloud – much like the electrical power grid we all tap into.

1.6 Cloud and Virtualization

Virtualization has been around for 30 years. Yet, how many users have really truly virtualized all the layers of the stack? You really cannot expect the cloud to produce what it is expected to produce if it is not virtualized, standardized, and automated, because people expect scalable services. The cloud environment is assumed as a self-service experience to quickly start the services with respect to on-demand services. This requires a fundamental platform to meet these demands.

The only way you are going to be able to get efficiency is by virtualizing, standardizing, and automating (Fig. 1.4). And that is going to drive down costs and improve service. This is really

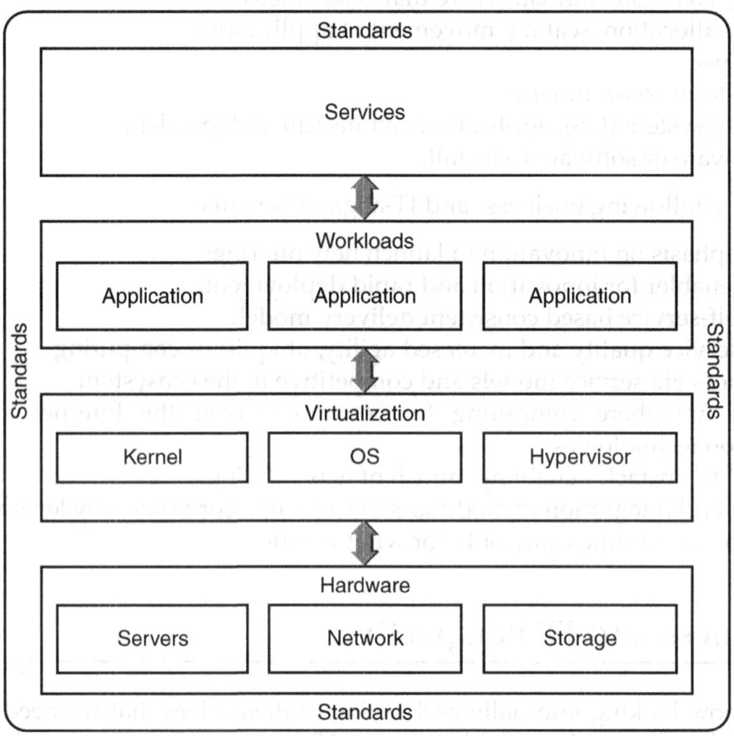

FIGURE 1.4 Datacenter clouds.

a pretty simple equation and we are seeing organizations that are doing this to achieve very real measurable business results. These results include:

1. **Server/Storage:** IT resources from servers to storage, network, and applications are pooled and virtualized to help provide an implementation-independent, efficient infrastructure, with elastic scaling – environments that can scale up and down by large factors as demand changes.
2. **Automation using self-service portal:** Point-and-click access to IT resources.
3. **Automated provisioning:** Resources are provisioned on demand, helping in reducing IT resource setup and configuration cycle times.
4. **Standardization through service catalog ordering:** Uniform offerings are readily available from a service catalog on a metered basis.
5. **Flexible pricing:** Utility pricing, variable payments, pay-by-consumption with metering and subscription models help make pricing of IT services more flexible.

1.7 Cloud Services Requirements

Cloud computing is being touted as the next best thing for cutting the cost of providing first-class IT services. You can decide which workloads are right for the cloud and which are not through an examination of your workloads – usage of IT resources for particular activities or tasks. You can also decide which workload can go on the vendor cloud [via the Internet or a virtual private network (VPN)] and which need to remain onsite (behind the organization's firewall). This focus on outcomes and delivery models presents a new opportunity to open up competitive accounts and expand the IT optimization conversation with existing clients.

Most cloud computing vendors offer point-solution and product offerings. In contrast, one should offer comprehensive, asset-based solutions that help deploy dynamic infrastructure, which is required for a cloud delivery model. These services along with workload solutions are designed to deliver business outcomes to the clients. Any approach to cloud computing should offer the following powerful advantages:

1. A proven service management system embedded with cloud services to provide visibility, control, and automation across IT and business services.
2. Services targeted at certain infrastructure workloads to help accelerate standardization of services, supporting significant productivity gains and rapid client payback on the investment.

Infrastructure strategy and planning services for cloud computing should be designed to help companies plan their infrastructure workloads, via appropriate cloud delivery model. Specific assistance includes cloud strategy, cloud assessment, design and development of a cloud roadmap, and return on investment (ROI) assessment by workload. Cloud leaders can help clients identify the right mix of public, private, and hybrid cloud models for infrastructure workload. Clients should be encouraged to get started with a strategy and plan consulting engagement as well as a pilot implementation of a key workload.

1.8 Dynamic Cloud Infrastructure

Through cloud computing, clients can access standardized IT resources to deploy new applications, services, or computing resources rapidly without re-engineering their entire infrastructure, thus making it *dynamic*. Cloud dynamic infrastructure is based on an architecture that combines the following initiatives:

1. **Service management:** Offers business transparency and automation across the pillars of business for consistent delivery.
2. **Asset management:** Maximizes the value of critical business and IT assets over their lifecycle with industry-tailored asset management solutions.
3. **Virtualization and consolidation:** Reduce operating costs, improve responsiveness, and fully utilize the resources.
4. **Information infrastructure:** Helps businesses achieve information compliance, availability, retention, and security objectives.
5. **Energy efficiency:** Offers green and sustainable energy solutions for business.
6. **Security:** Provides end-to-end industry customized governance, risk management, and compliance for businesses.
7. **Elasticity:** Maintains continuous business and IT operations while rapidly adapting and responding to risks and opportunities.

1.9 Cloud Computing Characteristics

Cloud computing uses commodity-based hardware as its base. The hardware can be replaced any time without affecting the cloud. Cloud computing uses a commodity-based software container system. For example, an instance or service can be migrated from one provider to other service provider with zero impact.

Cloud computing also requires a virtualization engine and an abstraction layer for the hardware, software, and configuration of systems. Cloud computing also has the multi-tenant feature where multiple customers share the underlying infrastructure resources without compromising the privacy and security of their data. Clouds implement the 'pay-as-you-go' pattern with no lock-in and no up-front commitment and are elastic as the service delivery infrastructure expands and contracts automatically on the basis of the capacity needed.

1.9.1 Cloud Computing Hurdles

There are various hurdles in adopting the cloud for large-scale cloud deployment services. The first and foremost is security. Now because of new paradigm, the data security concern is more hyped for cloud, but in some manner it is same as securing the datacenter services, network, storage in hosted and utility-based solutions. As the services are opened and delivered over the network between the cloud service provider and the consumer, the security in this model is perceived at higher levels. Other inhibitors can be location-independent resource pooling where consumer does not know where his services are running or where his data is stored. It is also believed that multi-tenant models are somewhat less secure than dedicated models. Limited service management and monitoring capabilities in the public cloud model also add to the complexities.

The second hurdle is of regulation and compliances. There is a need of data governance models to be established in the enterprises and federating data privacy. In large organizations, IT delivery is taken with the concerns of reliability, performance, and availability. There are different levels of maturities for organizations seeking different levels of service-level agreements (SLAs) but cloud service providers are not equipped to deliver the services. There is a need of stringent recovery point objective (RPO) and the recovery time objective (RTO) with the agreed number of mins/hours down-time. There is a very less chance to take any corrective actions after any impact and it does not cover the consequences happened due to outage. It is also difficult to cater to different type of SLAs for various tenants by the service providers as it is very difficult to tailor the SLAs based on the customer interest and requirements. Also it is observed that if the service delivery is for a complex application bundle, there is a risk of poor performance. There are few components in the cloud ecosystem that are beyond the control of a consumer or a service provider such as bandwidth.

Cloud migration is the next hurdle in cloud computing. This requires the property of powerful interoperability of platforms that should identify the appropriate application that can be migrated to the cloud. It is important to identify the interdependencies and integration points with standards and interfaces that are lacking today among service providers.

Cloud migration becomes more complex if the service bundles are integrated from multiple cloud service providers. This can also become the deal breaker or the reason for downgraded performance. There can also be the licensing problem in the cloud environment. Also there are issues related to multi-geography-based application platforms deployment and implementations in the cloud-based model and get some hits with respect to the desired levels of service for multiple offerings.

Last hurdle is the workload suitability for cloud. It is also a big question whether the workload is seasonal for the cloud deployment or not. Not all the applications are suitable candidates for the cloud. It depends on the function of the business, enterprise policies, application architecture, scalability, suitability, usage patterns according to pay-per-use-model, or infrastructure requirements in the service model.

1.10 Cloud Adoption

Business functions that suit cloud deployment can be low-priority business applications – such as analytics, against partner and field service-based functions – and other low-priority business functions. Cloud favors traditional Web applications and interactive applications that comprise two or more data sources and services, and services with low availability requirements and short life spans; for example, enterprise marketing campaigns need quick delivery of a promotion that can just as quickly be switched off. It is also helpful when high-volume, low-cost analytics and disaster recovery scenarios, business continuity, and backup/recovery-based implementation are required. It is like a boon to one-time batch processing with limited security requirements, record retention, media distribution, and mature packaged offerings, such as e-mail, collaboration infrastructure, and collaborative business networks.

Based on technical characteristics, we can say that cloud adoption is suitable for applications that are modular and loosely coupled, isolated workloads, single virtual appliance workloads; software development and testing, and pre-production systems. It gels well with research and development projects, prototyping to test new services, applications, and design models and applications that scale horizontally on small servers, that is, by adding more servers, rather than by increasing a server's computational capacity.

Applications that need significantly different levels of infrastructure throughout the day, such as those used almost solely during the business day, should be deployed through the cloud. Applications that need significantly different levels of infrastructure throughout the month, or that have seasonal demand, such as those used primarily during the end-of-the-quarter or during a holiday shopping season, are the best examples of cloud deployments. Applications for which the demand is unknown in advance, for example, a Web-based application for a start-up organization, will need to support a spike in demand when they become highly demanding and will need to reduce once all the users turn away from the workload.

Cloud adoption is not suitable for mission-critical and core business applications, transaction processing, and applications that depend on sensitive data normally restricted to the organization or requiring a high level of auditability and accountability as these processes cannot share the high-importance data, processing power, and hardware with the third party. Applications that run 24 × 7 × 365 with steady demand and applications that consume significant amounts of memory – including applications dependent on large in-memory caches, databases, or data sets – are not suitable for the cloud. Applications that take full advantage of multiple cores, such as those that do a significant amount of parallel processing and thus benefit from many cores on a single server, are not recommended for cloud deployment.

Cloud adoption is also not recommended for applications that require high-performance file system I/O which needs high-bandwidth interserver communications, for example, highly distributed applications. The cloud does not work well with applications that scale vertically on single servers, that is, by increasing a server's computational capacity rather than by adding more servers and applications dependent on third-party software, which does not have a virtualization or cloud-aware licensing strategy.

1.11 Cloud Rudiments

The cloud delivers a software platform that will enable the customer's IT department to build an Infrastructure-as-a-Service (IaaS) cloud. The cloud is built on capabilities of existing virtualization management and physical server provisioning solutions to deliver an application infrastructure to users that can be consumed in a self-service manner.

The cloud optimizes the usage of the physical and virtual infrastructure through intelligent resource allocation policies, and adds the ability to flex applications elastically based on demand. The high-level capabilities of any cloud include the following:

1. **Resource aggregation and integration:** The cloud solution operates on the top of existing virtualization management, physical server provisioning, and system management environments. It retrieves inventory information about machines and software

templates from multiple locations, and aggregates this information into a central logical view of all resources in the infrastructure.

2. **Application services:** Rather than providing access to resources directly, cloud solutions' application 'Definitions' describes packages of machine capacity and software images that can be allocated by resource consumers. Applications can range from individual machines provisioned with an operating system image through to full multi-tier application environments that consist of collections of machines and software stacks provisioned in a specific order with network and storage dependencies handled through integration with third-party management tools. Application instances represent an agreement between the cloud provider and the consumer to use capacity on a reservation or on-demand basis. Reservations allocate capacity in the resource inventory, guaranteeing that the capacity will be available to the consumer at some defined point in the future. On-demand allocations provide access to resources but do not guarantee availability. Reserved and on-demand capacity can be combined in an application where a baseline of capacity can be elastically increased or decreased according to metrics and policies defined by the consumer.
3. **Self-service portal:** An important principle of a cloud solution is to enable self-service access to resources with minimal IT involvement. It should support the notion of account owners signing up for contracts and then being able to delegate the use of the purchased capacity within their own groups or departments. Users can request machines or entire multi-machine application environments and monitor and control them using a Web-based self-service portal. The system will drive the workflows necessary to create the environment and provide run-time environment management in order to support application elasticity.
4. **Allocation engine:** Dynamic Resource Management (DRM) is an automated allocation and reallocation of IT resources based on policies that express business demands and priorities. DRM is a key component of any cloud solution that maximizes the efficiency of the IaaS infrastructure. DRM policies should be applied both when initially placing applications onto machine resources and when selecting applications to migrate in order to preserve SLAs around application performance. Some of the allocation and migration strategies include advance reservation of resources, load-based placement and migration, application and resource topology constraints, and energy usage optimization. The use of sophisticated DRM helps to increase the utilization of cloud resources, reduces overspending by effectively using existing resources, and saves costs in terms of operations, power, and cooling.
5. **Reporting and accounting:** To close the loop and determine how the cloud is behaving, metering information on resource allocations as well as on actual usage is collected in an accounting database. Data are centrally available to create reports on inventory capacity, capacity allocated versus capacity used by contract, and usage-billing reports based on consumed resources.

The following are the *cloud features* that would help to bring in *agility* and *transparency* along with an increase in the utilization of the existing resources at the datacenter of any customer.

1. **Self-service:** This feature presents an interface for separate authenticated end-users – via role-based access controls (RBAC) – to select options for deployment. It should have unique policy controls per tenant and user role, and the ability to present unique

catalogs per user or group. The self-service portal is a Web interface also accessible in other ways, such as through a mobile client.

2. **Dynamic workload management:** With the cloud solution implemented, datacenters are enabled with automation and orchestration software that coordinates workflow requests from the service catalog or self-service portal for provisioning virtual machines. Also each provisioned virtual machine is enabled with a life-cycle for deployment expiration which increases the efficiency of resource utilization.
3. **Resource automation:** Using cloud solution, administrators or engineering team members of the datacenter can control the heterogeneous environment on a single pane. This feature establishes secure multi-tenancy, isolates virtual resources, and helps prevent contention in the load aware resource engine which intelligently does the workload packing or load balancing across hypervisors automatically.
4. **Chargeback, showback, and metering:** Using this feature, administrators can bring out the usage reports for cloud infrastructure service consumption, which serve as a basis for metering and billing system. Using this, administrators will be able to determine if the virtual machines are attached with appropriate resources. Enabling *chargeback*, *showback*, and *metering* in any organization would bring in transparency to the business and the environment for the management to clearly see the usage and the dollar value associated to it and take decision-making steps.
5. **Open architecture:** The cloud should be integrated with existing third-party products that are already installed in the datacenter. It should also be integrated to a public cloud to enable the use of additional resources and should be managed through a single cockpit. It is also possible to meter the public cloud resource usage.
6. **Image pools:** The cloud solution should have a full-blown service catalog and support to most of the operating systems. It should be possible to vary the hardware configuration for the templates. The cloud should also integrate with existing templates and images used by the development and testing teams.
7. **Role-based access administration:** The cloud solution should have the capability to integrate cleanly with any of the existing Lightweight Directory Access Protocol (LDAP), or other authentication and identity mechanisms. These features are crucial for providing secure multi-tenancy. This would also bring in security to the self-service portal.
8. **Virtualization:** The cloud should extend support to the virtualization layer. This implies that the cloud should support most of the industry-proven hypervisors. This enables the administrators and the engineering team of the datacenter to control the hypervisors over a single pane.

1.11.1 Cost Savings with Cloud

Faster Time-to-Market (Missed Business Opportunity)

Deploying new application environments quickly and reliably can have a direct impact on the competitiveness, enabling organizations to take market share. The cloud will enable automated delivery of application environments exponentially faster than current practices.

With the cloud model, teams could be delivering fully configured, multi-component application environments to users in just a few minutes. This makes an immediate impact on user efficiency as well as eliminates much of the manual labor previously required of both the IT and the application team. In addition to this, ability to remove a physical or virtual compute, will have a similar performance efficiency. This once again allows computing power to be available for other users.

Public Cloud Interfaces

Cloud infrastructure with its policies should manage workload placement optimally by looking at several metrics. The cloud should also offer the capability to burst out to a public cloud or internal resources when needed and cut off that link when done. The cloud should also be able to meter the usage of the deployed instances in the public cloud. Customer datacenters could use resources in the public cloud for testing and development environment if there are no resources available on the premise, which will also help them to defer from new hardware procurement.

Automated Scaling

The cloud solution should provide an out-of-box functionality to flex-up or flex-down an application instance or resource based on performance metrics and should also flex-up and flex-down an environment automatically or manually. The cloud solution should offer policies that can be customized to look at any metric and take action based on the threshold. These policies must be embedded in a service catalog to monitor an application or the entire environment and flex-up or flex-down with more resources.

Business Transparency

Service accounting helps improve the utilization of datacenter infrastructure, with accurate visibility into the true costs of physical and virtualized workloads. It enables decision makers to have cost transparency and accountability for usage, metrics, roles, and definitions. This would also help an administrator to understand whether a machine is equipped with right resources or not.

1.11.2 Benefits

The cloud brings a lot of benefits for any enterprise. These benefits are given in brief as follows and will be discussed in detail later in the book.

1. Increased agility on the IT datacenter resources and innovation.
2. Enabling of self-service portal and thus ensure virtual machines (VMs) in less lead-times.
3. Adherence of SLAs as the VM lead-times and down-times are significantly reduced.
4. Trial and error configuration tests can be done at ease.
5. Complete control over cloud usage for administrators is possible.
6. Scalability and flexibility allow the IaaS cloud to almost deliver the promise of unlimited IT services on demand.
7. Usage-based payment and not getting billed when the utilization decreases.
8. Significant reduction in the costs for IT datacenter.
9. Dynamic sharing of the resources available in IT datacenter through private cloud so that demands can be met cost-effectively.
10. Considerable increase in the utilization of resources of IT datacenter.

11. Increase in the operational efficiency of the resources in the IT datacenter.
12. Achieve a greener datacenter (server consolidation and virtualization enables over committed machines).
13. Support for heterogeneous hardware vendors. Avoids vendor locking.

It will help the enterprises by

1. Reducing the number of administrators required to manage a more diverse IT resource pool.
2. Dramatically reducing in cycle times to provision new assets.
3. Realizing an infrastructure 'pay-per-use' model.
4. Reducing planned capital spending and maintenance.
5. Increasing end-user satisfaction with the help of IT services.
6. Reducing physical server count.
7. Consolidating enterprise application licenses.
8. Flexibility to meet future demands on infrastructure goals that can be leveraged.
9. Increasing the capacity on demand (pre-provision, automate).
10. Consolidated, streamline change control.
11. End-to-end application provisioning.
12. Allowing developers to provision development application environment autonomously.
13. End-to-end performance measurement.
14. Consumption-based charge back.
15. Plan for active/active datacenter operations.
16. Plan for increased datacenter density.
17. Separate production and development networks.

1.12 Summary

In this chapter, we explored cloud computing, its benefits, and its services. The chapter also gave deep insights into cloud computing models that are put into practice.

CHAPTER

2 Cloud Deployment Models

CONTENTS

2.1 Introduction

Cloud computing is an emerging style of computing in which applications, data, and resources are provided to users as services over the Web. The services provided may be available globally, always on, low in cost, 'on demand', massively scalable, and on 'pay-as-you-grow' basis. Consumers of a service need to care only about what the service does for them and not on how it is implemented. Cloud computing is a technology that allows users to access software applications, store information, develop and test new software, create virtual servers, draw on disparate IT resources, and more – all over the Internet (or other broad network).

Cloud computing is a model-driven methodology that provides configurable computing resources such as servers, networks, storage, and applications as and when required over the Internet with minimum efforts. The cloud also indicates essential uniqueness, service models, and deployment models.

This chapter visualizes several models for cloud computing, including private clouds (where the deployment is within the organization's firewall) and public clouds (where application services and data are hosted by a third party outside the firewall). Consistent data availability and security are critical success factors for any cloud deployment. Businesses need to ensure that data are adequately protected and can be restored in a timely fashion following any disruption event.

When we deploy the cloud from the service provider's point of view, it requires a datacenter; but from the consumer's point of view, it is expected not to think about the datacenter. A datacenter is a facility house of servers, storage, security devices, networks, and telecommunications. It includes power supplies, redundant power backup options, communication setups, cooling, fire suppression, floor space, etc. with environmental controls.

All datacenters are designed on the basis of geographies and local requirements with redundant power, cooling, resources security, and environmental controls. However, clouds are not bound to location and possess the characteristics of location independency. The cloud provides the abstract view that it is not specifically tied to any datacenter for the self-service request of compute, storage, and disaster recovery options. Availability and redundancy of the datacenter come from the service provider, from which the resources are pooled and services are catered. In this way, the cloud is achieved and spanned from multiple datacenters, but there is no datacenter itself.

2.2 Cloud Characteristics

The cloud carries the basic infrastructure characteristics that are helpful to deploy the cloud service in a fast and cost-effective way (Fig. 2.1). The characteristics discussed in the following subsections set apart the cloud from other computing techniques.

2.2.1 Self-Service On-Demand

As a cloud consumer, users are privileged to request and provision computing capabilities bundled with services with or without approval process powered by automation and workflows.

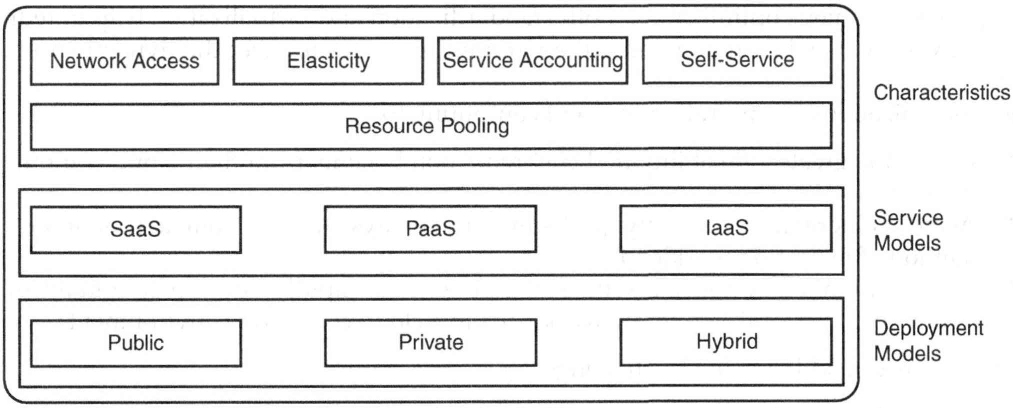

FIGURE 2.1 Cloud model.

2.2.2 Ubiquitous Network Access

This is the characteristic by which end-user and server computing devices can be accessed over the network even using the next generation heterogeneous devices such as smart phone, tablets, phablets, thin and thick clients.

2.2.3 Resource Pooling

This characteristic refers to the pooling of resources across multiple datacenters. These pooled virtual datacenters are then divided into multiple pools to provide their services to various consumers in a multitenant model. These pools can have both physical and virtual resources. Also the devices provided by this pool give the notion of location-independent compute (storage, servers, processing, network bandwidth, virtual machines, etc.), where the consumer does not have control or visibility about the service location and its geography.

2.2.4 Rapid Elasticity

This characteristic make the provisioning rapid and elastic. This provisioning can be automatic and can flex-up and flex-down on the basis of spikes of utilization. The consumer can view the infinite capacity available as a service, which can be bought at any point of time.

2.3 Measured Service Accounting

The cloud environment is optimized by effective workload management. This management requires measured service, monitoring, metering, and chargeback capability with the required abstraction, and optimization at user level. The usage of resources can be controlled, reported, monitored, charged, billed, and invoiced on actual from provider to consumers.

The measured service is directly proportional to standardization and to the economies of scale for operating expenses. The more the virtualization is practiced in the environment, the more it helps to achieve optimization. Both standardization and virtualization help to reduce the cost investments while maintaining the required resources to meet the dynamic need of the infrastructure.

Now organizations are migrating to cloud computing to

1. Derive the greatest flexibility and cost-reduction benefits from their cloud computing investments.
2. Avoid vulnerability to costly problems and delays arising from a trial-and-error method of migrating workloads.
3. Augment limited in-house resource or experience to rapidly develop an optimization roadmap and smoothly migrate workloads to a cloud computing environment.

Cloud vendors can address client's challenges by

1. Prioritizing workloads for cloud adoption on the basis of business impact and risk.
2. Maximizing business return by identifying applications that are well suited for cloud computing and have high business impact.
3. Addressing problematic workloads to improve their propensity for cloud computing.
4. Avoiding costly implementation issues by identifying and addressing potential difficulties during the migration.
5. Mitigating the risk of costly implementation delays by identifying potential problems and addressing them before the migration.
6. Avoiding inadequate performance of highly complex and integrated workloads.
7. Leveraging the expertise to deliver an actionable roadmap to successfully migrate applications to a cloud computing environment.
8. Accelerating the cloud initiatives.

2.3.1 Cost Factor

There are a number of reasons why cloud computing is popular with businesses. One of them is the cost aspect. By virtualizing and standardizing your environment, you can deliver more services with fewer resources and drive up the utilization. By adding automation, you can reduce the labor cost which gives you an additional cost benefit. These advantages give you a lot of flexibility because you can access cloud workloads services without thinking about the location and the time of their execution. So cloud computing allows an organization to free up the budget so that money can be diverted to new innovations and development of new capabilities rather than just keeping the lights on and running the IT enterprise.

The growing complexity of IT systems and soon a trillion connected things demand that sprawling processes should become standardized services that are efficient, secure, and easy to access. In order to get the control, transparency, and automation of the system, a service management platform is required for consistent delivery. Self-service plus standardization will drive lower operational costs, unlock productivity, and ensure better security.

The cloud allows businesses to be smarter in services delivery. The first aspect of this is a self-service portal that allows your end consumers to see only the services they are allowed to have; however, it also allows them to initiate the process of getting those services. Behind that service request, you could put either a very light or no-touch approval process, or you could put a more complex one in which you may need multiple levels of signature.

This allows you to really fit what the business needs. In some cases, where you have high security, you have high-level service-level agreements (SLAs) – you really want to be able to control how those services are distributed. In other cases, let us say you do not have a research and development team and you want the ability to have as much flexibility as possible. It allows you to be very productive if you adopt the cloud platform which allows you to really make your infrastructure more dynamic and get the resources to the teams that really need them at any point of time.

Let us look at some of the major factors that are driving cloud computing economics. If you look at the infrastructure layer, first comes virtualization. By virtualizing workloads and being able to stack multiple workloads on a system to drive up the utilization, you can lower your capital requirements. In a number of cases, businesses have hundreds – if not thousands – of physical servers and unless they have used the virtualization and are really driving that utilization, the utilization could be as low as 10%. So, in a lot of cases, organizations that use cloud computing are able to drive the utilization up, lower the future capital requirements, and even retire the antiquated equipment and drive their costs down.

From the labor perspective, using a self-service portal allows your clients to help themselves. So there is less support and it makes the offering more available from a service availability perspective. In terms of automation, cloud computing takes the tasks which are manual and repeatable, and their automation reduces your IT operations cost. In a development or test environment, you need multiple skills – such as operating system skills, middleware skills, database skills, and application skills – to get that environment to the end-user. This allows you to define environment as a repeatable, deployable resource, and it drives down your labor cost. Of course, you need to standardize the workloads. Standardization has labor cost and quality benefits so that you can ensure consistency from one environment to another environment.

In many cases, you may want to use multiple models for different types of services that you want to deliver. Starting with private cloud services, the first model (which is also the most popular currently) is the private on-premise cloud. If the cloud is within the organization's datacenter, it is operated and managed by the organization itself.

One of the daunting task in the field of infrastructure management is to optimize the capex and opex cost. This task can be efficiently handled with the help of cloud computing. Cloud computing aims to guarantee the consistent service delivery with economies of scale with the infrastructure powered by the internet. The cloud gives the flexibility for a new model of business by optimizing the IT business while maintaining consistent self-service delivery.

2.3.2 Benefits

We can enjoy many benefits by adopting the cloud:

1. **Self-service capability:** When somebody deploys the cloud services, he becomes capable of self-service. Now testing teams do not have to buy computing services as they can enjoy the same services over the cloud. It also reduces the procurement process. Hence, the testing teams can concentrate on the testing services and efforts.
2. **Resource availability:** It is one of the most common benefits facilitated by the virtualization. It also helps to track and leverage the resource pool under the same umbrella of resource units.

3. **Operational efficiency:** Sometimes conventions and configurations followed by the test and operation teams may differ from those followed by the development teams. This difference may cause the application behavior to be different from what was intended as well as result in delayed services. The template-based approach, with its solution stacks of hardware, configurable applications, and operating systems, is more transparent and can help the teams to understand the environment better.
4. **Hosted tools:** In cloud computing, the developers and testers need not to install, configure, run, or maintain tools on their systems as they can log into the network maintaining these tools from any machine.

These four benefits help the developers and testers to concentrate on their core work and retain focus without worrying about other jobs. This increases quality and productivity; and therefore results in more developer innovation, increased test quality and coverage, which are beneficial for an organization.

There are a number of major challenges that developers face today in getting started and rolling out new applications and services faster. Innovative new products and services are the lifeblood of rapidly growing companies and represent a substantial portion of corporate sales and profits. In an environment of heightened competition, the inability to roll out new applications and services quickly means declining market share and lost revenue.

A growing application backlog leaves lines of business and end-users frustrated because they consider IT as a bottleneck and look for ways to work around IT to roll out new products and services more quickly. Testing backlog is often very long and a major factor in the delay of new application deployments.

A major reason why testing takes so long, on an average it takes weeks, is because of the time taken to set up the application environments for testing and QA as well as production. The testing phase becomes longer because of the time required to procure new hardware and software, and then schedule the time with the IT to configure and set up the systems. Configuration and setup are manual processes where errors are easily introduced. An average new application takes six to nine months to be deployed. The whole process application development is affected by a number of factors ranging from poor governance to poor collaboration between business users and development to inflexible infrastructure and tools. Almost 30% of the defects are caused by wrongly configured test environments. This is a result of following manual processes without any automation to replicate testing environment along with challenges organizations face in finding available resources to perform tests in order to move new applications into production. Test environments are seen as expensive and provide little real business value.

2.4 Cloud Deployment Models

Let us talk about cloud computing and different types of cloud deployment models and services that can be delivered using these models. Cloud computing is a style of computing in which business processes, application, data, and any type of IT resource can be provided as a service to the users.

Cloud delivery models can be briefly classified into the following three types (Fig. 2.2):

1. **Public:** In a public cloud, a business rents the capability and pays for what is used on-demand.
2. **Private:** In private clouds, a business essentially turns its IT environment into a cloud and uses it to deliver services to their users.
3. **Hybrid:** Hybrid clouds combine elements of public and private clouds.

Private cloud is good when the control and customization are bigger concerns to drive the efficiency. Today public clouds are also process-oriented and easily standardized with lower risk problems. There are many standardized functions that can be moved to public cloud such as collaboration, search, CRM, and sales force management.

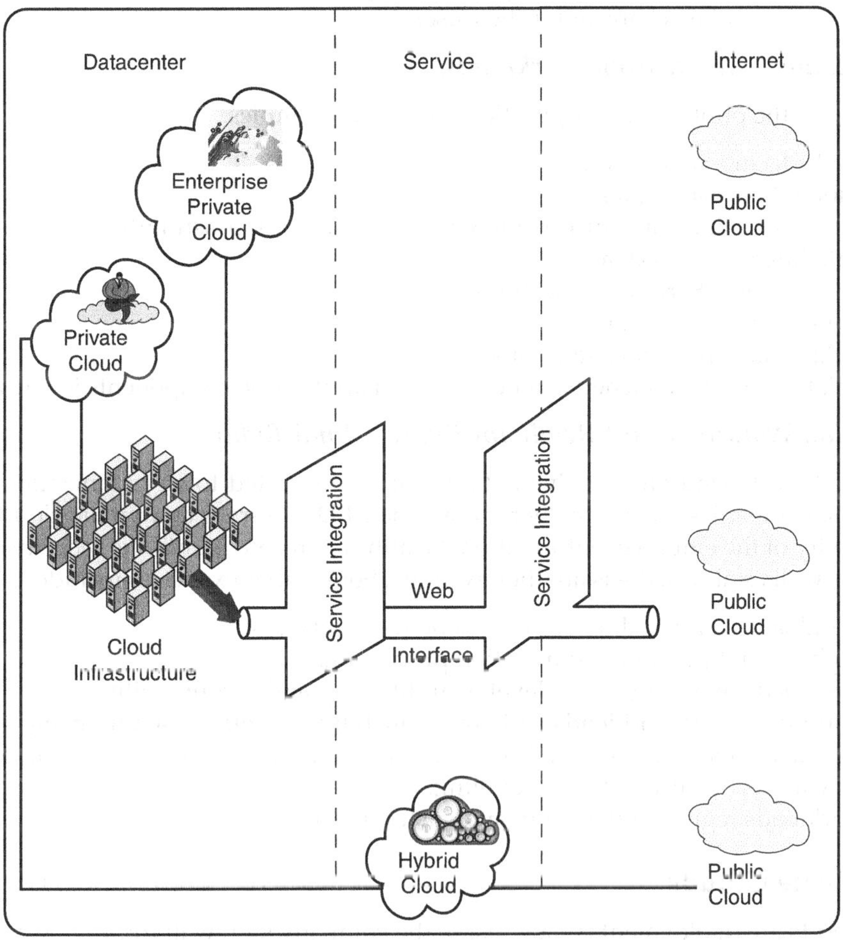

FIGURE 2.2 Private, public, and hybrid clouds.

There is no one-size-fits-all model; in a number of cases, businesses may end up using all these models eventually based on the business model for different services.

2.4.1 Public Clouds

Public cloud services are offered by third-party datacenter provider to end-user consumers over the Internet. Public cloud offers resource pooling, self-service, service accounting, elasticity, multi-tenancy to manage the solutions, deployment, and securing the resources and applications. Companies can use it on-demand and with the pay-as-you-use option, it is much like utility consumption. Enterprises are able to offload commodity applications to third-party service providers (hosters).

The term 'public' does not mean

1. That it is free, even though it can be free or fairly inexpensive to use.
2. That a user's data is publically visible – public cloud vendors typically provide an access control mechanism for their users.

Public Clouds – Application Workloads

Following are the public cloud application workload examples:

1. Public facing Web pages.
2. Public Wiki's and blogs.
3. Jobs resembling batch processing with lower security constraints.
4. Data intensive workloads.
5. Software-as-a-Service applications.
6. Online storage solutions.
7. Online backup/restore solutions.
8. Isolated workloads where latency between application components is not an issue.

Application Workloads not Ready for Public Cloud Today

Workloads that depend on sensitive data, normally restricted to an organization, are public today. Most companies are not ready to move their LDAP server to a public cloud because of the sensitivity of the employee information. Health care record – until the security of the cloud provider is well established – is another example. Some other examples include:

1. Workloads composed on various, dependent services.
2. High throughput online transaction processing.
3. Workloads requiring a high level of auditability and accountability.
4. Non-virtualized workloads and non-availability of cloud-based licensing strategy.
5. Workloads looking for complex service accounting mechanisms for different services for various departments based billing.
6. Workloads requiring flexibility and customization.

2.4.2 Private Clouds

Private clouds are deployments made inside the company's firewall (on-premise datacenters) and traditionally run by on-site servers. Private clouds offer some of the benefits of a public cloud computing environment, such as elastic on-demand capacity, self-service provisioning, and service-based access. Private cloud is suitable when the traditional requirements, such as control, security, and resiliency, are more emphasized by an organization with the restricted and designated user access and authorization.

Services in Private Cloud

This section highlights the services provided by a private cloud and the services consumed from public cloud, specifically:

1. Virtualization.
2. Government and management.
3. Multi-tenancy.
4. Consistent deployment.
5. Chargeback and pricing.
6. Security and access control.

The services consumed from a public cloud are as follows:

1. Security and data privacy.
2. Ease of access.
3. Discovery of services.
4. Restful interface support.
5. Lower cost.
6. Speed and availability.

High 'Cost of Privacy'

Many experts believe that a private cloud implemented with internal hosting/running of the infrastructure makes it difficult to realize many key benefits of clouds, including

1. **Eliminating capital expenses and operating costs:** Ownership of the hardware or software eliminates the pay-per-use potential, as these must be upfront purchases. The full cost of operations must be shouldered as there is no elasticity. If the private cloud hardware is sized for peak loads, there will be inefficient excess capacity. Otherwise, the owner will face complex procurement cycles.
2. **Removing undifferentiated heavy lifting by offloading datacenter operations:** Utility pricing (for lower capital expenses and operating expenses) usually implies an outside vendor offering on-demand services. It relies on the economies of multiple tenants sharing a larger pool of resources. These higher costs might be justified if the benefits of quicker and easier self-service provisioning and service-oriented access are large.

Private Clouds Provide More Control

In traditional security models, location implies ownership which in turn implies control when security is location-specific. Then location, ownership, and control are aligned. Strong requirements for control and security usually drive a preference for a private cloud, where they own the cloud resources and control the location of those resources. For example, government may not want their applications or data to reside outside certain borders. Clouds rely on virtualization; and in the public model, this loose coupling breaks the link between location and application, and reduces the perceived ownership and control.

When we talk about the information control, it is not related to fixed geography or total ownership of the information. One example is public key encryption – the ownership of the key means control over the information without owning the rest of the infrastructure. The information control can be managed over the infrastructure that is trustful on the basis of the contracts, regulations, SLAs, standards, and imposition of the security mechanism on service providers. Compliance is difficult outside of traditional security models. As long as control through technology and contracts can be clearly demonstrated, it is possible to make a public cloud computing environment as compliant and as secure as a privately owned facility. Auditors and regulators are continuously adapting to new technologies and business models. Ownership can have multiple avenues as follows:

1. Full-implementation ownership.
2. Lack of full ownership.
3. Controlled ownership.

There are many possible approaches in between, such as partial control and shared ownership. There are also different levels of limited access – specific departmental access, industry-only access, and controlled partner access.

2.4.3 Hybrid Clouds

A hybrid cloud is a combination of an interoperating public and private cloud. This is the model where consumer takes the non-critical application or information and compute requirements to the public cloud while keeping all the critical information and application data in control. The hybrid model is used by both public and private clouds simultaneously. It is an intermediate step in the evolution process, providing businesses an on-ramp from their current IT environment into the cloud.

It offers the best of both cloud worlds – the scale and convenience of a public cloud and the control and reliability of on-premises software and infrastructure – and let them move fluidly between the two on the basis of their needs. This model allows the following:

1. Elasticity, which is the ability to scale capacity up or down within minutes, without owning the capital expense of the hardware or datacenter.
2. Pay-as-you-go pricing.
3. Network isolation and secure connectivity as if all the resources were in a privately owned datacenter.
4. Gradually move to the public cloud configuration, replicate an entire datacenter, or move anywhere in between.

2.4.4 Community Clouds

This is the cloud managed by groups of people, communities, and agencies especially government to have the common interests – such as maintaining the compliance, regulation, and security parameters – working on the same mission. The members of the community share access to the data and applications in the cloud.

2.4.5 Shared Private Cloud

This is a shared compute capacity with variable usage-based pricing to business units that are based on service offerings, accounts datacenters. It requires an internal profit center to take over or buy infrastructure made available through account consolidations.

2.4.6 Dedicated Private Cloud

Dedicated private cloud has IT Service Catalog with dynamic provisioning. It depends on standardized Service-Oriented Architecture (SOA) architectural assets that can be broadly deployed into new and existing accounts and is a lower-cost model.

2.4.7 Dynamic Private Cloud

Dynamic private cloud allows client workloads to dynamically migrate to and from the compute cloud as needed. This model can be shared and dedicated. It delivers on the ultimate value of clouds. This is a very low-management model with reliable SLAs and scalability.

2.4.8 Cloud Models Impact

Clouds will transform the IT industry and profoundly affect how we live and how businesses operate. Cloud computing

1. Offers the scalable compute model to be accessed from anywhere.
2. Simplifies service delivery.
3. Provides rapid innovation.
4. Provides dynamic platform for next generation datacenters.

Some say it is grid or utility computing or Software-as-a-Service, but it is all of those combined.

Public Clouds: Benefits

There are various benefits of public clouds. Following are some of the benefits of public clouds:

1. No big upfront investments.
2. Offer self-service for rapid-start development.
3. Deliver new pricing models for hardware, software, and service consumption.
4. Flex-up and flex-down capacity in short span.
5. Demonstrate proof of concept (POC), collaboration, workload management.

Internal Private Clouds Drive Cost Savings

There are significant cost savings in implementing an internal private cloud instead of using a usual traditional infrastructure. With a traditional infrastructure, each server typically runs a single application and the hardware is sized to meet peak demands. This setup leads to very low average hardware utilization and high software costs due to the number of servers that are deployed and the lack of resource sharing. The internal private cloud uses virtualization on larger servers and leverages advanced service management capabilities to drive efficiency. The servers can be dynamically provisioned to adjust to workload changes and end-users can request the services they need through self-service portals, which drive automation.

Significant cost savings can be achieved by leveraging these capabilities to automate test and development environments. Automation drives down IT labor cost by automatically responding to the changes in the environment and taking action before the problems occur. Virtualization coupled with service management greatly improves server utilization and reduces software license costs since fewer machines need licenses. Automated provisioning and standardization allow systems to be provisioned within minutes by scripting the install process. In addition, end-users can now interface with IT through self-service portals to request services similar to ATMs that are leveraged to improve banking service. So the virtualization can

1. Reduce IT labor cost by configuration, operations, management, and monitoring.
2. Reduce license cost by utilizing the capital effectively.
3. Lower administrative costs.
4. Reduce end-user IT support costs.
5. Reduce provisioning cycle times from weeks to minutes.
6. Provide benefits of cloud economics with security within your firewall.
7. Provide self-service for rapid-start development.
8. Provide consistency of application environments.

2.4.9 Savings and Cost Metrics

The use of virtualization in cloud computing consolidates systems, which drives reductions in hardware costs. This is often the initial appeal of funding virtualization projects.

Savings on manual efforts are also bigger. Today enterprises are involving human resources to provision the compute resources, which require longer cycles sometimes even week, hence they suffer cost. In this way, highly skilled resources are doing the administration work and not focusing on important higher value jobs. This can be avoided by the automation of the tasks that are highly repetitive. This automation can save good amount of labor cost while removing the errors, enhancing agility, and improving quality.

Cloud computing features two delivery models, namely, private cloud computing and public cloud computing. Private cloud computing exists behind the firewall, while public cloud computing is accessed through the Internet. Cloud vendors believe that these three models – traditional IT, private cloud services, and public cloud services – can co-exist as the part of an overall strategy, based on the application type and the business need that would dictate which model to use.

Hybrid clouds services, delivered to the end-user, are composed of both private and public cloud computing elements.

2.4.10 Commoditization in Cloud Computing

When businesses started taking advantage of IT, the first organizations to computerize their business processes had significant gains over their competitors. As the IT field matured, the initial competitive benefits of computerization fell. Computerization then became a requirement just to stay on a level of the playing field. In essence, there was an increasing amount of IT that operates as a commodity.

For example, a paper products company needs a certain amount of unique IT to run its business and make it competitive. But it also runs a huge amount of commodity IT. The commodity 'technology' takes time, money, people, and energy away from their business of producing quality paper products at a competitive price.

As executive management realizes that the company is operating a lot of commodity IT, which is not core to their competency, the debate shifts from whether cloud computing will take hold on the enterprise to a debate on how much of the organizational IT will be left internal, on-premise. For this process, IT functions should be evaluated and a determination be made of what is a 'commodity' and what is not. Then it also needs to be determined where to place that function in the new IT organization.

2.5 Security in a Public Cloud

Let us now discuss some of the security concerns that should be considered for the cloud deployments.

2.5.1 Multi-Tenancy

As long as the cloud provider builds its security to meet the higher-risk client requirements, all of the lower-risk clients get better security than they would have normally. A bandage manufacturer may have a low risk of being a direct target of malfeasants, but a music label that is currently using file sharers could have a high risk of being targeted by malfeasants. When both the bandage manufacturer and the music label use the same cloud (multi-tenancy), it is possible that attacks directed at the music label could affect the bandage manufacturer's infrastructure as well. So the cloud provider must design the security to meet the needs of the music label – and the bandage manufacture gets the benefits.

2.5.2 Security Review

As the time passes, organizations become lenient with their security policies. In order to tackle this, cloud service provider should conduct regular audits, review, and assessments for the security. This should be done by security specialists who are able to identify the issues and fix them. The report should be provided to each client immediately after the assessment is performed so that the clients know the current state of the overall cloud's security.

2.5.3 Mutual Risk

There can be a situation where the cloud service provider may not be the cloud operator, but providing a value-added service on top of another cloud provider's service. Like somebody wants to offer the SaaS-based services, it is good to lease the infrastructure of an IaaS provider and offer the SaaS-based services instead of building the infrastructure from the scratch. In this way, the tiers of IaaS and SaaS are developed on top of each other. In this setup, there is a risk associated to each operator and service provider and it is shared among them. They share the security risks at different levels. Therefore, a holistic risk mitigation plan should be devised to suit the architecture of the cloud provider.

2.5.4 Employee Physical Screening

In this outsourcing world, it is common for the organizations to hire the contract services. Same thing works for the cloud service providers. Like regular employees, contract employee background verification should be done by a third party for cloud service provider.

Service provider should publish its policy to all type of employees and report should be generated for the employees once the background verification is accomplished. This screening establishes the trust between the user and the service provider.

2.5.5 Multi-Geographical Datacenters

Disasters, whether manmade or natural, are part of life. They can be hurricanes, earthquakes, fire, or cable cuts. In practice, the cloud is a reliable model as it is not based on single or one location-based datacenter. Cloud datacenters are distributed and hence less prone to disasters. But sometimes organizations sign up the public cloud services for one location only. In this case, it is more important for the providers to test their disaster recovery option as they are heavily tied with SLAs and penalties. At the same time, organization as a consumer should also check and test the disaster recovery options with mock drills of failover.

2.5.6 Physical Security

Physical threats are also important to be analyzed when opting for cloud services from a provider. There are various points to be analyzed:

1. Whether all the facilities of the cloud provider have the same level of security?
2. Is it possible that only one site is secured and there is no information available for the data residency?
3. Whether datacenter is having the all the necessary physical security components such as biometric access, surveillance cameras, logbook, escorts, and automatic alarms?

2.5.7 Regulations

If any of the service provider says that they never had a security issue, it means they are either misleading or not aware of the consequences of the incidents. So all cloud service providers should have a special task force for any incident response based on the policies and regulations. These policies should be shared with the end customers also.

2.5.8 Programming Conventions

Whether it is IaaS, Saas, or PaaS, cloud providers still use their own software that may be prone to security threats and bugs. It is recommended to the cloud providers to use the secure coding and programming practices. It should be written based on standards that are well documented, reviewed, accepted, and adhered.

2.5.9 Data Control

Today in the security arena, an organization's greatest risk is data and information control. All governments and corporate organizations have laid down compliances and regulations to handle the situation.

Therefore, the cloud service provider should be able to adhere to the guidelines laid by the region or agency. The cloud provider should own the policies to meet the regulation and compliances. There should be strong encryption mechanism for the in-flight data. The cloud provider should also call for a rigorous risk assessment of the data at least once a year. The report should be published periodically once the audit and assessment are completed. The cloud provider should maintain the security incident policy.

2.6 Public Versus Private Clouds

A public cloud is a shared cloud computing infrastructure that anyone can access. It provides hardware and virtualization layers that are owned by the vendor and are shared between all customers. It is connected to the public Internet and presents an illusion of infinitely elastic resources.

Initially, it does not require upfront capital investment in the infrastructure. For consumption-based pricing, the user pays for the resources used, allowing for capacity fluctuations over time.

Now the new request-based provisioning is done on the basis of self-service portal. If one applies economies of scale, service provider can save on cost. This operation cost is also included in the chargeback models. Here consumers do not directly have any say in the SLAs and the data also moves outside the organization firewalls. The service provider location distance can also create problems because of the bandwidth and latency issues.

A private cloud is a cloud computing infrastructure owned by a single party. It provides hardware and virtualization layers that are owned by or reserved for the business. It, therefore, presents an elastic but finite resource and may or may not be connected to the public Internet.

2.7 Cloud Infrastructure Self-Service

The cloud infrastructure has to be provisioned and paid up-front in private clouds. Users pay for the actual compute usage, allowing the spikes over the period of interval. Self-service provisioning of infrastructure capacity is only possible up to a point in private clouds. Standard capacity planning and purchasing processes are required for major increases. For a large, enterprise-wide solution, some cost savings are possible from providers' economies of scale. The enterprise maintains ongoing operating costs for the cloud, and the cloud vendor may offer a fully managed service (for a price). SLAs and contractual terms and conditions are negotiable between the cloud vendors and the customers to meet specific requirements.

The sensitive data and information stay behind the organization's firewall and there is no connectivity to other clouds. Private clouds can also be designed on the basis of preferred and supported operating systems, application, and usage and business use cases. It can be based on the geographic location, compliance, and regulations. Actually , there is no best model or right model for any organization. It depends on the use, organizational policies, application behavior, geographic location, and government compliances and regulations. Likewise public cloud can be a good option for the testing and development cloud as the provisioning requirement in the development and test environment is very rapid and for a shorter period of interval. It requires to decommission the service frequently. Also for this environment, SLAs are not very stringent. At the same time, the private cloud can be a good option when the environment requires lots of information and data controls, and the sizing is known with the capacity forecast and resource availability.

Cloud computing employs a structured technique to holistically leverage IT industry best practices to uncover areas of relative strength and weakness across multiple IT domains (strategic alignment, computing system and storage, applications and data, processes, organization, finance/environment, and network) to determine readiness for a cloud computing deployment.

Infrastructure strategy and planning for cloud computing gear the clients who are looking for assistance in understanding the business value that the cloud computing model can bring. It is designed to help the clients evaluate their readiness for cloud computing and possible cloud computing usages within their infrastructure. The goal is to develop a high-level vision strategy, value case, and roadmap for cloud computing.

2.7.1 Infrastructure Strategy and Planning Features

The strategy and planning has the following three major features:

1. Evaluation to know the gaps, readiness, and strengths of the existing environment.
2. Development of the value proposition for cloud computing in the enterprise.
3. Strategy, planning, and roadmap to successfully implement the selected cloud delivery model.

Cloud architected solutions have introduced new set of characteristics, like scalability and unique service delivery model, for consistent delivery. They help to reduce the capital investment and operational cost with meeting the high SLAs. It heavily relies on the services that make the environment highly available and redundant all the time in case of disaster whether natural or manmade.

It should be ensured by the administrators that minimum data should be impacted while taking the backup to face the challenges of hard numbers of recovery point objectives and downtime impact should be minimum for recovery time objectives after the outage recovery. Emerging models, where users can have access to applications or compute resources from anywhere with their connected devices through a simplified user interface (UI), are best suitable alternatives for the ease of use. These models help applications to reside in massively scalable datacenters where compute resources can be dynamically provisioned and shared to achieve significant economies of scale. The 'pay-as-you-go' usage model enables the users and companies to predict and manage expenses, reduce costs, and simplify operations better.

2.7.2 Cloud Computing Steps

The process from virtualization to cloud computing can have the following phases:

1. **Stage 1 – Server Virtualization:** Companies usually start virtualization as a consolidation attempt. The focal point tends to be reducing capital expenses (such as server, storage, and networks), reducing energy costs, and perhaps avoiding or delaying a datacenter build-out or move.
2. **Stage 2 – Distributed Virtualization:** Once companies start down the virtualization way and start to achieve capital expense improvements (such as server, storage, and networks), the next focus tends to be on elasticity, operational improvements, rapidity, and organizing downtime more efficiently.

3. **Stage 3 – Private Cloud:** Once the processes are designed for alacrity and the standards are in place to enable broad automation, the company is ready to look at introducing self-service capabilities based on the virtualization architecture.
4. **Stage 4 – Hybrid Cloud:** Private clouds will not be the only answer for any enterprise. The self-service portals and interface introduced by private clouds should enable the IT enterprises to leverage public cloud services when they make logic without affecting the end-users.
5. **Stage 5 – Public Cloud:** Virtualization is not the must thing or the stepping stone before companies use public cloud services. Actually, some companies will attempt with the cloud in the public cloud arena first, and use their lessons to establish private clouds for their enterprises.

2.8 Summary

We have discussed several models for cloud computing, including private clouds (where the deployment is within the organization's firewall) and public clouds (where the application services and data are hosted by a third party outside the firewall). Consistent data availability and security are critical success factors for any cloud deployment. Businesses need to ensure that data are adequately protected and can be restored in a timely fashion following any disruption.

CHAPTER

3

Cloud as a Service

CONTENTS

3.1 Introduction

In today's economy, many businesses face the challenge of 'taking cost out' of their infrastructure while continuing to deliver new, innovative business services – basically they need to 'do more with less'. Many businesses face the necessity to bring fast changes to their IT infrastructure to manage requests during peak times. In order to overcome this situation, organizations are dealing with IT resource optimization and lowering the IT cost, and are looking for a way to manage these resources to meet such requirements. They are also trying to add rental-style capability to the IT resource usage.

Cloud computing defines a new way to manage IT resources by enabling self-service provisioning of IT resources, metering-style accounting based on use/time, the automation of IT management in a standard process environment.

Cloud computing is an emerging style of computing where user experience is utmost important while adopting a correct business model. Cloud computing is offered with compute and application in an appropriate service model over the Internet or a network. Cloud computing is based on infrastructure management coupled with platform development and is achieved by maintaining massive number of servers in a virtualized fashion from the same pool to deliver the services.

This chapter visualizes different cloud models with respect to services. The chapter also takes into account what service is all about and different types of infrastructure services that can be offered on the cloud as a service.

Common attributes of a cloud infrastructure are defined as follows:

1. **Flexible pricing:** It means utility pricing, variable payments, and pay-by-consumption; subscription models make pricing of IT services more flexible.
2. **Elastic scaling:** It means resources scale up and down by large factors as the demand changes.
3. **Rapid provisioning:** It means IT, and network capacity and capabilities are – ideally automatically – rapidly provisioned using Internet standards without transferring the ownership of resources.
4. **Standardized offerings:** It means uniform offerings readily available from a services catalog on a metered basis.

Cost optimization can be done in two ways, that is, by controlling operating and capital expenses. The problem is not to minimize the cost but to manage it for maintaining an equilibrium between the two expenses.

When you look at different cloud types, the common terminology that comes up is 'as a service', with infrastructure as a service being the most basic type of service. It includes compute power, storage, and file systems as services. At the next level, you have platform as a service, where a compute platform or middleware is provided.

At the next level, we have software as a service. Here the software capability is offered in a package – such as customer relationship management or e-commerce – and is delivered as a service. At the highest level is business process as a service. This is where a business can take a function that is considered to be a commodity, and not a differentiator, and can be completely outsourced in a service-based model. So cloud computing has really taken a hold because of the fact that you take virtualization, standardization, and automation, and drive this automated delivery of services at a reduced cost.

Cloud computing introduces the concept of 'IT-as-a-Service'. To support this service, the cloud infrastructure must perform the following tasks:

1. **Abstraction:** Alleviate IT consumers from the operations of applications and allowing the end-users to focus instead on the execution of high-value activities.
2. **Virtualization:** On-demand access to services irrespective of location and resource availability.
3. **Dynamic workload management:** Workload placement, provisioning, and de-provisioning based on available resources and capacity management.
4. **Data management:** Fast, secure, reliable data access and mobility with integrated data protection and recovery management.

Because all the data reside on the same shared storage systems, effective and efficient data storage management becomes critical in a cloud deployment.

3.2 Gamut of Cloud Solutions

There are a variety of cloud offerings in the broad spectrum of services (Fig. 3.1). Below are the common types under which most of the services can be viewed:

1. **Platform-as-a-Service (PaaS):** This refers to provisioning the developer's platform who writes custom application using the hardware, operating system (OS), database, and middleware. There are some software policies using which developers write and balance the scalability for application development.
2. **Software-as-a-Service (SaaS):** This refers to provisioning a purpose-built software over the Internet that uses underlying hardware, OS, and distribution capabilities.
3. **Infrastructure-as-a-Service (IaaS):** This is the provisioning of hardware or virtual computers where the organization has control over the OS, thereby allowing the execution of arbitrary software.
4. **Storage-as-a-Service (StaaS):** This is the provisioning of database-like services, billed on utility computing basis, for example, per gigabyte per month.
5. **Desktop-as-a-Service (DaaS):** This is the provisioning of desktop environment either within a browser or as a terminal server.

The distinction between these five categories of cloud offering is not necessarily clear cut. In particular, the transition from Infrastructure-as-a-Service to Platform-as-a-Service is a very gradual one.

3.2.1 Platform-as-a-Service (PaaS)

Instead of just offering applications over the Web in the form of SaaS, public cloud players are actually offering an entire PaaS. They provide the foundation to build highly scalable and robust Web-based applications in the same way the traditional operating systems such as

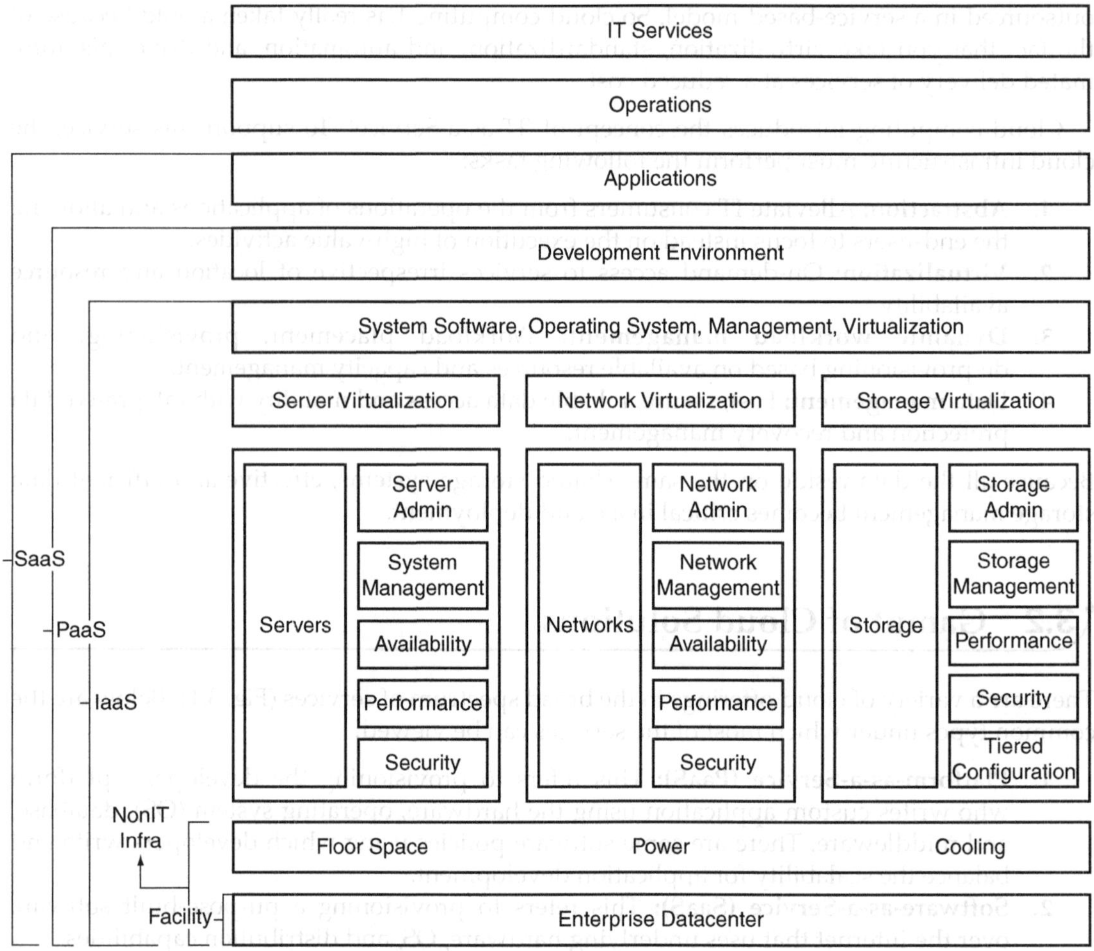

FIGURE 3.1 Cloud@datacenter.

Windows and Linux have done in the past for software developers. What is very different about this model is that the platform itself is no longer 'sold' to the customer who is then responsible for running and maintaining it. This model becomes more attractive with its operation on the hosting platform capabilities and with more capabilities in self-service model and billing. So PaaS has far-reaching implications on the business models of both PaaS vendors and their customers. One can use private clouds to speed up application deployments within minutes. It will help in tracking the usage for the chargeback and will give the option of cost-effective and secure appliance.

In order to optimize deployments, many organizations are looking to extend SOA to cloud services.

Cloud capabilities can improve the productivity of development and testing teams to roll out new applications and SOA services faster, and reduce the application backlog. The cloud provides a catalog of virtual images and patterns all ready for immediate use and these patterns define a cluster of servers working together.

PaaS saves costs by reducing upfront software licensing and infrastructure costs as well as ongoing operational costs for development, testing, and hosting environments.

PaaS enhances the capability of development platforms and helps to remove the problem of integrating the development software and tools such as OS, database, middleware, security mechanism, frameworks, and virtually shared infrastructure. PaaS also reduces the cycle time of delivery and development iterations by providing development, testing, QA, and staging on the same platform. It brings collaboration between the developers and operation team. It actually helps to achieve bigger goals of project management and remove the gaps between the development and operation communities.

Currently, PaaS is in the maturity stage. There is a requirement to bundle the application services with the platform to make it more portable and create a standard platform across vendors to choose the services. The collaboration and component models should be adopted by all vendors and should support the legacy application on the same platform for the same cloud-based services.

There are different set of users for SaaS, PaaS, and IaaS. SaaS looks for the users who want to simplify the provisioning process of business services using hosted applications. PaaS is meant for the development community to support rapid development, testing, and delivery. IaaS is a managed services platform where infrastructure is provisioned to provide compute, storage, and network services.

3.2.2 Software-as-a-Service (SaaS)

SaaS reduces the investment by removing development effort, software licenses configuration, installation maintenance, infrastructure cost, delivery and release, and reducing operational cost and administration.

The SaaS platform takes lesser time to build the service compared to the traditional way of doing it. It becomes easier as all the tedious work of management, software maintenance, and support is passed to a vendor. This gives time to workers to focus more on the business' value-based features.

SaaS application does not need extensive customization and should not look for complex business-process applications. So, it is not well-suited for service-based deployment.

There are some issues in SaaS related to migration also. While moving from one on-premise network infrastructure to publically available network infrastructure, SaaS requires an upgrade in the infrastructure. It also requires upgradation of software versions and this can become a big problem for the vendors offering these services.

3.2.3 Infrastructure-as-a-Service (IaaS)

IaaS eliminates the cost by handling the provisioning process with the automation during the peak loads. So IaaS helps the server to flex-up and flex-down to meet the demands by

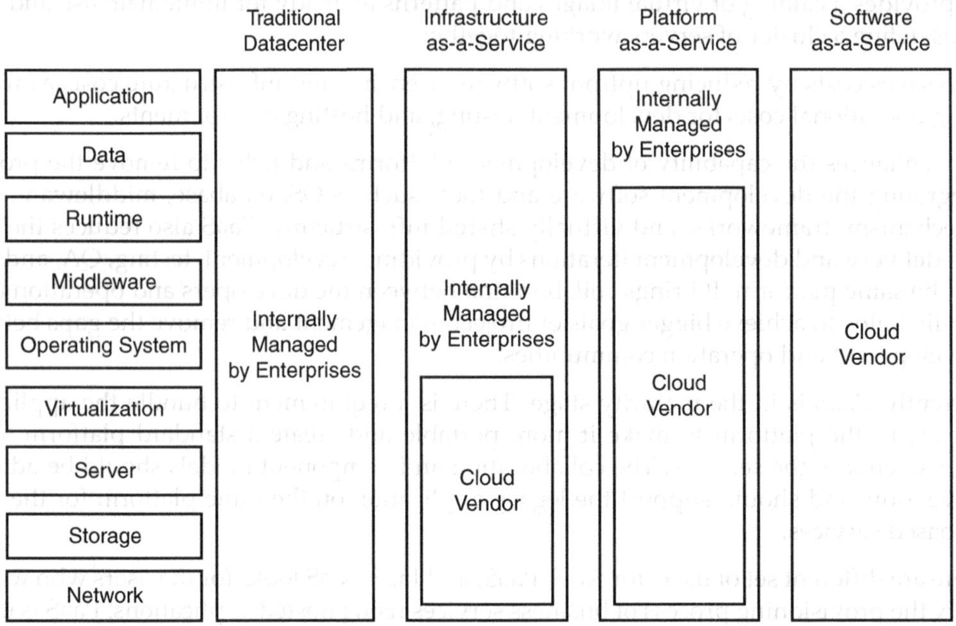

FIGURE 3.2 Cloud taxonomy.

reducing the operation cost and optimizing the support, administration, and maintenance cost. Organizations can manage their infrastructure requirements without increasing their infrastructure footprint. This also helps to control the resources required to manage the environment (Fig. 3.2).

The biggest drawback with the infrastructure provisioning is lengthy procurement cycles. IaaS helps to reduce the duration of these cycles from months to minutes. It is like shopping in an online store where one submits a request, gets it approved, and receives the services at his doorstep. These platforms follow open architecture with diverse set of supported operating systems, hypervisors, frameworks, and middlewares.

These compute resources are available on lease on the basis of pay-as-you-go model, typically based on the usage in terms of days, hours, and even in minutes. The application that needs 100% availability may not be the perfect suit for these types of services, but today even this can be managed as cloud service provides these services with the help of high availability and disaster recovery mechanisms. This infrastructure provides scaling options and therefore it is recommended to have the architecture and design of applications which can support scaling. There is no proper standardization mechanism currently for the integration and deployment of third-party software applications. This will be done in the coming years when all independent software vendors (ISVs) and cloud service providers will have a common understanding of standard software licenses and APIs to talk to diverse set of interfaces.

SaaS is considered to be more mature as a cloud offering than PaaS or IaaS. Even then, mainly small and medium businesses have adopted cloud services. Adoption by larger enterprises is still extremely low. A perception of cloud services as a high-risk technology option has led the large organizations to restrict the use of cloud services to a limited number of projects. PaaS is a more sophisticated service platform, and is still an emerging product. It needs to stabilize and mature before developers can use it for the extensive development of new SaaS applications. For IaaS, the entry of large vendors, such as Amazon and other cloud vendors, is driving up the maturity of the offering rather quickly, with Amazon leading the efforts to define the IaaS market.

There are now hundreds of vendors offering some new services of cloud computing. Other vendors have attached themselves to the 'Cloud bandwagon' by providing ancillary services to available offerings.

3.3 Principal Technologies

The key to provide a dynamic cloud infrastructure is the virtualization layer that sits between the cloud instances and the physical hardware it runs on. The platform virtualization software – the hypervisor – allows multiple operating system instances to run as guests on the same server.

The main drivers for cloud computing are *cost*, *agility*, and *time to market*. By building cloud infrastructures using a cloud orchestrator and a provisioning engine, one can realize cost savings and improve time to market. The cloud orchestrator and a provisioning engine sit on top of the virtualization layer working on the network, server, and storage. It is a layer of software that (a) interacts with multiple servers, (b) enables IT departments to pool resources together across servers, and (c) defines standardized tiers of services called *virtual compute centers*. This helps break down infrastructure silos and drives the sharing of infrastructure.

Using the cloud orchestrator and provisioning engine, IT departments can define organizations and on-board users that can share the underlying cloud infrastructure in a secure multi-tenant environment. It can then create standardized collections of virtual machines (VMs) and set policies on how users can use these VMs. The users can login into the orchestrator and self-provision respective workloads which IT has setup already.

These orchestrators also transport with the API, which allows the cloud administrator and users to inter-relate with the cloud infrastructure in a systematic way. In addition, the cloud orchestrator and the provisioning engine allow writing workflows to automate the creation of the cloud infrastructure.

The increased pooling and sharing of resources, self-provisioning, and increased automation deliver greater savings in agility, IT infrastructure, and faster delivery of applications. So one can deliver the cloud benefits for today's applications and for the applications which will be developed in the future as the cloud orchestrator and the provisioning engine build the top of the hypervisor layer.

Virtualization is the foundation for the cloud. It consists of physical hardware with hypervisor layered on the top of it. The cloud orchestrator and the provisioning engine consist of one or more cells that communicate with a single database and offer a Web portal. Using this

Web portal, cloud administrators create the cloud infrastructure resources and the users' self-provision the cloud infrastructure resources in a secure multi-tenant fashion, thus enabling IaaS.

Chargeback and metering are a key area of on-premise cloud solution. In this process, the server talks to

(a) own database, (b) server database, and (c) cloud orchestrator and provisioning engine databases and allows to associate costs with the cloud and generate usage and billing reports. The server also needs to integrate with workflow systems, Lightweight Directory Access Protocol (LDAPs), approval process, etc. to provide the lifecycle management of the cloud environment.

3.4 Cloud Strategy

This section provides a high-level guidance to define the cloud strategy and the artefacts that capture the architecture of a cloud-enabled application. These architectural artefacts are meant for the implementation planning phase of the cloud for enabling an application. Only the high-level architecture of the system that is to be cloud-enabled is captured in these artefacts.

The implementation planning phase of the cloud enables an application lying between the business strategy definition for the adoption of the cloud and the design, development, and implementation phases of the application that are being implemented to be offered on the cloud platform. This phase also takes care of linking the business strategy that is defined for a business to adopt a cloud-based strategy and the IT requirements for the applications on the cloud that are needed to support this strategy. So, this critical piece of the implementation planning translates the business intent to a set of IT requirements for the cloud-based application, deriving the high-level structures of the cloud-based application and defining a roadmap for the implementation of the application.

So, the primary input for the cloud implementation planning phase comes from the cloud strategy for the business that is driving the cloud-based implementation of one or more applications on the cloud.

The key steps in the cloud implementation planning are as follows:

1. Understand the cloud strategy.
2. Define the cloud application requirements.
3. Assess the cloud readiness.
4. Define high-level cloud architecture.
5. Identify changes in management requirements.
6. Develop a roadmap and implementation plan.

Of these phases, the artefacts defined here relate to the phase of 'defining the high-level cloud architecture'. In this phase, the high-level structure of the cloud-based application is defined from the inputs of the previous step, the 'define cloud application requirements'.

The first step in the architecture development is the usage of existing asset analysis to understand which of the components, including components of the existing application, can be used for building the application and how they can be leveraged in the cloud environment. The next step is to derive the high-level structure of the solution from the IT requirements for the cloud in the form of the following artefacts. The non-functional characteristics that the application must support and deliver are captured in the artefact 'Non-Functional Requirements'.

The roadmap for strategy and planning for cloud deployment helps in:

1. Identification of the business justification for adopting the cloud.
2. Starting the architectural work for cloud computing.
3. Application readiness and fitment based on workload.
4. Workload assessment and recommendation for the steps of migration.
5. Selection of correct solution and implementation.
6. Acquiring required skills and bridging technology gap.
7. Management of roles, responsibilities, and customer-relationship.
8. Development of high-level cloud roadmap and value proposition.

This roadmap helps in cloud deployment with the following benefits:

1. **Reduced risk and faster deployment:** It leverages cloud vendor assets, skills, and experience to reduce the risk. It also accelerates the development and implementation by identifying gaps, activities, and risks, and defines mitigation strategies within an implementation roadmap.
2. **Improved service:** It identifies the optimal delivery model, mixes and prioritizes the workloads to migrate to the cloud to achieve the business and IT objectives.
3. **Lower cost:** It identifies the opportunities to reduce capital and operating expenses across the infrastructure.

3.5 Cloud Design and Implementation Using SOA

SOA is a very useful architectural style for implementing applications in the cloud. Adoption of SOA is the best way to leverage and consume the application services provided by the cloud. A cloud-based application consists of many granular coarse-grained services offered on the cloud. These cloud offerings may in turn integrate and leverage services and systems from different environments. The coarse-grained services that cloud offerings leverage can come from the traditional IT environment in the form of standard services that are already provided and are internal to the cloud.

Standardization across these different IT environments is not possible; hence they mostly consist of heterogeneous environments. So a cloud service offering should be based on open standards that can be consumed and leveraged by this environment. Language- and platform-independent services can be provided using standards-based, platform-agnostic SOA architecture with the support for appropriate industry and technology standards.

The cloud-based application services consist of a coherent set of business processes that are aligned to the business boundaries, provide a coherent, integrated set of operations that adheres to the business intent and provides value to the users. These services also comprise consumable interfaces which may be user interfaces on different devices, coarse-grained Web-service interfaces, feeds, or widgets.

The cloud application services should be mapped to the business processes that they consist of. These business processes could be at different levels. Drill down the processes to the levels that make business sense.

These processes – along with the business strategy, the modular business alignment model, and the process scenarios to be supported – form the input to Service-Oriented Modeling and Architecture (SOMA) methodology. SOMA is applied with a meet-in-the-middle approach. Business processes and the business strategy along with business goals stated are used to arrive at the service portfolio using SOMA. While deriving the services, a bottom-up approach is also followed, taking into consideration the existing assets, which consist of existing application components and services available on public clouds and internal to the cloud, as well as industry cloud component maps.

3.5.1 Architecture Overview

The purpose of the architecture overview artefact in a cloud-based implementation is to communicate to the sponsor and external stakeholders a conceptual understanding of the architectural goals of the cloud implementation. It offers a layered conceptual model of the application services to be cloud-enabled and provides a high-level vision of the cloud architecture and its scope to developers. It is easy to explore and evaluate alternative architectural options for the cloud implementation. This stage enables early recognition and validation of the implications of the cloud-based architectural approach and facilitates effective communication between different communities of stakeholders and developers.

This developed document will help to understand the conceptual points of the cloud implementation and its dependencies on internal or external cloud ecosystem. The document may include both the cloud and non-cloud infrastructures such as offerings, components, relationships, external systems, and elements for support systems.

This artefact can also provide key stakeholders with the first high-level view of the cloud architecture landscape of their transformed cloud-based implementation.

Typically, the artefact is produced after multiple iterations and as the project moves through the solution definition and design phases, the conceptual models get clearer and this document is kept up-to-date and governed to always have the current conceptual elements.

An architecture summary depiction represents the governing ideas and candidate building blocks of a cloud-based offering and enterprise architecture. This depiction also provides an overview of the main conceptual elements and relationships in the architecture. The main purpose of such a depiction is to communicate a simple, brief, clear, and understandable overview of the target IT system.

At the enterprise-level, the architecture summary depiction is often produced as a part of an overall IT strategy to move to a cloud-based offering model. At this instance, it is used to describe the vision of the business and IT capabilities required by an organization that needs the offering to be hosted on the cloud. The architecture summary depiction provides an overview of the main offerings and the relationships with other offerings, external systems, components, nodes, connections, users, and systems, and a definition of the key characteristics and requirements.

At the system- and component-level, the architecture summary depiction is developed very early in the project (possibly pre-proposal) and influences the initial cloud hosting vision with the component model and operational model. It is intended that design commitments should be based on this conceptual overview, while the (more detailed) component model and operational model are developed and validated. Subsequently, the component model and the operational model are the primary models used for implementation activities, while their compliance with the architecture summary depiction is maintained continually. Changes to the architecture summary depiction are made using a governance process.

For most infrastructure cloud engagements, the project scope is something less than the client's enterprise architecture. Therefore, the depiction will represent the governing ideas and candidate building blocks of the offerings that are to be hosted on the cloud, and the focus of the engagement. There can be, then, multiple views of the cloud-based IT environment represented by architecture summary depiction the current and future view, views by waves of transformation, or views by types of clouds – for each alternative solution.

3.6 Conceptual Cloud Model

So far, we have discussed different service paradigms for cloud deployment. Now let us discuss the conceptual cloud model based on cloud services.

This model gives the structure of offerings in the cloud on the basis of the components of hardware and software with their relevant roles, interdependencies, and interfaces to provide the functionality. The cloud component model for implementation planning is specified at the conceptual level.

The highest level of the conceptual model is the set of cloud-based offerings that make up the cloud-based business solution. These highest-level conceptual components are derived on the basis of business intent and business functionality. These conceptual components, which form offerings, align tightly to the business intent that initiated the creation of cloud-based offerings.

Conceptual offerings that provide the cloud-based implementation of the solution can be further broken down and depicted in a layered composition. The next level of conceptual component model broken down below the offering consists of the following elements:

1. High-level service components that form the services provided by the offerings.
2. Resources that support cloud services.
3. Technical components that provide technical underpinnings of the cloud service and support non-functional needs of the cloud application.
4. External and internal services that are leveraged by cloud application services.

The high-level conceptual component model is the main artefact that provides an abstract view of the design of a cloud application to business stakeholders. This abstract view describes how the business needs will be met by the cloud application components without delving into their technical details. Components identified can be decomposed into further layered conceptual component structures to convey further details of the respective components (Fig. 3.3).

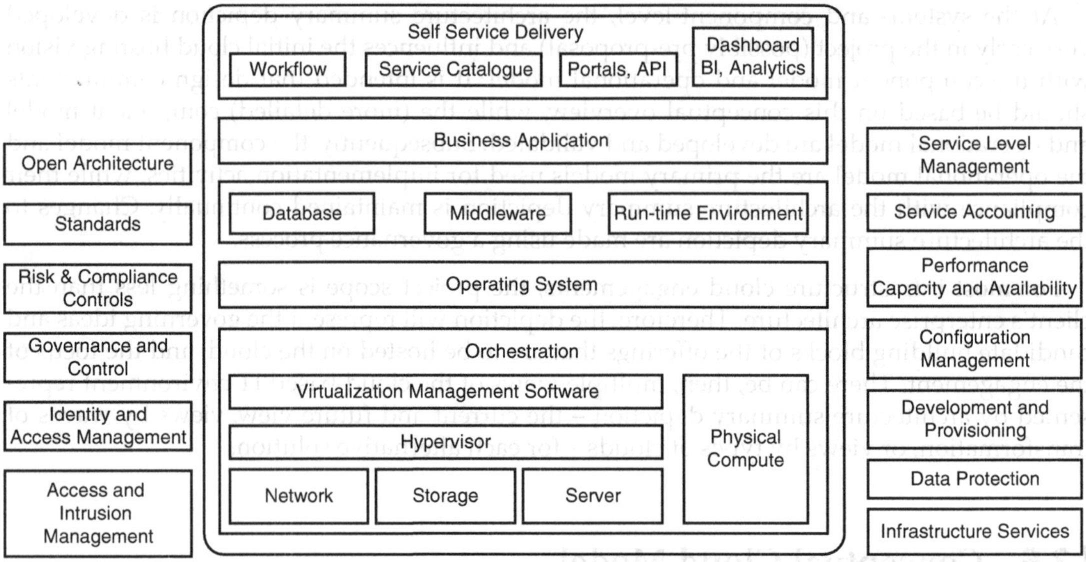

FIGURE 3.3 Cloud model.

The cloud conceptual component model should contain the following elements:

1. The conceptual structure of the cloud application.
2. Dynamic interactions and dependencies between various conceptual components.
3. Components that comprise the cloud services provided by the application, each of which may be made up of sub-components.

At this level, the conceptual components are not converted to physical components but retained at the conceptual level only.

3.6.1 Cloud Application Security and Privacy Principles

Cloud application security principles contain the high-level guidance to cover the security and privacy characteristics identified in the Information Asset Profile. This is a summary document of the information asset required for the architecture. Cloud application security principles deliverable contains a number of security principles that occur in a typical application. Typically, quite a number of the characteristics identified in the information asset profile effort will relate to the existing enterprise security elements of the client.

In addition to the elements from the existing enterprise security program, consider the following areas that tend to change during the transition to the cloud environment.

3.6.2 Governance

How will the decisions like different SLAs be made between cloud vendors and cloud customers for the cloud environment? These decisions are typically made by either another infrastructure group within the client IT organization or an external vendor who provides cloud infrastructure management for either a managed private cloud or a public cloud environment.

Authentication and Access Control

As an application moves to the cloud, the methods used to authenticate and authorize users require examination. Existing methods may require additional support to work in the cloud environment, such as providing connectivity to an existing server, and may require significant extension to accommodate the requirements of an external vendor providing infrastructure support.

Data Protection

With the move to a cloud environment, the existing methods of data protection – protecting the data from disclosure or modification both on the network and on a storage medium – are likely to require changes with the move to a virtualized storage and with the introduction of additional infrastructure administrators, often from a vendor organization.

Logging and Alerting

Logging is the ability to tie actions to an individual. Alerting is the method of recognizing activities that may indicate a malicious act and bringing those to the attention of the security staff. With the move to a cloud infrastructure, with different network and additional administrators, often from an external vendor, the process of tying actions to specific individuals requires additional attention.

3.7 Cloud Service Defined

This section highlights the aspects of service, its scope, and cloud-based different platform integration and deployment services.

3.7.1 Service Definitions

Let us begin with a cursory glance on what 'service' is:

1. **Service:** A specific IT deliverable that provides customer value. It is measurable in 'customer' terms and provides the basis for doing business with the customer. It is delivered through a series of processes and/or activities.
2. **Service portfolio:** The collection of services provided by IT in aggregation to represents all the 'value add' activities performed by IT.
3. **Service component:** A logically grouped set of activities that represent a part of a service that touches the customer. Service components are grouped together to create deliverables that form the basis for doing the business with customers.
4. **Service owner:** The individual who is accountable for ensuring that the customer receives the identified value of the service. They take customer's end-to-end view of IT activities by working with process owners to ensure that all the required delivery components fit together smoothly.
5. **Process:** A collection of related activities that take inputs, transform them, and produce outputs that support an enterprise goal.
6. **Enablers:** The decomposed components of a service (process, organization, and technology) that are combined to create *service deliverables*. The collection of activities (and their supporting roles and technology) become the workflow needed for *service delivery*.

7. **Service-level agreements:** It is a grouping of services or service components that have specific delivery commitments and roles identified with the customer. SLAs can be grouped together in different ways to represent various products. Examples would include e-mail and service delivery.
8. **Service-level management:** It is the governing mechanism for coordination, agreement, monitoring, reporting, and reviewing the steady-state operations service agreements, so that the service is maintained at a given level and with continuous improvement. It is the trust building activity between provider and consumer. This mechanism is required in any organization to maintain the IT service level needed to support the business. Service-level management also keeps a check on what is achieved or what is not, and the reason behind that.
9. **Service-level management objectives:** The objectives related to SLA maintain the quality, agreement clauses, penalties with the help of constant monitoring and reporting. This also helps to investigate the causes for not meeting the SLAs because of the poor service. It develops a better relationship between the IT department and its customers.

SLAs should be established for all IT services being provided. Underpinning Contracts (UCs) and Operational Level Agreements (OLAs) should also be in place with those suppliers (external and internal) upon whom the delivery of service is dependent.

SLAs are likely to be a service if the 'what' is separated from the 'how', and we can change the underlying assets – processes, technologies, data – as well as suppliers, but still provide the promised business outcomes and value. It is a service if its description and design highlight separate roles for customers, users, providers, and suppliers, and is offered with a pre-defined value proposition stating specific price points and performance metrics tied to business (not just IT operational) outcomes. It is something that makes sense as a customer/user-selectable item with corresponding service requests available in a menu or service catalog.

3.7.2 Services Scope Overview

In this section we discuss about the service scope for platform-based management operations.

Platform Development Services

These services provide a set of project services for planning, design, procurement, assembly, integration, site installation, and project management of the deployment mainstream and special-purpose end-user devices, and also include a number of asset lifecycle services. These services integrate and customize multiple devices – including PCs, wireless and mobile devices, kiosks, ATMs, point-of-sale (POS) devices, and printers – as per end-user specifications. These services follow a factory approach for off-customer-site build and integration services, using build and integration centers around the globe.

Software Platform Management Services

These services provide a set of project and annuity services to manage end-user software platforms, including image development and management, application software packaging and distribution, and services to manage the availability of the end-user platform proactively. This includes services to design and migrate end-user platforms, for example, Microsoft XP to Vista or Linux. These services follow a factory approach for off-customer-site platform management services, using management and configuration centers.

3.7.3 Platform Integration and Deployment Component Services

This section discusses some of the very important platform integration and deployment component services.

Order Management

This service handles the procurement of hardware and/or software on behalf of the customer (regardless of asset ownership), and the fulfilment (delivery) of that hardware and software to a central build facility prior to platform build and pre-load.

Warehousing and Stock Management

This service gives provision of central warehousing facilities to store hardware and other agreed components before and after build, and before the shipment to the site. It provides services for receiving and warehousing, and ensures that the inventory is efficiently maintained and protected while the products are in the storage.

Platform Build and Test

This service provides services to build, integrate, customize, prepare, and test the hardware and software platforms before the shipment to the customer site or the end-user location.

Base Backup

This service provides a base backup to be taken during platform pre-build (assuming that the software platform supports this feature).

Data and Personality Migration

This service migrates data and personal settings (e.g., desktop wallpaper, Internet favorites, desktop layout, etc.) from the original to a replacement platform.

Asset Tagging and Custom Labelling

This service provides custom asset tagging of hardware components during build and pre-delivery preparation at a central build facility.

Asset Inventory Update and Report

This service includes adding a new asset to the customers or managed asset database.

Logistics and Delivery

This service includes the shipment of the hardware to a respective site for building the platform.

Installation

This service provides the deployment of the platform into the customer's operational environment. This could be either at the end-users' desk or at the agreed deployment center location for the machines that are to be collected or deployed by the customer.

Extended Project Management

This is an extension to base project management services that cloud uses to manage internal functions and activities. This service extends project management scope to cover overall management of the platform deployment program, including customer and customer third-party resources and activities.

Platform Removal and Return

This includes decommission of platform from the customer location and return to cloud vendors for refurbishment or disposal (but not including refurbishment or disposal activities).

Asset Refurbishment

This service checks the suitability of the hardware platform, refurbishment and upgrade as appropriate, and integration into the deployment process.

Asset and Data Disposal

This service provides removal of sensitive data from the hardware platform to varying levels of security (e.g., to the department of Defense standards), as well as safe environmental disposal to international standards and/or asset value recovery.

Emergency Replacement

This service provides the emergency replacement of hardware platforms (pre-built to the customer's standards) to agreed service levels.

Software Platform Services

This section explains the software platform management services in detail.

1. **Software platform design consulting:** This service helps the client to understand the business and technology needs for a new software platform, and provides the design specification.
2. **Software platform creation and customization:** This service creates and tests a software platform to support the needs of the business.
3. **Software support and maintenance:** This service provides ongoing support and maintenance of the client's software platform, including platform updates and management, and ongoing problem support.

Application Scripting

This service creates application software unattended installation scripts to accommodate the customer environment. This service also includes new software applications and updates for existing packages.

Application Discovery

This service discovers which applications are in use across the organization.

Application Portfolio Management

This service helps the clients to manage their application portfolio.

Software Delivery

This service schedules and transports application packages to target end points. It includes the capability to PUSH software out to user PCs from a central distribution and/or the ability for the users to PULL software to their PCs using a Web interface.

Antivirus Management

These services manage the delivery of antivirus signature files. They provide real-time protection from malicious virus attacks that can cause potentially disastrous system.

Patch Management

This service ensures that end-user devices have the latest patch releases installed. This service also provides real-time deployment of critical operating system patches for protection against flaws and vulnerabilities.

Health Check Services

These services ensure that end-user devices are in a good state of health of the system, such as infrastructure and PC checks. They also perform remote monitoring of supported workstations for critical hardware alerts and initiate scripted responses as alerts are received. Examples of health check services are identification of low memory, detection of spyware, identify low disk space, etc.

Compliance Services

These services ensure that end-user devices are compliant with client standards. They perform remote monitoring of supported workstations to perform activities such as detecting peer-to-peer software detection of games. Until there is an agreement to industry standard definition of what an IT service is, one must agree with the client on a definition of 'service'. So, different type of the services visibility with respect to the customer will be considered.

External Services

These services are visible and seen by the customer, and include business services (business intelligence, logistics, receiving orders, marketing services, invoicing, accounting, etc.) and user services (desktop support, maintenance, education, etc.).

Internal Services

These services are invisible or less visible to the customer, but essential for the delivery of IT services. They include infrastructure services (hosting services, storage, availability, data retention, or recovery) and network services (network, remote access, mobile or wireless services, etc.). Internal services also take care of application services (integration, testing, design, maintenance, optimization, etc.).

User-Initiated Service Request

This request includes service request handling in incident management, for example, the service request progresses through its lifecycle exactly as an incident. Most companies separate user service requests and incidents, for example, a service request follows a different process and use a different tool to track it throughout its lifecycle. Users request services for which their businesses have already contracted with a service provider and to which they are already entitled. Some people have referred to the list of services from which a user can order services as a service catalog. Perhaps it is a 'User Services Catalog'. These service requests and this type of listing of services are appropriately offered through a single point of contact for the users of IT support, that is, the service desk.

Customer-Initiated Service Request – A Service Catalog-Based Request

It includes the concept of a service catalog as a list of services that the customer can order. The customer is the one who pays for services. When customers order a service, their users are entitled to receive services under that agreement. Each individual request made by a user is a user initiated service request. The user is entitled to services that their business has ordered through a service catalog request. This type of request is from the customer to some account representative or 'business relationship manager' who responds to this request and initiates the service provisioning for that customer.

3.8 Summary

This chapter visualizes different cloud models with respect to services. The chapter also takes into account what service is all about and different types of infrastructure services that can be offered as the cloud as a service.

CHAPTER

4

Cloud Solutions

CONTENTS

4.1 Introduction

The cloud environment presents an opportunity to enhance user experience by providing a broader communication path for reaching out to the user or providing a series of business services to the user via application features.

Deploying an application to the cloud is somewhat different since the deployment process will not be done locally within the enterprise and the existence of the provisioned image as well as a series of deployment steps are needed to deploy the application and validate the deployment.

Development and testing environments are readily available within the cloud environment. The advantages of these environments, especially from a cost perspective, are numerous as there is no need to purchase and deploy servers within the normal enterprise environment. If a proof of concept (POC) was being developed and the project was cancelled, no software, hardware, or even development tools would have to be purchased, only to be thrown away later, as the cloud supports development and testing of applications.

4.1.1 Cloud Application Planning

Cloud application design and planning exercise requires many unique considerations, which are as follows:

1. Business functions.
2. Application architecture.
3. Security for cloud computing.
4. Cloud delivery model.
5. User experience.
6. Development, testing, and run-time environments.

Application architecture is selected through an appropriate criteria evaluation. The key thing to talk about from the security aspect is the enhancement to the existing security model where data protection and isolation of the data becomes important from other areas of the cloud environment. Encryption is one possibility to further enhance the security model; however, the enterprise would not necessarily invoke that option. Another aspect of security would be to further authenticate and authorize users of the application and services they have been entitled to use.

4.1.2 Cloud Business and Operational Support Services

The elements that are required by the cloud service provider to run the business operations are called business support services (BSS). These elements are mostly associated with service providers having a utility-based service model. These services include:

1. Accepting customer orders.
2. Managing customer data.
3. Managing order data.
4. Billing.
5. Service offered.

The IT system used by service providers comes under the category of operational support services (OSS). It is mostly associated with the network infrastructure and maintenance services such as:

1. Provisioning.
2. Installation and configuration.
3. Fault management.

BSS and OSS components need to be externalized so that the application's supporting services being transformed to the cloud environment can capitalize on the various functions provided by OSS and BSS. For example, provisioning can be adapted to support the application's provisioning requirements instead of creating self-provisioning service from scratch. The ability to tap into the monitoring and metering events and keep track of the activity within the cloud environment can assist the application to continue to provide service levels and quality of service. Each of the OSS and BSS offered by the cloud environment will continue to support the application and its consumers in maintaining the key characteristics of cloud computing.

Applications built for the cloud have a layered architecture and are composed of infrastructure, security, business services, application programming interfaces (APIs) to devise the optimal solution. The service provided in the cloud model is offered by service providers to their consumers. Typically, the services offered in this area are infrastructure, software, platform, and business processes, and they come with rapid deployment, scaling, self-service, pay per use and a shared infrastructure model.

The service provider is accountable for offering service instances of various categories to cloud service consumers. This also requires ongoing operations, with an option of self-servicing, to manage cloud service instances. All technical configurations are standardized and capsulated in a template that also describes the OSS, an artifact to describe the services with respect to the service provider and cloud services.

To fulfill these services, specific tools and software are required over the cloud layers. For infrastructure as a service, a hypervisor, cloud orchestration and a provisioning engine are needed; whereas for platform as a service, middleware and development platforms are required; similarly for software as a service, multi-tenancy–enabled distribution software is required. Based on services, various cloud service instances represent various entities.

Cloud services can be built on top of each other, for example, a software service could use a platform service or infrastructure service as its foundation, and a platform service could use an infrastructure service as its foundation. However, this is not always true because a software service could also directly be built on top of the 'traditional' infrastructure, clearly inheriting all the constraints associated with such an infrastructure. In general, the basic cloud architecture postulates to share as much resources as possible across cloud services with respect to the management platform and underlying infrastructure. However, the cloud does not require to have only one single, fully homogeneous infrastructure. Of course, this would be the ideal goal, but given different infrastructural requirements, this is not possible. For example, if a particular cloud service has very specific infrastructure needs, then this cloud service will be allowed to run on a dedicated infrastructure (e.g., the Google search engine or HPC cloud services would always run on a purpose-built physical infrastructure due to performance and efficiency reasons; however, they would not run on a virtualized compute cloud service).

When we build cloud services in a layered fashion, it is very important to understand the difference between OSS and BSS available on a common platform. These differences should be studied across multiple cloud services and their usage capabilities.

Whatever be the scenario, any cloud-based service can be treated as an OSS or BSS for cloud vendors. Therefore, a service is developed after gathering a lot of requirement data and standardization based on business decisions. It is followed by go-to-market (GTM) activities with appropriate and proven business models for the development and operations of cloud services.

4.2 Cloud Ecosystem

It is very important to understand the relationship between a cloud service and the artefacts that can be developed on the basis of and within the boundaries of an ecosystem-focused infrastructure-as-a-service (IaaS) or platform-as-a-service (PaaS) cloud service. Taking any service to a potential market requires huge budget allocation and then needs to be enabled with appropriate chargeback and metering mechanism to support the business model. At the time of development, it is difficult for developers to understand the need to make it as flexible as possible for unpredictable scenarios. A cloud ecosystem is shown in Fig. 4.1.

Once a service provider thinks of launching services, it calls the exercise of illustrating all the requirements of its functional and non-functional relationships. Once the ecosystem is developed, there is a limited scope of change as most of the components existing on the top layers of the cloud ecosystem are frozen. This is not a negative phenomenon as it provides stability to the system. It also helps in providing strict guidelines for the ecosystem and lays down the principles for using the services to reduce the overall cost of the system. The more time it takes to create the service instance, the less will be the chances of it being successful in the market.

Therefore, it is very important to first visualize the relationship between the business and the technical understanding and then develop the artifacts on the existing layers of the ecosystem that will focus on the service based on boundaries. Also, most of the time, cloud service

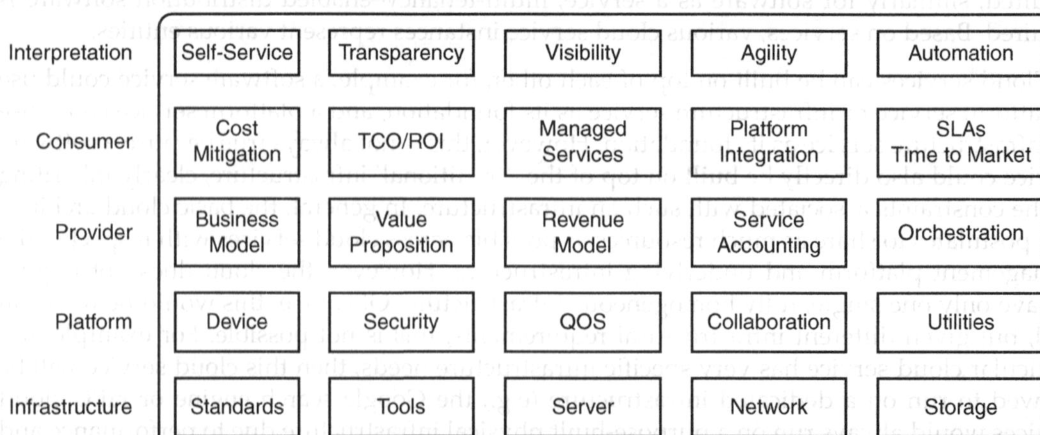

FIGURE 4.1 Cloud ecosystem.

is termed as a service product with the deployment capability in various environments and comes with the benefit of choosing suitable services that fit best in the business function.

This means that an organization is not tied to one solution for cloud computing, but can rather use multiple solutions. So, depending on business needs, the application, and what the application has to offer, cloud requirements help in selecting proper cloud environments.

Cloud-based environments come handy especially when used to develop, test, and run your application for the following reasons:

1. Easy availability in your own private cloud environment or on the public cloud.
2. Rapid access to a configurable development and test environment to speed time to market.
3. A self-service portal for multi-tenancy, provisioning, and account management.
4. Pay as you go pricing, with capacity and workload management.
5. Security with compliance and regulations to protect the environment.
6. A rich service catalog with images.
7. Faster provisioning to reduce the cycle time.

4.3 Cloud Business Process Management

Business process management (BPM) looks after business processes across the organization which may be cross-functional and directly or indirectly customer focused. BPM is implemented by the strategy based on the core business objectives and deployment of resources across the organization to create customer-centric values. It integrates all vertical-based core functions such as supply chain and product development in an integrated way within multiple line of businesses (LOBs). In this way, BPM is distinguished from other traditional approaches.

BPM is based on the principle of continuous improvement to increase value for market sustenance of the organization. It defines and aligns operations, IT, and organization. Therefore, the cloud can help in the following ways:

1. **Integration of core business:**
   - Is holistic.
   - Crosses organizational functions and boundaries (height and breadth).
   - Includes business and technology.
2. **Value-focused efficiency:**
   - Customer-centric perspective.
   - Bottom-line success.
   - Return on investment (ROI) delivery speed.
   - Performance measurement.
3. **Continuous:**
   - Based on longer period of intervals pertaining to cloud business.
   - Continual improvement.
4. **Cultural:**
   - Cultural considerations of the organization
   - Geographical and cultural factors at the time of due diligence of requirement.

4.3.1 Identifying BPM Opportunities

This section discusses the opportunities required for successful cloud BPM and the characteristics of cloud deployment offerings. The answers to the following questions can help you identify cloud opportunities better:

1. Are the strategic value proposition and capabilities defined for your organization?
2. How does your overall strategy drive the design and execution of your business processes? Is there a traceability of execution to goals?
3. How do you manage your core business processes?
4. What are your current process initiatives?
5. What are your current process governance facilities?
6. Are your existing organizational structures aligned to enable efficient process operations?
7. How do your customers measure and assess the performance of your processes?
8. How does your process performance compare with that of your competitors?
9. How effectively does your current technology (information, systems, tools, machines, etc.) enable the enterprise's core business processes?
10. What risks and challenges does your current technology present for current and future process capabilities?
11. What type of products does your organization have?
12. What are the notable pieces of your IT portfolio?
13. Has your organization adopted service-oriented architecture (SOA)?
14. How are the processes currently modelled in your organization? What is included in this model?
15. What design/development tools are currently used in the organization?
16. What testing tools are currently used by the organization? What are the strengths/weaknesses of these tools?
17. Please describe the different business processes that are automated in the organization.

Cloud application development offerings provide

1. Cloud application reference architecture.
2. Unmatched experience of developing high-performing, secure applications across a wide range of technologies of the cloud vendor.
3. Unmatched application security expertise.
4. Leadership in cloud-related technologies such as multi-tenancy, virtualization, and pervasive computing.
5. Significant expertise with cloud business models.
6. Ability to integrate a portfolio of related cloud services.

4.3.2 Cloud Technical Strategy

This section describes the technical strategy on how cloud customers can enable cloud deployment.

Cloud services enable our cloud users to build middleware clouds in their datacenter and utilize public clouds, where it makes sense to provide the following cloud-enabled middleware services:

1. Infrastructure services.
2. Platform services.
3. Application services.

Cloud strategy enables our organizations to do the following:

1. Build middleware clouds in their datacenter.
2. Utilize public clouds where it makes sense.

4.3.3 Cloud Strategy Support Areas

The cloud strategy does so by providing support in the following areas:

1. **Cloud-enabled middleware services:**
    - Infrastructure services.
    - Platform services.
    - Application services.
    - Serving on-premise and public clouds.

So, what does it mean to develop an application service for the cloud? For one, it means product features development similar to on-premise software. This means:

1. **Enabling the software for cloud essentially implies**
    - Support for collaborative multi-tenancy.
    - Self-service registration.
    - Customers and their entitlements management.
    - Single sign-on.
    - Additional security concerns.
2. **Integration with the datacenter:**
    - Firewalls and reverse proxy configurations.
    - Certificate and domain names.
    - Management of services and patch procedures.
    - Isolation, recovery, and backup issues.

4.3.4 Cloud Use Cases

IaaS or Test/Development

Problem: Development teams require unpredictable amount of infrastructural facilities to get their job done. In the majority of cases, getting all of these resources in place before they are actually required in the development cycle can be quite a challenge. Purchasing the hardware consumes project budget, and procurement of it is often quite slow. Static development and testing resources require manual re-provisioning to re-purpose resources for use, or new resources need to be purchased to meet demand. In cases where project timelines are short, project managers often choose not to set up much of an environment because it depletes their budget or jeopardizes the project's delivery schedule. Actual usage of the system(s) can be quite short in terms of absolute time. Different types of projects require different kinds of development components (such as SQL server, SharePoint, and BizTalk) depending on the architecture of the solution. Besides the testing environment, the team usually needs a system that looks quite similar to the production environment. This system helps to perform various simulations for load, stress testing for various deliveries and training.

Solution: Companies can create standardized service catalog items for common infrastructure requirements and enable development and test teams to access infrastructure in a self-service model (IaaS). Overall control over the process is maintained with business policies around quotas, reservations, reclamation, and standardized offerings.

Standardized Development Platforms/Middleware (PaaS Enabled)

Problem: Developers deliver their code without involving operations into architectural decisions or code reviews. Enterprise architects recognize the large costs associated with non-standard development platforms. To simplify the ongoing maintenance and streamline development operations, many companies are creating corporate standards around development stacks that include middleware/applications. However, most companies are hesitant to an external PaaS offering due to the constraints of having to rewrite their internal applications to fit the external PaaS API sets.

Solution: Companies can create standardized development platform definitions for use by development teams to standardize and streamline their efforts. This improves corporate IT productivity by helping them build a 'private cloud' that provides a common foundation for building custom applications running securely behind their own firewall.

Application Cloud

Problem: Companies want to move beyond self-service for infrastructure and provide application owners the ability to define, instantiate, and manage complex multi-tier applications. This includes configuring the application for production usage and monitoring performance within the application for Service-Level Agreement (SLA) optimization.

Solution: End-users can access complete application definitions and manage them according to their quotas and preferences defined by cloud administrators. Applications in production can be monitored across multiple factors and automatically scaled up or down according to business policies.

Software-as-a-Service (SaaS) to End Customers

Problem: Many companies or independent software vendor (ISVs) want to deliver their applications to end-users as a service. However, creating a multi-tenant SaaS offering requires substantial development to support security, performance, and scalability needs. Due to these high costs, companies cannot offer new services based upon existing applications.

Solution: Companies can provision a unique application instance per customer, with private cloud automation capabilities. Environments are provisioned according to business policies, and unique SLAs can be delivered per customer according to the business arrangements.

The cloud engine should provide the automation to provision on-demand complex application and configuration environments required along with the dynamic application scaling. The cloud engine should also deliver unique business policy selections, including custom placement and high availability across multiple datacenters.

4.4 Cloud Service Management

The cloud service management system offers standardization, operation control, support desk, monitoring, and consistent service delivery required for public, private, and hybrid cloud platforms.

1. **Simplify user interaction with IT:**
   - Self-service portals speed up the delivery consistently.
   - Service catalog enables standards which drive consistent service delivery.
2. **Enable policies to lower the cost with provisioning:**
   - Automated provisioning and de-provisioning speed up service delivery.
   - Provisioning and de-commissioning of assets.
3. **Enhance system administrator efficiency:**
   - Migration from various management isolations to full-fledged service management system.

The emergence of cloud deployment is prompting enterprises to either assemble in-house teams to manage specialized cloud service providers or look for third-party cloud brokers chiefly due to the following reasons:

1. Every service-oriented approach needs a mechanism to enable discovery and end-point resolution.
2. Registry/repository technology provides specialized cloud service and third-party cloud brokers where the service delivery is inside the firewall.
3. Cloud services delivered across firewalls need something similar – a third party that serves as a 'service broker'.

Leveraging service brokers will probably become a critical success factor in cloud computing as cloud services multiply and expand faster than the ability of cloud consumers to manage or govern them. The growth of service brokerage businesses will increase the ability of cloud consumers to use services in a trustworthy manner. Cloud service providers are expected to begin to partner with cloud brokers to ensure that they can deliver the services they promote. These brokers help companies to get the right platform and deploy applications among multiple service providers as well as arbitrage services to migrate and move from one platform to the other based on the best pricing model. There can be three categories of opportunities for cloud brokers:

1. **Cloud service intermediation:** This requires the right cloud platform and becomes the basis for building new services.
2. **Cloud aggregation:** Deploying customer services over multiple cloud platforms.
3. **Cloud service arbitrage:** Supplying flexibility, providing 'opportunistic choices', and fostering competition between clouds.

It will be similar to cloud services under one umbrella except that services being aggregated will not be fixed. This flexibility will be important while doing chores such as providing multiple e-mail services through one service provider or providing a credit-scoring service that checks multiple scoring agencies and then selects the best score.

The ability to federate an application across multiple clouds will become important as in the case when one service goes down, another can be started and the service broker will just simplify it. To help federate the clouds, a 'storefront' site can be created with services that are pre-screened to meet government procurement guidelines. The new site can be expected to cut red tape and make it easier for government agencies to quickly deploy the latest technology.

4.4.1 Key Cloud Solution Characteristics

The key characteristic capabilities of cloud orchestrator and provisioning engine are as follows:

1. **Scalability:** The cloud orchestrator should maintain an index of the resources that are acquired from the hypervisor, giving the master a low overhead and enabling it to scale across tens of thousands of machines across multiple geographies.
2. **High availability:** The cloud orchestrator should play for the master node to support 'Active–Passive' as well as 'Active–Active' scenarios for availability and disaster recovery (DR). It should also monitor individual physical servers for availability, and in case of a physical resource server failure, it should restart the virtual machine (VM) on another running server to meet the requirements.
3. **Application life cycle:** The cloud orchestrator should offer complete application life cycle support, from the creation of infrastructure to installation, configuration, and launching an application to its deletion or expiration. This allows applications to be instantiated, removed, or flexed very quickly to respond to real-time demand for the same.
4. **Multi-tenancy/Role-based administration:** The cloud orchestrator should also support multi-tenant capability with specific user permissions. It should have multiple personas such as cloud administrator, account owner, and user. Application definitions are only 'published' to specific users. The application owner or administrator logs in with his/her credentials and can view (user) the application VMs that have been allocated to him/her as well as perform admin operations (account owner) on those VMs if needed. Role-based administration allows fine-grained control of what each person can or cannot do in terms of cloud orchestrator features.
5. **Policies:** The cloud orchestrator should provide a rich set of policies that can be enabled. These policies can be modified or new ones can be created to take effect at the global level on applications, VMs, hosts, etc. These policies can also be embedded in service definitions to take effect of automatically depending on the metric threshold. For example, a policy can be created to allow an application to flex up to 10 VMs during high load or demand and to be reduced to only 2 running VMs during low load or demand. This policy frees up resources which can be used by other applications that are experiencing high load.
6. **Alarms:** The cloud orchestrator should provide pre-defined alarms that can be set at the global level for applications, VMs, hosts, etc. These alarms can be used to notify individual users or application owners regarding the application thresholds being reached. For example, an alert can be sent if the response time of an application is below the SLA but there are no more resources for the application to flex up.

7. **Application awareness and policy-based allocation:** The cloud orchestrator should be aware of application requirements and optimize the placement of the application accordingly, such as placing the VMs running the application close to each other to reduce latency. Cloud orchestrator should also support major application servers.
8. **Resource awareness and policy-based allocation:** The cloud orchestrator should optimize the usage of the cloud infrastructure through intelligent resource allocation policies and allow load balancing of VMs.
9. **Elasticity based on performance (flex-up/flex-down):** The cloud orchestrator should provide out-of-box functionality to flex-up or flex-down an application instance or resource based on performance metrics.
10. **Reporting and accounting:** The cloud orchestrator should also provide metering and billing reports on resource allocation and actual usage. Additionally, this data can be used to create reports on inventory capacity and consumption. This allows different business owners to create reports on how much or how little the application is used, and administrators can then adjust the resources allocated to each application accordingly.
11. **Self-service portal:** The cloud orchestrator should enable a self-service portal for application owners. Application owners can request machines or entire multi-machine application environment, and monitor and control them through this portal. The portal should drive the workflow necessary to create the environment and provide run-time environment management to support application elasticity. For example, the owner of the auditing application may request more resources for his application during a busy period.

4.5 On-Premise Cloud Orchestration and Provisioning Engine

On-premise cloud orchestration and provisioning engine can be a bundled offering that includes hardware, software, and all the services one needs to get started with cloud computing. This bundled offering should include all the elements in a service ecosystem. The offering must have a self-service portal which should include automation and should track as well as control all the resources.

The other objective is to completely integrate and include a service and, allow users to add other services to do integration or other types of cloud work. It can be a pre-packaged private cloud offering that can bring together the hardware, software, and services needed to establish a private cloud or to accelerate selling efforts and effectiveness.

Cloud orchestration and provisioning engine should be designed from client cloud implementation experiences and integrated with the service management software system along with servers, storage, and services to enable a private cloud in the IT environment. This approach will help in doing away with the guess work of establishing a private cloud by pre-installing and configuring the necessary software on the hardware and leveraging services for customization as per the environment. This is required to install applications and utilize the benefits of cloud computing such as pooling, self-service, agility, and service accounting.

4.5.1 Benefits/Value Proposition

1. Powers faster time to innovation and lowers cost per unit of innovation.
2. Dramatically improves business values and IT's effect on time to market by enabling business workloads to be deployed rapidly as well as accurately, when and where they are needed.
3. Helps in improving productivity and reducing the capex investment.
4. Minimization of human error based on automation.

4.5.2 Cloud Orchestration and Provisioning Requirement Analysis

To know cloud orchestration and provisioning engine requirements, we need to understand the test and development requirements of cloud deployment. Therefore, we should be sure about the automation of testing and development cycles to reduce the deployment time. To do so, we can initiate discussion with the cloud customer about the opportunity for the deployment of the cloud orchestration and provisioning engine. After this, we can set the boundaries of the environment. About 30–50% of any given IT environment is devoted to test/development purposes. It can take developers days, weeks, or even months to procure and configure appropriate hardware, networking, management software, storage, etc. for testing. With cloud orchestration and provisioning engine, a developer can log into a self-service portal, select the required resources along with the time frame, select an image to provision from the service catalog, and be ready to go within hours, as opposed to months. Customer datacenters support hundreds or thousands of distinct composite applications representing business workloads. They leverage multiple types of servers, storage, networks, middleware, and operating systems. About 70% of the IT datacenter budget is spent on assembling and re-assembling existing infrastructure, thus leaving fewer resources for innovation.

Cloud solutions are based on its service management solutions. The first solution in a series of cloud orchestration and provisioning engine solutions that should be considered is workload-specific deployment. It will be a great entry point for users who want to get into cloud computing, as users can roll out cloud orchestration and provisioning engine into their environment without adversely effecting anything else in the environment, and use it as their initial pilot project to start running cloud services.

Cloud orchestration and provisioning engine in any IT environment represents an alternative entry point into cloud computing. So, in some cases, the users want to turn their existing environment into a cloud. In that case, we go into the datacenter, install a cloud management platform, and assign the existing resources to the cloud. One reason behind this transition may be that the organization already has plenty of equipment that are not being used efficiently and the organization sees a lot of benefit in turning its existing investment into a cloud. So, cloud orchestration and provisioning engine can work as the established platform to start the cloud-based services and can then be bundled with the compute and storage to jumpstart the services.

Entry points:

1. **Turn existing environment into a cloud:**
   - Install a cloud management platform and assign existing resources to the cloud.
   - Scenario – you already have enough equipment or the cloud orchestration and provisioning engine offering is not the right platform.

2. **Jumpstart your cloud:**
   - Hardware, software, and services required for a quick startup.
   - Can use a 'seed and grow' model – start with the cloud orchestration and provisioning engine and then add more.

So what solution should one use? Let us look at some scenarios. When can you opt for a cloud orchestration and provisioning engine? The answer to this question is that one can opt when you wish to get started with cloud computing and recognize the advantages of having a cloud management platform bundled with the resources. This is the most rapid way to get a cloud platform up and running. In a scenario where you want to transfer your existing resources into a cloud, you use this service. Also, a user who uses cloud orchestration and provisioning engine will be benefitted when the cloud vendor can help him plan, design, and implement services, whether he wants to implement either infrastructure or platform as a service, or else turn it into a production cloud.

So, in some cases, it is appropriate to opt for cloud orchestration and provisioning engine, business development and test services, because if you just start with the provisioning engine only, you may eventually want to build out your service catalog, integrate it into your directory, cloud vendor or third-party service management products, and extend the capability of the platform.

4.5.3 Cloud Infrastructure Security

The security aspect of the cloud infrastructure goes side by side SOA security. It can be introduced as a layered approach. At the top, the service layer with the run-time-secure virtualized environment can be seen. This layer is available as a distributed service environment. These services include administrative and security aspects across different clouds as well as within a single cloud. This environment should gel with the Web services stack, and it is important that we bind the internal resources with other cloud services to offer better hybrid cloud services for successful cloud deployments. We will discuss more about this in Chapter 9.

SOA helps to integrate multiple services from different providers. Cloud computing is the biggest buyer of this characteristic as cloud accommodates various tenants, sub-providers, standards, and distributors.

This type of support is required to manage the SOA system based on mutual trust and agility, and by adopting dynamism within it. The audience may be open, which makes it really difficult to establish the relationship between the provider and the consumer.

The virtual system layer has secure access to the data store. This run-time system differs from classic run-time systems as it operates on VM images, rather than on individual applications. This run-time system provides security services such as anti-virus, introspection, and externalized security services around virtual images. While the foundations of secure virtualized run-time pre-date SOA security and are built on decades of experience with mainframe architectures, the development of secure virtualized run-time is still very much in flux. Cloud vendors continuously invest in research and development of stronger isolation at all levels of the network, server, hypervisor, process, and storage infrastructure to support massive multi-tenancy.

Cloud orchestration and provisioning engine–integrated service management is offered with network, servers, storage, services, and financing as an integrated offering for client test platforms. It

1. Delivers consistent and rapid services from a preloaded system.
2. Helps to improve the value of the business system by effective freedom of choice and faster services.
3. Reduces capital expenses and optimally utilizes the resources.
4. Based on automation and standardized platform, minimizes the chance of human error.
5. Has open architecture–based workload management.
6. Is a complete platform with infrastructure, service management, middleware and distributed system.
7. Is scalable and modular.
8. Offers virtualization for compute and storage.
9. Offers self-service–based delivery.
10. Works as 'lights-out' or 'without human intervention' operations.

Cloud orchestration and provisioning engine is offered as a service engagement which can build a solution to the client's needs, including creation of custom virtual images for dispensing. Summary points are given below:

1. Reduction in configuration and installation time.
2. Creation of new environments in minutes.
3. **Reduction in risk by codifying infrastructure:**
   - Freeze-dry best practices for repeated, consistent deployments.
   - Life cycle–based security.
4. **Simplify maintenance and management:**
   - Flexibly manage and update the components of your patterns.
   - Ensure consistency in versions across development, testing, and production.
5. Spend less time in administrating and more time in developing new solutions.

4.6 Computing on Demand

On-demand computing (CoD) is the need of the hour. It is very essential even in the supercomputing environment. On-demand computing can be implemented using various virtualization techniques. The cloud gives an option to leverage the computing infrastructure without actually buying the hardware. This helps to transfer the workload, if the resources are not able to support it; and at other times, others can utilize the resources that are lying idle. In this way, it is possible to use the resources in the most efficient manner. There may be many spikes in the utilization, but cloud experts can make it smoother.

The uniquely rich set of features offered by on-demand computing enables the service seeker to deploy a true utility. The platform allows users to:

1. Align cost with utilization so that users can scale costs down as well as up. This allows a workload to start with minimal upfront costs and scale the cost as the demand grows,

without paying a penalty to increase capacity. Additionally, users can benefit from not incurring the disruption to move to a larger machine.

2. Increase end-users availability significantly. As the workload can be moved dynamically, it is possible to move the workload from one server to another without any interruption, so the remedial work can be carried out if server downtime is required.
3. Balance workload dynamically across multiple servers without taking applications offline. Using workload mobility features, customers can align their costs by ensuring that the workload is deployed in such a way so as to optimize the system's resources.
4. React to short-term resource requirements almost instantly. If a workload has to be deployed at a short notice, a VM can be created on the server and resources can be allocated instantaneously using the dynamic capacity model.
5. Reduce the physical footprint in the datacenter. Consolidation of the workload on to a smaller number of servers will improve space, power, and cooling metrics.
6. Confidently increase system utilization to over 75%, without the fear of degrading performance for end-users.
7. Develop a simple charging model that reflects usage for end-users as the service delivery culture continues to mature.
8. Double the workload delivered in the power and cooling envelope.

4.6.1 Pre-Provisioning

For the on-demand computing requirement, pre-provisioning is a viable option as it helps the organization in meeting dynamic datacenter requirements. Organizations would like to reduce the time they take to commission servers when new workload is to be deployed. This approach is ideal when

1. The sizing and capacity planning is fully understood.
2. The workload is fairly constant, ensuring good utilization levels are being achieved.
3. There are business reasons that require physical separation of the workload.
4. The workload can be scaled horizontally.

4.6.2 On-Demand CPU/Memory/VM Resources

In the dynamic environment, it is important to track the requirements of CPU, memory, and VMs. It is based on the common pool concept, where resources are allocated and de-allocated as the requirement is over. This approach is ideal when

1. Workloads are trending upward so that investment can be aligned with utilization.
2. Peaks in workload are long term.
3. The workload scales vertically.
4. There is a chance to 'buy out' dynamic capacity, as it proves advantageous then.

4.6.3 Dynamic Capacity

Dynamic capacity is based on utility where the additional processing power for a short period of time can be shared from the resource pool. The service is measured via a service accounting tool based on the utilization and finally the billing is done on the basis of the usage. This approach is ideal when

1. The workload is very variable and multiple workloads can be hosted on to a single machine, thus leveling out the utilization.
2. The workload has short periods where system utilization increases massively, but for the majority of the time, it is not resource intensive.
3. Workloads can share a physical platform.
4. The workload is designed to scale vertically only.
5. Users want to dynamically balance workloads across servers.
6. Users want to continue to run very small workloads without incurring the overheads associated with running a physical server to support it.

Benefits

1. Partition mobility, significantly reduced power/cooling footprint, donation of unused processor cycles of VMs with dedicated processors to uncapped partitions, and, at the same time, guaranteed performance of these VMs.
2. Very short deployment time (time-to-market optimized).
3. Lowest possible cost for the deployment of small workloads.
4. Less management effort, for example, when using VMs.
5. Most granular charging scheme, for example, pay for the CPU and memory cycles when actually used.
6. Complete decommissioning of partitions, with resources being available for other purposes.
7. Flexible workload management where workloads can compensate for each other, thus reducing overall utilization.
8. Ideal for environments with identical systems management, utilities for development and testing.

Limitations

1. Dynamic capacity shows short peaks, must not exceed certain limits, and needs to be monitored (via Web interface) to ensure that the best value is obtained.
2. Utility CoD provides processor resources only to the uncapped partitions.

However, one of the most important advantages of the dynamic capacity model is the flexibility, that is, to allow the switching of CPU capacity on and off as needed, which can reduce costs significantly. This is not reflected in the calculation as it requires input from application owners.

4.6.4 Cloud Platform Characteristics Based on CoD

This section discusses cloud platform characteristics on the basis of low-end, on-demand, and dynamic-capacity–based servers.

Low-End Servers

1. Physical segregation of servers.
2. High administration cost due to the management of more physical servers.
3. Limited and complex scalability – maximum eight processors per server, slower turn-around time for server deployment.

4. Longer lead time for server deployment from ordering of servers to setting up of infrastructure.
5. Non-ideal for short product life cycle application due to fixed-cost expenditure for the hardware.
6. Wastage of hardware resources for applications that react to a volatile market.
7. Inability to share resources between applications.
8. Wastage of unused processing cycles if the application does not fully utilize the resources.
9. No hardware/application interdependency forcing downtime on application owners.
10. No capacity on demand capability. Downtime is required for adding new hardware.
11. Low price per CPU cycle purchased, but higher cost per CPU cycle actually used.

On-Demand Platform

1. Physical or logical segregation of servers or partition implementation.
2. Lower administration cost due to less physical server management.
3. Possibility to lead to quick turnaround time for new application deployment or increase the capacity according to business requirements.
4. Enhanced time to market for new product launch, with immediate availability of CPU/memory capacity.
5. Non-ideal for short product life cycle application due to fixed-cost expenditure for the hardware.
6. Wastage of hardware resources for applications which react to a volatile market.
7. Ability to share I/O, CPU, and memory resources between applications.
8. Ability to take advantage of unused CPU/memory if dynamic VM reallocation or share pool methodology is implemented.
9. For provisioning of a platform of independent hardware and application forcing downtime on application owners, careful capacity planning and management is required.
10. Capacity on demand capability – no downtime is required if COD CPU/memory is sufficient.
11. Higher price per CPU cycle, but lower cost per CPU cycle actually used.

Dynamic Capacity Platform

1. Choose VM or workload VM implementation for application consolidation.
2. Lower administration cost due to less physical and logical server management.
3. Can cater to quick turnaround time for new application deployment.
4. Enhanced time-to-market for new product launch, with immediate availability of infrastructure and setup.
5. Ability to scale up and down, which is ideal for applications with short product life cycle.
6. Ability to cater to applications which react to a volatile market, that is, scaling-up and -down capacity.
7. Ability to share I/O, CPU, and memory resources between applications.
8. Ability to take advantage of unused processing cycle of other applications.
9. No hardware/application interdependency forcing downtime on application owners as workload can be dynamically moved to facilitate maintenance, etc.

10. Capacity on-demand capability. No downtime is required as the machine is fully configured.
11. Higher price per CPU cycle, but lower cost per CPU cycle actually used. Average price due to the ability to optimize utilization and rapidly deploy workload.

4.7 Cloud Sourcing

Today, we are living in an era of optimizing hardware resources and moving toward larger enterprises day by day; so, cloud computing is becoming the major ingredient of infrastructure deployments. Now you may not just need cloud computing, you also need the entire consulting, implementation, and management solutions.

The new wave that is igniting cloud deployments in the service industry is cloud sourcing – outsourcing an end-to-end solution using cloud methodology through public cloud, infrastructure, and platforms. This will be a more planned approach as it will comprise the whole service cycle of outsourcing business with cloud principles through the help of strategized connected cloud platforms matching the overall enterprise requirements.

This includes the whole cloud implementation, IT business consulting, integration, and configuration of the business. This will give the option of enjoying the benefits of service industry with the benefits of the cloud, thus providing an innovative approach of paying resources over subscription.

Real deployment of cloud sourcing will require a business model with the impact of cloud customer and cloud vendor requirements.

With respect to cloud customers, it is important to note that there is no control on the infrastructure layout of cloud deployments or over the place from where data services are offered by the cloud vendor. It is also known that cloud customers do not have to think about the operational staff for the deployments.

Thus, cloud sourcing will play a vital role in the next generation of cloud implementation. With the availability of new open-source tools, it is like icing on the cake, integrated with partner cloud solutions, platforms, and infrastructure. Also, the new charging models, such as services on both project and subscription basis, will generate a new wave to deploy and adopt cloud sourcing models. This will help to customize applications on cloud infrastructure. This will be primarily offered as a public cloud, and all these offerings will be available as managed services. These services will be prototype-based, that is, developed internally on the product and working applications. Therefore, they will provide a good opportunity to use intellectual property for developing different business vertical solutions easily.

4.8 Summary

In this chapter, we have pointed out the main features of cloud orchestration and provisioning engine, BPM clouds, cloud sourcing, and requirements of service management. The next chapter will discuss different types of cloud offerings.

CHAPTER

5

Cloud Offerings

CONTENTS

5.1 Introduction

The growth of information is at an exponential stage. It is growing day-by-day and is being generated by millions and millions of people with billions of smart devices, M2M, sensor networks, machines, and instruments. Today, there is a massive growth in unstructured data where the images, music, scans, and medical data are flowing more than the speed of imagination.

Until now, organizations could not fully or quickly synthesize and interpret all the information out there – they had to make decisions largely on the basis of instinct. But now, there are mechanisms that can capture, organize, and process the entire data scattered throughout an organization, and turn it into actual intelligence. These mechanisms enable organizations to make better business decisions.

5.2 Information Storage, Retrieval, Archive, and Protection

There are various stages of an information management cycle. The information gets processed, managed, migrated, protected, retrieved, staged, and archived for business data. Organizations manage the data on the basis of characteristics of the data such as age, usage, compliance, policies, regulations, protection, disaster, and availability. It is done by the established practice of Information Lifecycle Management (ILM). ILM becomes even more important for cloud deployments as the process requires sharing data services between the cloud vendor and the subscribers.

ILM is not a latest data storage, retrieval, and protection solution; piece of hardware; or some software, but rather an approach to assess and manage the information across the enterprise. ILM is based on how data is used and how readily it must be available to the people who use it. It is focused on managing and storing data according to its value to business operations at any given point in time. It is concerned with the placement of data at the appropriate level of storage with an appropriate retention and retrieval policy. In response to these challenges, organizations are defining the following objectives to support and improve their information management:

1. **Cost reduction:**
   - Controlling demand for storage.
   - Reducing hardware/software costs.
   - Reducing storage personnel costs.
2. **Better system performance and personnel productivity (i.e., improved efficiency):**
   - Doing the 'right' storage activities.
   - Improvement in people, community, processes, and technologies to deliver storage services.
   - Defining and enforcing policies to manage the lifecycle of data.
3. **Increased effectiveness:** Defining and implementing an appropriate storage strategies to address current and future business requirements.

They are also coming up with new ways to generate, enhance, and sustain higher savings. These include:

1. **Activities for gaining initial savings:**
   - Reduce the amount of used storage as a result of initial clean-up.
   - Validate storage area network (SAN) requirements and reclaim used switches and switch ports.
   - Validate data replication requirements in order to reclaim used storage space and offset future growth requirements.
   - Develop and document information classification.
   - Develop and document classes of service.
   - Design and implement the tiered storage architecture.
   - Migrate existing information to lower-cost storage using a tiered storage architecture.
2. **Activities for maximizing savings:**
   - Reconfigure the current storage environment effectively to improve the available raw utilization.
   - Reclaim available storage that has been over allocated.
   - Enhance the information classification, classes of service, and tiered storage architecture.
3. **Activities for sustaining savings:**
   - Develop a storage model based on policies.
   - Implement changes to existing storage management processes, such as capacity planning, and provisioning to effectively improve capacity utilization on an ongoing basis.

While designing a target storage environment, the estimated financial impact is calculated on the basis of the following key cost components:

1. **Operating cost categories:**
   - ***Personnel:*** Storage support and contractors.
   - ***Facilities:*** Current floor space consumed by the storage. Telecommunication charges attributed to storage and tape vaulting services.
   - ***Storage hardware maintenance:*** Existing maintenance and incremental maintenance resulting from growth.
   - ***Storage software maintenance:*** Existing software maintenance and incremental requirements resulting due to innovation and development.
   - ***Outages:*** Cost avoidance associated with the reduction in unplanned outages.
2. **Investment cost categories:**
   - ***New hardware required:*** Typically includes disk, tape, and array cost but not the incremental cost of adding SAN fabric. Investment is either upfront or over a period of time if the client leases equipment.
   - ***New software required:*** New storage software required to support the target environment.
   - ***Hardware refresh:*** Investment required to refresh the existing hardware is often considered in the base case.

- *Transition services:* Incremental cost required to transform the current environment to the future environment. Not typically estimated until the scope of the third-party implementation services has been defined.

When more than 90% of the data stored on hard disks is not actively accessed by the users or applications, it is good to go for more intelligent management and migration to a less expensive storage. But the savings can go significantly beyond disk acquisition costs and annual hardware maintenance costs. Some points in information management are

1. **Data:** Discrete element, reasoning, discussion, or calculation of content created through the interactions between applications or between computing devices.
2. **Information:** Organized and structured collection of data.
3. **Information lifecycle management:** It is a combination of policies, processes, tools, and management practices to align the value of the information with the infrastructure needs, right from the time when the information is created till its disposition.
4. **Information taxonomy:** Data described in the context of business process requirements and lifecycle characteristics.
5. **Information classes:** Groups of information taxonomies with associated business value that provide the basis for storage management and service delivery.
6. **Value-driven data placement:** An event correlation framework that 'senses' the value of data changes and based on business policies 'responds' by moving data to the appropriate storage tier.
7. **Storage process:** A documented set of storage-related tasks and activities required to support a storage infrastructure.
8. **Storage service:** Capabilities provided to a customer base that is designed to meet their business requirements, wants, and needs, and enabled by a storage infrastructure.
9. **Enterprise class of service (COS):** A common set of storage services that are delivered to meet a corresponding set of storage requirements based upon key information management characteristics, and the features, functions, capabilities, processes, and governance required to deliver the required enterprise storage services.
10. **Storage tier:** A subset as a set of storage devices that are identified to store and/or maintain information for a predefined period of time based on key information management characteristics, such as performance, configuration, residency, retention, and value.
11. **Tiered storage infrastructure:** An organized collection of storage tiers reflecting the flow of all the information managed in the enterprise storage architecture.
12. **Utility-based service delivery:** The 'just-in-time' delivery of standardized storage processes, management, and infrastructure as a measurable service on a 'pay-as-you-go' basis.

5.3 Cloud Analytics

Cloud analytics is a new offering in the era of cloud computing. Cloud analytics will help in the consulting domain and will ensure better results. It provides users with a better forecasting technique to analyze and optimize the service lines, and provide a higher level of accuracy. Cloud analytics can help the users apply analytics principles and best practices to analyze different business consequences and achieve newer levels of optimization (Fig. 5.1).

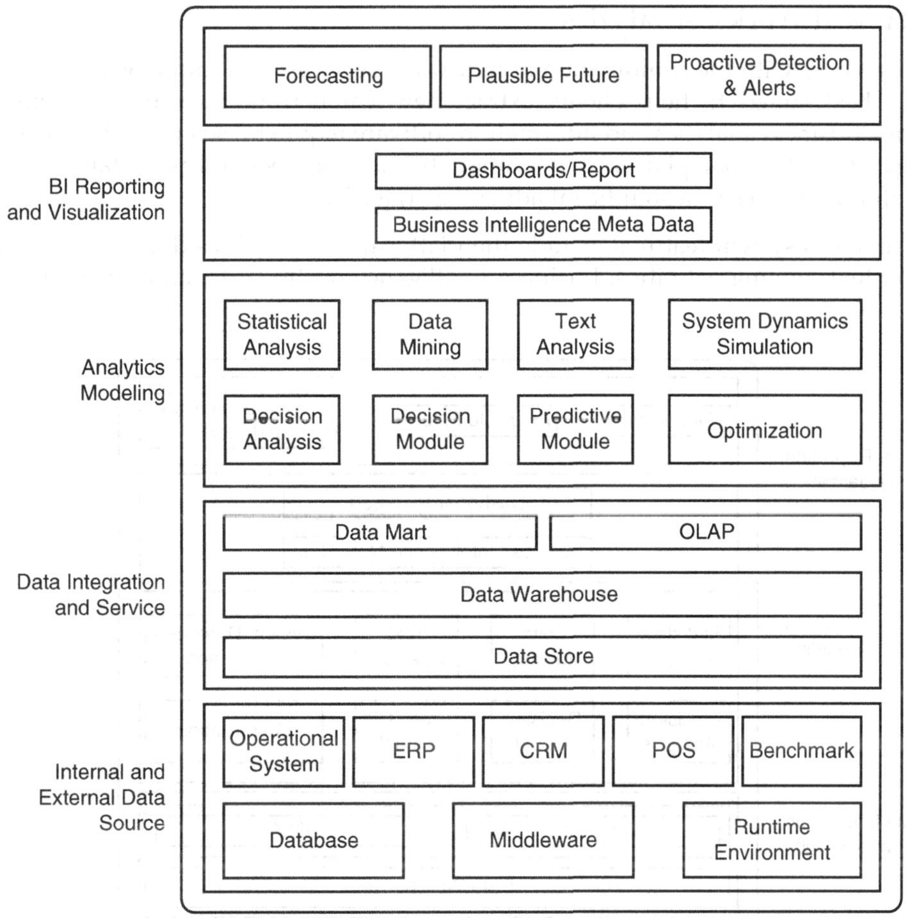

FIGURE 5.1 Cloud analytics.

It can combine complex analytics with the newer software platforms and will lead towards the predictable business situation out of every business insight.

5.3.1 Cloud Business Analytics Competencies

The practice of cloud analytics requires multiple service lines to strategize how client can achieve the goals in faster manner coupled with less risk. The aligned competency features business intelligence and performance management that help increase performance by providing accurate and on-time data reporting. The next is competency comprises of analytics and optimization that provide different types of modelling techniques, deep computing and simulation techniques to check for different types of 'what if' analysis to increase performance. Another competency is enterprise information management that helps in applying different architecture related to data extraction, archival, retrieval, movement, and integration. Content management system is another competency that is required for cloud analytics and includes different service architecture, technology architecture, and processes related to capturing, storing, preserving, delivering, and managing the data. It also helps to provide access in the global environment and makes it easy to share data with stakeholders across the globe.

5.3.2 How it Works: Analytics

Analytics works with the combination of hardware, services, and middleware. This expertise makes it best suited to help clients extract new value from their business information. Delivering business analytics and information software requires a seamless flow of all forms of data regardless of format, platform, or location. Its focus on open industry standards is the key to this effort and gives us a significant advantage (Fig. 5.2).

The analytics system features include the platform that provides data reporting, analytics based on text, mining activities, business intelligence dashboards, and perceptive analytics

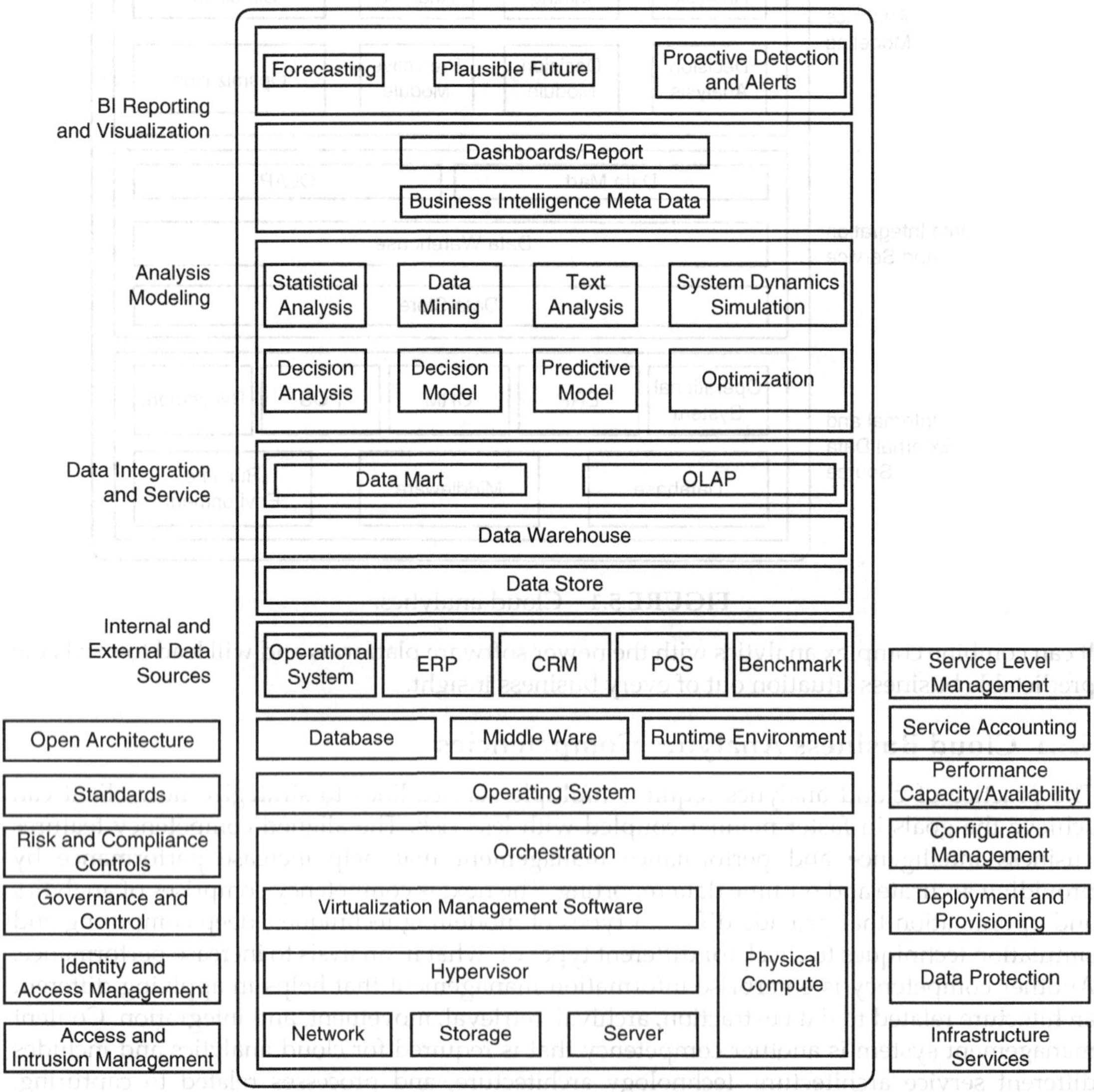

FIGURE 5.2 Cloud analytics business outcomes.

techniques. This also takes care of the storage optimization and different high-performance data-warehouse management techniques. It also involves the umbrella activity of different installation services and a highly reliable system platform.

Analytics Business Outcomes

Analytics systems help to get the right information as and when required, identify how to get it, and point out the right sources to get it. Therefore, analytics also helps in designing the policies faster as decisions are based on the information available in the organization and decision-makers work with the exploration services available within the organization. This system also helps in gauging the business results by measuring the different metrics generated with the help of analytics. Analytics give options through which the organization can increase profitability, reduce cycle time, and reduce defects.

5.4 Testing under Cloud

Private cloud deployments need virtualized servers that can be used for testing the resources for the cloud. This ensures more secure and scalable solutions where consumers can access the IT resources in the test environment. Therefore, testing under the cloud environment gives a very good insight by decreasing the manual intervention and reducing the processes that are involved in typical testing environment. By enabling access to resources as and when required, the cloud reduces the investment on capital, as well as enables the business to handle the ups and downs of the testing requirements. With this feature, organizations can reduce the test cycles, minimize IT costs, reduce defects, rationalize the testing environment, and hence, improve the service quality. This provides a good return on investment (ROI) on moving the typical testing environment to the cloud. This also gives the flexibility to play with the surrogate of the real system without the actual risk.

5.4.1 Benefits

1. Cut capital and operational costs, without affecting the mission critical production applications.
2. Offer new and innovative services to clients, present an opportunity to speed up the cycles of innovation, and improve solution quality.
3. Facilitate a testing environment based on the request, and provide a request-based service for storage, network, and OS.

5.4.2 Value Proposition

Business test cloud delivers an integrated, flexible, and extensible approach to test resource services and management with rapid time to value. This is an end-to-end set of services to strategize, design, and build request-driven delivery of test resources in a cost-effective and efficient manner.

These test tools allow you to orchestrate and build your services and development projects, and permits to catalog and organize all of the various software assets. These can be provisioned by the administrators, development team leads, or project team members who are permitted to do the same.

5.4.3 The Biggest Benefiters

The biggest problem for the finance heads are to reduce the operational and capital expenses of the development and testing environment. Testing under the cloud environment comes as a boon to implement this in an organization. So testing under the cloud not only helps in reducing the financial burden on the company, but also reduces the cycle time for testing and development environment without buying the infrastructure. The cloud environment provides test tools to synchronize and build the services for the project, and helps to arrange the project resources, assets and various versions of deliverables. Also, permission can be set on the basis of the roles in the organization to provide access to the assets.

So why is testing under the cloud a great on-ramp to cloud computing for organizations that want to embrace cloud computing and are trying to figure out where to start? Well, the test and development environment is rarely optimized and is usually like a low hanging fruit in terms of getting ROI and benefit out of cloud computing. These are environments that have a high degree of dynamic change. Hence, the environment is tested and developed after having gone through a lot of build-up and teardown as it moves from project to project. Typically, 30 to 50% of all servers in an IT environment are dedicated to test and development, which is a significant amount. A number of these servers are positioned at very low levels of utilization, and in fact, sit idle for a period during the project life cycle. So, a better utilization of those systems can be a huge benefit for the organization.

Many defects are introduced into test and development environments because of the fact that there is a high degree of manual configuration that typically goes on. Often, projects are backlogged because of the limited access to test environments. Thus, if you do a lot of test and development, or even if you buy your products, you still have to integrate those in a test environment before moving them into production. This intends to be an excellent entry point into cloud computing.

It is important to take a holistic look at the problem you are trying to solve. Are you building a development cloud? Are you building a test cloud? What pre-existing service management or enterprise management tools exist, so that you can identify the starburst opportunities that come off business development and test cloud services or at the cloud strategy and planning consulting workshop service? Some of the things to consider include:

1. What are the types of service management integration (SMI) that need to happen?
2. Do they want to integrate with discovery?
3. Does the SMI want to integrate with the service desk?
4. Does it want to create a help ticket whenever a provisioning step occurs?
5. Do these SMIs want to create an asset every time a new virtualized environment is created?
6. Do they want to do usage and accounting chargeback?
7. Does the SMI want a test optimization service?

These and many other possible opportunities exist in the organization, so make sure that this is the part of the discussion regarding the requirements so that it can make its way into the design and implementation piece of the engagement.

Organizations engaged in the development and testing share a common challenge in executing fluid projects within rigid infrastructures. Development projects are initiated to meet specific 'needs' that may include introducing new applications into the market, updating or patching existing software, or developing in-house assets. There is no way to 'schedule' needs; identification and application development can be as much an art as a science with an intrinsic unpredictability that makes resource allocation very difficult within traditional infrastructures.

As needs arise erratically and projects slip within their individual timelines, there are inevitable overlaps and gaps in development resource requirements. Organizations are often faced with frustrating delays as projects wait idle due to the unavailability of the infrastructure. Alternatively, maintaining enough capacity to accommodate peak demand will leave large windows of severe under-utilization. Even the best compromise represents unwelcome cost and inefficiency.

With the ability to deploy virtual environments quickly and automatically, and redirect capacity as per the needs of the projects, cloud computing offers an ideal solution for testing and development. Cloud vendors make the transition even more appealing with solutions that allow your clients to experiment with cloud in what is already, by definition, an experimental environment–a low risk introduction to cloud and a first step toward addressing other IT challenges across the business.

The cloud testing services give the overall business transformation value that helps you to reduce the cost associated with the IT operations by prioritizing your business requirements. A strategic roadmap is required to enjoy the benefits of application virtualization for testing in the cloud environment, and requires different assessments.

The first assessment is to consolidate the server and conduct a comprehensive virtualization assessment. Getting the requirements of a cloud infrastructure is a very difficult task; hence, the first assessment provides an opportunity to study the initial requirements of the cloud environments that help to provision automatically, and gives the reason to adopt the cloud infrastructure, and appreciates the best practices of cloud. The other assessment is to determine what type of software models can be applied to the available infrastructure to win over the constraints and increase the schedules.

Any business that relies on software development for revenue probably has some benefits to gain from reducing its cycle time and improving the quality. This offering, through its automation and change, and configuration management, can reduce errors and speed up the deployment.

Businesses with a dedicated development and testing organization can be benefitted by the reduction in capital and other expenses that are the result of automation and utilization improvements. There are a growing number of organizations that no longer have space or power to expand their datacenter. By using standardization, consolidation, and virtualization, they can maximize the use of their existing assets.

Businesses that are looking to change their business model to be more line-of-business focused may, instead of doing straight allocation, want to do chargeback and have customers pay for only what they use. They may also be able to smoothen out the resources across different departments so that each department does not have to maintain an account of its own peak demand, and smoothen that demand across the peaks and valleys of different departments and different projects.

5.4.4 Cloud Offering Key Themes

Today, the enterprise datacenters are managed by infrastructure specialists and administrators working in the operations team. This team is responsible for the availability, archiving, security, disaster recovery, service management, and ongoing operations. The main objective of this team is risk, release, and change management, and promoting standard infrastructure requirements for the applications. Adoption of virtualization technologies has brought a significant change in enterprise datacenters over the last several years, as it has fundamentally started to change the way IT is delivered and serviced. Enterprise IT operations managers are tasked with serving two main constituencies:

1. **Application teams:** Delivery of production internal and/or external applications according to service-level requirements in a cost-effective manner. Application infrastructures are often deployed in silos and provisioned for peak demand, resulting in capacity capabilities far beyond their normal requirements.
2. **Development teams:** Development departments are usually driven by user needs for frequent delivery of new features. Development teams often want to quickly test new ideas and/or features in a realistic environment. However, there is often a significant delay between requests to IT for new environments and actual delivery (often can be several weeks). Development teams frequently request and then hesitate to return IT environments into the centralized pool due to the fear of losing access to resources needed for their development cycles.

Due to the history of delivering dedicated environments to support both groups, infrastructure resource utilization metrics are typically below targets. The IT infrastructure managers are no longer being pushed solely to reduce cost, but also to improve end-user responsiveness. The operations team wants to become more responsive to business needs and reduce the application provisioning time by some great percentage (e.g., 90%), increase the resource utilization from what are typically very low percentages (e.g., <20%) to an exponentially greater reduction (e.g., 50–60% or higher), and reduce IT operational costs by some percentage (e.g., 25% or more), all this while avoiding vendor lock-in and regaining control of their applications and infrastructure so they can use it in the most efficient manner to meet the needs of the business.

Virtualization has its benefits, and it does modestly improve resource utilization and delivery times within its hypervisor domain, but nearly all datacenters have multiple hypervisors in use as well as many other computing resources that are not virtualized. Operations teams face significant challenges with manual provisioning and management, VM sprawl, and difficulty in scaling when needed.

Key Themes

1. **Infrastructure to applications:** The most commonly used case for private cloud is Infrastructure-as-a-service (IaaS). This can often be as simple as managing VM images to prevent VM sprawl. The vision is to support complex multi-tier application provisioning such that the applications can be fully configured and ready-to-run. In some cases, these applications are then delivered as a Software-as-a-Service (SaaS) model. In between, enterprises create their own Platform-as-a-Service (PaaS) catalog to enforce consistency in development platforms and middleware. Since companies are using this

for their internal use, they do not need to rewrite their internal applications to match an external PaaS custom application programming interface (API) set, that is required if a public PaaS service were to be considered.

2. **Development/testing to production:** In software development, there is a high-level lifecycle for applications. The beginning is development (dev), then testing/QA, staging, followed by production. Enterprises can also differentiate between the types of production applications between internal versus external production (customer facing) in terms of criticality. In development/testing, the orientation is toward many users with simpler requests (e.g., VMs or infrastructure) with a focus on shorter duration resource usage (reservation, quota management, and reclamation are keys to prevent sprawl). Production applications, in contrast, are more concerned about meeting runtime performance service-level agreements (SLAs) with dynamic scaling, and managing more complex, multi-tier applications. The solution should be unique in supporting the full lifecycle in one product offering in the enterprise environment (Fig. 5.3).

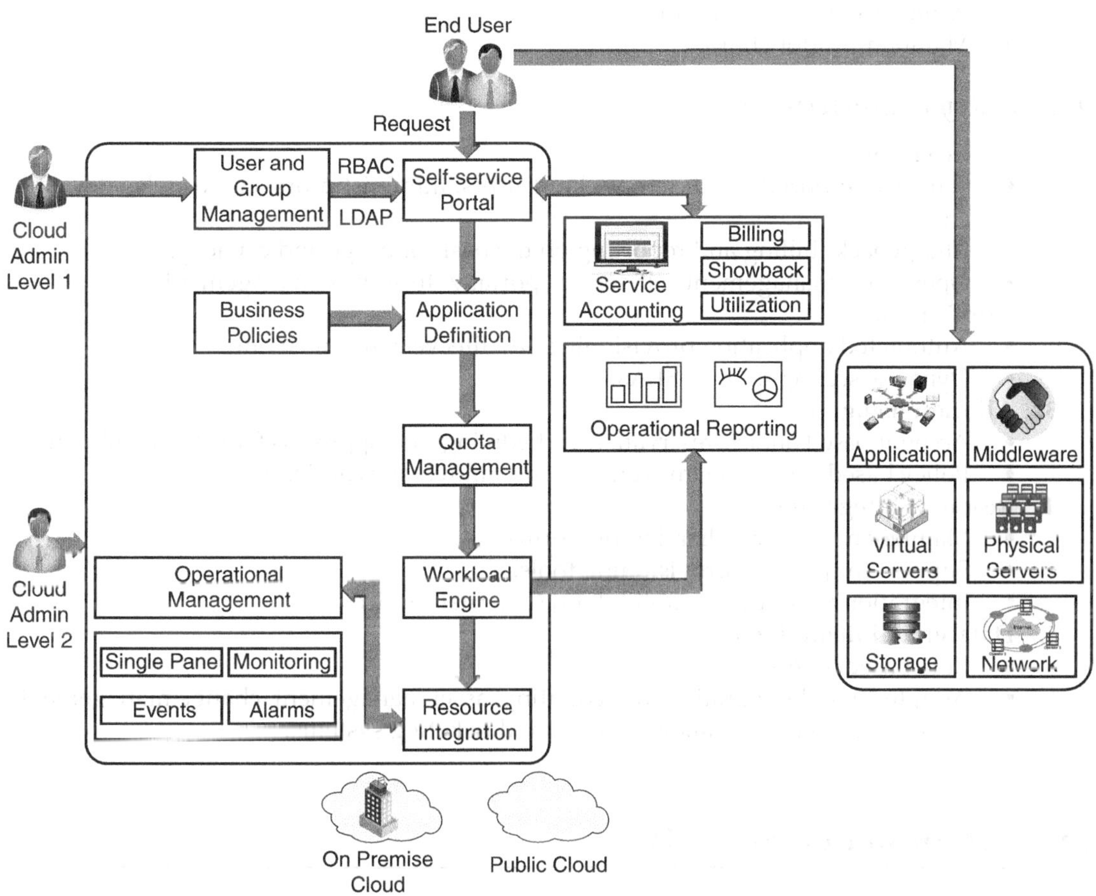

FIGURE 5.3 Cloud orchestration workflow.

3. **Allocation and run-time scaling:** Allocation is the process of instantiating a service catalog item: infrastructure, platform, or application. Run-time scaling is flexing-up or flexing-down of required resource elements to meet the SLA requirements defined by the application owner according to the standard corporate standards and business policies. The solution should be unique in providing both IaaS and runtime scaling/workload management in one product offering for the enterprise environment.

Benefits

1. **Increase agility and innovation**
   - Enable self-service delivery (within minutes).
   - Deliver on SLAs.
   - Simplify process for 'what-if' experimentation.
   - Gain control over public cloud usage.
2. **Decrease costs**
   - Increase utilization.
   - Increase operational efficiency (100 servers per admin).
   - Achieve a greener datacenter.
   - Maintain vendor choice.

Offering Key Characteristics

1. **Service layer**
   - Self-service portal for different cloud users: administrators, cloud delegates, and end-users.
   - Chargeback/billing and reporting on the basis of usage and capacity.
   - Operations management self-service portal with service management.
2. **Applications**
   - Automated application provisioning and lifecycle management.
   - Dynamic scaling to meet SLAs.
3. **Allocation engine**
   - Account-based quotas, reservations, scheduling, and approvals for resource allocation.
   - Policy based migration, movement, and failover of workloads.
4. **Resource integrations**
   - Maintenance of virtualization platforms.
   - Support for popular provisioning tools.
   - Integration for popular public cloud/external services.
5. **Datacenter integrations**
   - Role-based access.
   - Adapter-based integration to accounting, asset management, change management, entitlement, service catalog systems, and ticketing systems.

5.5 Information Security

Information security risks are potential damages to information assets. Successful organizations take a risk-based approach to information security. Nothing can be 100% secure – but by knowing your current state you can take a risk-based approach. You can focus on implementing mitigating controls to address your most significant risks. The remaining minimized risk is acceptable because the likelihood of exploit and the severity of exploit versus the cost of mitigation do not have a positive cost/benefit. Risk can be quantified by the following expected (average) damage:

1. **Value of asset:** What are your valuable information assets?
2. **Vulnerabilities:** What vulnerabilities exist in your systems that can be exploited and lead to the damage of your assets?
3. **Threats:** The level of threats that aim at exploiting vulnerabilities.

Security controls are protection mechanisms to avoid information security risk and have the following features:

1. **Must be effective:** Mitigate the given risk.
2. **Should be adaptive:** Adapt to changing risks.

Three main types of security controls are as follows:

1. **Preventive:** Prevent security incidents (e.g., patching vulnerability).
2. **Detective:** Detect a security incident (e.g., monitoring).
3. **Corrective:** Repair damages (e.g., virus removal).

Successful organizations recognize risks, implement the appropriate mitigating controls, and innovate to grow their business.

5.5.1 Expectation of Privacy

Consumers expect that security should be built into services themselves. Over 50% of potential cloud consumers still avoid online purchases due to the fear of financial information being stolen. Expectation drives regulation, and today, vendors like automakers are expected to take a greater share of responsibility. Enterprises must shore-up their weakest supply chain partners by insuring

1. More evenly distributed security responsibilities.
2. Increased transparency from start to finish.
3. Eased burden of customer-facing unit.

5.5.2 Security Challenges

As the information grows day by day, datacenters and infrastructures are stretching the upper limits of these resources. They are trying to maximize the use of the power, space, and personnel; hence, CAP-EX and OP-EX are also increasing day by day. Cloud computing and virtualization give an opportunity to meet these challenges. On one hand, it gives weapons to deal with these challenges; and on the other, it also gives rise to its own problems such as veracity of the virtual environment, data integrity problems, and even security challenge.

Another area to watch is security around Web applications. An average deployed application have dozens, sometimes hundreds, of defects and a bulk of security threats today target the application layer. Companies must take a proactive action to reduce the instances for their Web applications being exploited – before a hacker even has the opportunity to compromise their business. The most feasible and economic solution for the organizations is to catch vulnerabilities as early as possible and build a secure software from the ground up and not bolt it once it has been deployed.

We are moving toward a future where enterprises will adopt the services from cloud service providers externally. The most important point is that the workloads that will use these services will be rendering the low-risk workloads. This will also account for some of the assurances for the security, and the price of the service will be the key factor to decide whether to adopt the service or not. The workloads that possess medium-to-high risk factors will adopt private and hybrid clouds. This will also cover the workloads that contain proprietary contents and also those that need more security and depth of defense. Once these services mature and settled, the latter ones will also move towards the external cloud to enjoy the benefits of the external cloud, but without compromising the security.

5.5.3 Security Compliance

There is a need of policies and procedures for governance and risk factors with respect to cloud security. These services should include procedures to handle change management and incident management. These services generate reports for multi-tenant environments. Therefore, one has to bank on large log and audit files to do so. Transparency is an important factor as it is very important for public clouds and it is a black box for the service users.

It is also required to conduct third-party-based checks and audits for the agreements that are breached in the process. Also, third-party-based audits can issue non-compliance to the subjected violations. This process maintains visibility in the system.

Another method is to have strong SLAs so that the flexibility can be managed for the process based on the situations that will enable the traditional outsourcing model and service management to enjoy the benefits of the cloud.

5.5.4 Identity-Based Protection

The cloud environment requires extra protection levels as it works with a diverse set of groups. Therefore, it is essential to have proper authentication for getting access to resources for the environment. It also requires regulated monitoring of users, details regarding the logging to the resources, and check-up for the background verifications. One of the important aspects is to maintain the access that matches with the profile of the work and gauges the risk if something goes wrong due to the improper use of resources. There can be different classes of users, such as administrators who require the access based on the work they are doing with the cloud environment.

Maintenance of the identity is required to conduct smooth operation in the cloud deployments and authenticate the real users. This is required for both internal and external purposes for the hosted applications. The biggest hurdle is to secure the confidential data. In order to do this, one has to maintain a secure protocol over the networks and activate the firewalls to ensure the security of the confidential information and the information that is sensitive but not important for the business should be destroyed.

5.5.5 Data Protection@Cloud

Relevant terms that dictate the protection of data are: how it is stored, how it is accessed, what the compliances are, and what audits are required as per the SLAs. It also relates to the regulation of the breach of the data and its separation on the storage infrastructure. This even includes the archived data.

This is handled by the process of encryption and is managed by encryption keys, and the data are protected in the cloud datacenter. Another point that is not taken care of most of the times is the protection of the mobile data. It should be ensured that encryption is done for the mobile data as well. One of the biggest problems in Internet-based cloud is sending a large amount of data that is not possible with the Internet-based environments. Therefore, the data should be encrypted, and both the cloud service provider and subscriber should have the keys to encrypt it.

The movement of data between different locations of the organization depends on the cloud environment, support, SLAs, and business activities. There can be violations of the intellectual property law which should be kept in mind while working with different types of data. It must be ensured that the legal teams should review all the requirements of cloud environments and the methods to control the data that are collocated in a large geographical area.

Other important thing that can be classified is the data type and its associated risks for the protection of data. The risks levels and matrix breaches can be obtained and security mechanisms based on them can be derived. The measures can be different from domain to domain; for example, public services challenges will be different from financial services data.

5.5.6 Application Security@Cloud Deployment

It is incorrect to think that the protection mechanism in a cloud environment works only at the application level. In fact, it is required at the image level as well. Therefore, cloud vendors should have a clear and sound way to tackle the protection mechanism by meeting the demands of the subscriber for issuing licenses for the required period of interval, destroying them after use, and making sure that the sensitive unimportant data is also destroyed at the same time.

For maintaining and supporting the security, it is important for the customer to follow the standards that cloud subscribers demand. All the Web-based requirements should be coded to match the actual requirements, and the published content on the Web should adhere to the policies of the business.

In order to work with the successfully protected virtual environments, everybody in the cloud deployment should adhere to an agreed-upon basic security policy. Cloud vendors and subscribers should have the intrusion-based polices audited and should check the prevention system placed to handle this. This exercise becomes more valuable when we work in a shared environment because different subscribers on the same cloud environment should have the agreement for security and protection policies.

So far, we have talked about the security measures on the basis of software, policies, SLAs and audits; but we should also take care of the security in physical terms as well.

These security measures can include biometric systems and closed circuit television (CCTV) monitoring. These measures can restrict any unauthenticated entry into the system.

5.6 Virtual Desktop Infrastructure

Virtual desktop infrastructure (VDI) provides end-user virtualization solutions. This is designed to help in transforming distributed IT architectures into virtualized, open-standards-based frameworks leveraging centralized IT services. VDI combines hardware, software, and services to connect the clients' authorized users to platform-independent, centrally managed applications, and full desktop images that run as virtual machines on the servers in the datacenter.

The VDI solution introduces a new method of delivering and managing user desktop environments. In the IT industry today, several technology vendors provide components that enable building a VDI. VDI is generically used with reference to a collection of products and infrastructure components used to form a virtual desktop solution. This solution consists of the following:

1. Portal interface.
2. Thin-client.
3. PC with client components such as
   - Browsers with client messaging.
   - Security technologies.
4. IT infrastructure.
5. Varied client devices.

Project-based services provide IT consultants specializing in virtualization technologies, assistance to assess the organization's desktop and application needs, and subsequently develop a VDI solution that best meets these needs.

5.6.1 Architecture Overview

Desktop cloud virtualization services provide several advantages to an enterprise. One of very important advantages is the reduction of cost. By moving the core function of distributed end-user devices and applications to a centralized infrastructure, the lifecycle of the end-user device is extended, and the performance requirements are moved to a centralized infrastructure. The administration of a centralized IT infrastructure is more cost efficient than the administration of a distributed one. The implementation of virtualization with VDI solutions allows businesses to simplify their IT environment, reduce costs and complexity through consolidation of physical resources, and standardization of operating environments.

VDI creates a framework that offers many advantages to the enterprise such as follows:

1. **Cost reduction:** More efficient use of resources can increase utilization.
2. **Flexibility:** Common physical infrastructure can support a variety of end-users. New desktop images can be created dynamically without a hardware-procurement cycle. Multiple types of guest OSs can run on the virtual machines so that the physical

hardware can support a wide range of end-users without any costly integration or reconfiguration of the systems between user accesses.

3. **Security:** The data remain in the datacenter with the access control.
4. **Availability:** Higher availability as VM can be quickly migrated to a different physical server in the event of a hardware failure.
5. **Efficiency:** Service delivery is more efficient when IT processes are optimized for a centralized environment.

5.6.2 Enterprise Level

VDI provides a set of proven integration patterns and methods for implementing a client virtualization. The VDI team works with various tools and products to help the users with an assessment of their environment to develop VDI solution requirements and a solution design. The team then develops and deploys this solution into the client environment on the basis of a common architecture that supports the four VDI solution models (shared service, virtual client, workstation blades, streaming).

VDI solution is shaped by the component selection. The base VDI architecture is designed to integrate with existing client environments and, as the name implies, provide an access method to a highly scalable virtual infrastructure to the front-end clients. The VDI server farm's back-end integrates with existing infrastructure services and legacy applications.

VDI solution is designed to reduce the dependency on distributed PCs and laptops. By placing critical applications and data in a centralized datacenter with access from a variety of client device options, VDI can significantly reduce the cost and complexity of the management, and maintenance of desktop images.

VDI end-user desktops run on virtual machines hosted in a centralized IT infrastructure in the client datacenter. The end-users access their individual desktop image or a pool of desktops through a client access device such as PC client, a thin client, or a Web-based client. The applications run on virtual machines on host servers in the datacenter from resource pools rather than on the local machine.

Additional resources can be easily and quickly added to the IT infrastructure as business requirements arise. The VDI solution provides increased security as data remain in the datacenter. Optional secure encapsulation capabilities can allow network connections to be encrypted.

VDI's virtual client solution integrates into the organization's datacenter to leverage the existing network and infrastructure services. The solution provides access services to the virtual infrastructure hosted in the VDI server farm or datacenter (Fig. 5.4).

The desktop client devices can be new or existing thin client devices, PCs with an access client, a Web browser, or various combinations depending on the client environment. The desktop client devices can vary from organization to organization, and can be provided as a part of the VDI service engagement if required.

The VDI access service or 'connection broker' provides devices and user authorization, portal integration, session management, host monitoring, application streaming, and

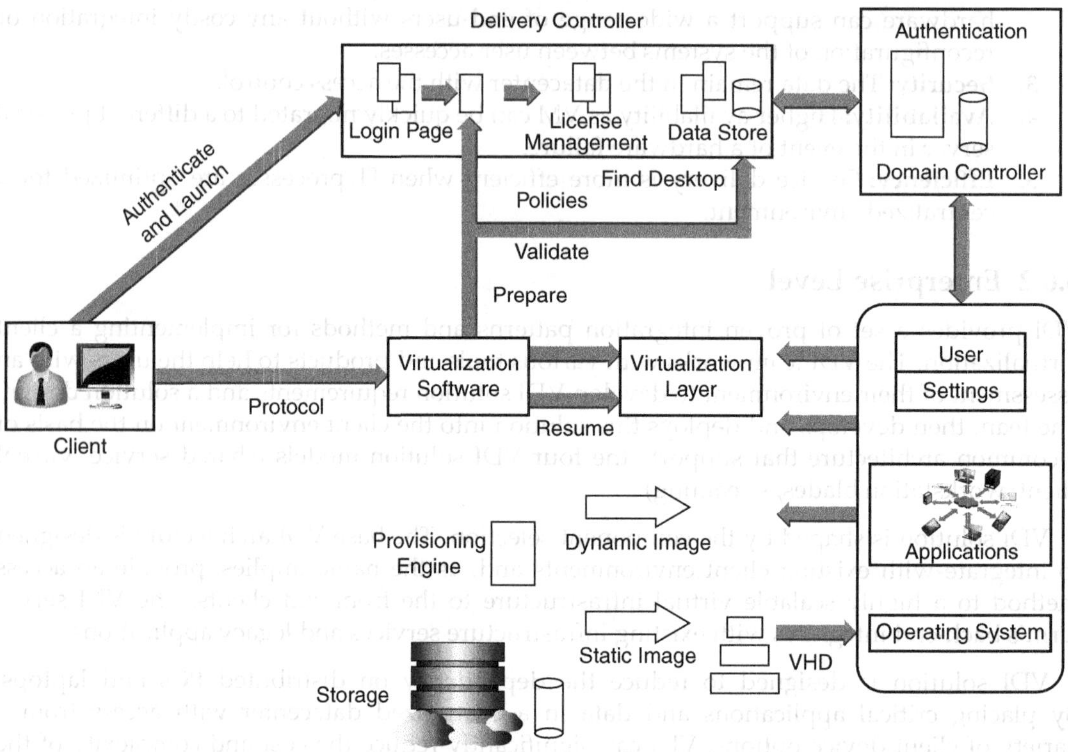

FIGURE 5.4 Virtual desktop infrastructure.

consumption-based metering. This access service also provides load balancing as needed for the front-end security servers, and for the connection servers. The security servers and connection brokers must have high availability as they are the single points of access to the virtual environment.

The VDI server farms, or datacenters, consist of a set of physical hardware platforms that facilitates the virtual environment to host shared OS, virtual machines, and dedicated desktop clients.

The infrastructure services include existing services such as activity directory, file, print, management, network, authentication services, and storage. This solution integrates with these existing services rather than introducing redundant features not required by the business. The service will not bundle in the components that are already available in the business's environment. If additional infrastructure services are required, they can be added to the project-based service for an additional charge. The cloud service project team integrates the VDI solution with the existing infrastructure services and desktop client devices as part of the project-based service engagement. Additional offerings may be combined with the cloud service product to meet the business requirements as needed.

The virtual desktop images can be configured to access the existing infrastructure services in the client datacenter as needed. The following sections briefly discuss the components of the VDI at a higher level.

5.6.3 Client Access

The users use their remote desktop client device to connect to their virtual desktop. This service is provided mostly by all virtual desktop vendors and is supported by a set of products that connect remote clients to the centralized virtual desktops. End users can use existing PC-running OSs where the user initiates a remote session to a VDI resource using a remote desktop client application or a Web browser. With some third-party products, one can have local desktop icons configured to access published applications or published desktops.

5.6.4 Desktop Virtualization Services

VDI can be viewed as a central-server-based resource pool with components connecting end users to applications, networking, and storage resources. VDI uses vendors to centrally host and deliver a cost-efficient desktop environment from the datacenter, and uses the management server to provide the virtual desktop management.

Virtualized clients and desktop management proactively manage diverse desktop environments and VDI server-based client technology. The end user retains the features and flexibility of the traditional desktop.

Management server authenticates users, determines the pool they belong to, and using predetermined policies provisions a desktop for those end users, with complete users' specifications and privileges, and finally deploys it. These pools can be persistent or non-persistent.

Individual desktop assignment is a static, one-on-one relationship between a user and a specific virtual desktop. This configuration is good for power users where the desktop is specifically configured for a particular user. This configuration can include specific applications, data access, and resource allocations. Individual desktops give users a high degree of customization.

A virtualized IT environment helps in providing security-rich, anywhere-anytime availability and access to applications, information, and resources. VDI is a unique end-user virtualization solution that helps businesses transform their distributed IT architectures.

Desktop cloud project-based service can substantially reduce the total cost of ownership by reducing the effort required for desktop PC deployment and management, software distribution, desk-side support, and help-desk required to support and maintain desktops. Businesses can avoid significant upfront investment and continuing cost for developing and maintaining the necessary skills, knowledge, and experience in systems management and desktop virtualization technologies.

5.6.5 Desktop Management

VDI brings together the desirable features of traditional terminal server while retaining the important features of distributed computing.

5.6.6 Pool Management for Virtual Desktop Infrastructure

The role of a management server is to maintain the authentication of the user, check the pool for the user, he belongs to, the policies he is entitled for, and ultimately provision the desktop for the specific user. These pools can be persistent or non-persistent. The connection server allocates entitled users to a virtual desktop from the non-persistent pool as requested. This allocation is not retained when the user logs off and the virtual desktop is placed back into the non-persistent pool for re-allocation to other entitled users. When the user connects to the non-persistent pool on subsequent occasions, the management connection server connects the user to any virtual desktop in the non-persistent pool. This is typically a many-to-many relationship.

When a group of users is entitled to the persistent pool, every user in the group is entitled to any of the virtual desktops in the pool. The management connection server will allocate users to a virtual desktop as requested. This allocation is retained for subsequent connections.

Maximizing the use of non-persistent pools for all users who do not have a desktop customization requirement is recommended. Typically, the task users could do with a non-persistent desktop.

VDI also offers managed services for businesses that wish to derive benefits of virtual infrastructure access but lack the necessary skills and expertise required for the ongoing management of the virtual infrastructure. Businesses can avoid significant up-front investment and continuing cost for developing and maintaining the necessary skills, knowledge, and experience in systems management and desktop virtualization technologies.

5.7 Storage Cloud

For any type of cloud deployment – private, public, or hybrid cloud – the environments are built using key foundation building blocks such as servers, storage, applications, and infrastructure. Storage and compute resources scale together, and the failure to manage them efficiently results in the failure of cloud services.

Storage management in the cloud can help organizations to address their challenges related to data and storage management in their clouds, for example availability of data at all times, storage resource utilization, application performance, longer restore times, higher storage costs, low productivity of storage personnel, and increased risk of data loss and downtime.

5.7.1 Value Proposition

Data and storage management within a cloud environment is a critical necessity to provide a reliable, on-demand service experience while at the same time reducing the costs and minimizing the risks. Streamlining the data to target applications plays an important role, which means the data has to be made available at all times and the storage should be provisioned rapidly to the applications built into the cloud for delivering efficient services. Often, storage administrators spend over 50% of their time on manual repetitive tasks. They find it difficult to meet stringent rules that are essential for restoring operations quickly after any disruption (database corruption, virus attack, disaster, and hardware failure) in a cloud. Failure to ensure data availability at all times can lead to a significant failure of a cloud service.

Also, the proper placement of data on different tiers of storage within the cloud, if done efficiently, helps to minimize the overall costs of hardware, software, and administration.

Cloud vendors offer technologies – storage, hardware, and software – as well as key storage services to support subscribers in their journey to leveraging cloud computing. They can assist in planning, designing, building, deploying, and even managing and maintaining storage solutions, whether on their premise or someone else's.

Cloud technology is helping organizations to build a smarter business infrastructure with immense flexibility and scalability – one that could result in improving service levels while reducing capital and operational costs. Today, many organizations in various industries including media and banking, which deal with large amounts of data, are increasingly adopting the cloud technology to address their needs of delivering faster services, protecting data in real time, seamless communication between employees, partners, and suppliers, for business continuity, and, of course, to become more energy efficient – to be a greener organization.

5.7.2 Challenges

Cloud services majorly focus on keeping the data and applications they are managing available at all times, and even more essential is to develop the ability to quickly restore the operations following any type of data disaster. Storage management is an important function to ensure that the data are available, capacity is provisioned rapidly, and storage resources are utilized effectively. Cloud administrators often find it difficult to meet all the following challenges they face concerning storage and data management:

1. Data availability and application performance.
2. High capital and operating costs, less ROI.
3. Utilization of storage resources.
4. Lack of automation – low productivity of storage personnel with specialists doing mundane tasks.

For customers, the drivers for adopting cloud technologies have been cited as follows:

1. Paying for only what they use.
2. Reduced costs.
3. Monthly payments instead of all up front
4. Having a standardized system
5. Always having the latest software version, since nothing is installed locally

5.7.3 Business Drivers

1. Need for standardization and automation of storage services.
2. Need to meet service levels consistently – provisioning on-demand computing capacity and storage capacity.
3. Need for simplified management of storage infrastructure – quick provisioning and redeployment of resources, built-in data reduction capabilities.
4. Data security and compliance issues.
5. Need to lower costs – lack of upfront capital, lower utilization of hardware resources
6. Recovery point objectives (RPOs), recovery time objectives (RTOs).

5.7.4 Benefits

1. Improved service levels by ensuring data availability and application performance and by quick provisioning through automation
2. Reduced capital and operational expenses by leveraging standardization and automation
3. Optimized utilization of storage resources and built-in data reduction capabilities to manage more storage with less hardware
4. Reduced hardware, software, and administration costs with policy-based data storage management.
5. Managed risk and streamline compliance through real-time data protection.

5.7.5 Product/Solutions Overview

Storage management software and services solutions for the cloud help in ensuring that business and IT are fully aligned and supported by integrated service management. They help in delivering a workload-optimized approach and offer a choice of implementation options for superior service delivery with agility and speed.

Cloud vendors offer second-generation storage management technology for cloud environments, delivering faster ROI. Cloud storage services include worldwide capability and capacity to provide integrated cloud service offerings to meet your storage management needs.

Cloud vendors reduce the complexity of managing cloud environments by offering a complete portfolio of automated solutions for managing data and storage infrastructure, enabling better efficiency for business resiliency, reducing costs, and improving security, while increasing visibility, control, and automation of the cloud storage infrastructure. There is a need of the broadest, most scalable, and reliable set of storage solutions available to keep the cloud services functional. These storage solutions should have the complete portfolio for protecting, managing, and virtualizing the environment.

5.7.6 Product/Solution Description

Cloud vendors should offer a complete portfolio of software solutions and services for the storage management in the cloud, designed to help in streamlining the storage resources in order to support cloud services, protection, and management of data, being able to virtualize the entire storage infrastructure, and offer it as a single resource to the cloud services bundle.

Cloud-based deployment and service models use new and scalable delivery models to offer cost-effective solutions. Data availability and application performance are critical factors to migrate the applications in the cloud. Additionally, a cloud environment cannot afford longer downtime as after any disruption, it is critical to restore operations quickly. Whether it is an organization managing its own private compute/storage cloud environments or a managed services provider offering cloud-based services (private or public), the key concern is how well the existing resources are optimized in their infrastructure, to improve end-user experience – whether they are able to provide flexibility, speed, reliability, and efficiency. Data and storage management play a critical role in improving on-demand service experience and reducing costs and risks in the cloud.

Often, the absence of sophisticated storage management systems in a cloud results in the lack of visibility into the storage utilization and provisioning, costs, and associated risks. Cloud administrators face difficulty in understanding how much capacity is available, where it is, which applications are accessing it, how secure they are, and whether they are able to meet stringent RTOs. Gaps that may exist between the unpredictable demand for data availability and the ability of the business to support the same in an efficient way, results in unmet service levels, additional downtime, new hardware and operational costs, and lower customer satisfaction.

5.8 Summary

Today, as we are becoming interconnected, instrumented, and intelligent – the world is becoming smaller – more data is being generated within the operations of all organizations, and they are struggling to manage the complexity in their storage environments. The costs of backup and recovery, archiving, expiration, and storage resource management are exploding. It is not just about increasing the capacity but managing the data efficiently, reducing the data, ensuring adequate protection of the data, and quick restoration of the data for better business performance. We need better implementation of VDI, test cloud environments, and analytics to handle cloud offerings.

CHAPTER

6 Cloud Management

CONTENTS

6.1 Introduction

Companies and their IT vendors are increasingly focusing on virtualization-based cloud services and consolidation solutions, and the potential benefits they provide businesses. But this growing popularity sometimes obscures the fact that managing cloud virtualized infrastructures can present organizations significant challenges in areas related to implementation and service management. In particular, it is often difficult for businesses to determine how and for what purposes the employees and groups are utilizing virtualized IT assets.

What is required is a cloud solution that aims to help overcome these problems by providing insight into the relationships between virtualized and physical IT assets – who is utilizing shared resources, and what and how much they are using. Such information is vital in a number of ways. For organizations such as IT outsourcers, a well-suited solution will serve as an accurate measurement tool underlying billing processes and service-level agreement (SLA) compliance.

Innovative cloud virtualization technologies from cloud vendors extend that service accounting concept far beyond simple partitioning on a single server to a systems virtualization platform. This platform includes server and storage technologies and common tools to deliver workload and platform management across your IT environment.

Over the past decade, the number of department servers and department storage has proliferated, creating a challenge for IT management. The top driver for consolidation is the reduced cost, followed by improved system performance, ease of management, high availability (HA), security, and disaster recovery (DR). In addition to consolidation, many enterprises are interested in managing the growth of their IT resources to maximize return on investment (ROI). To do this effectively, they require usage information of all resources on the network (storage, server, network, and application) to build a complete picture. This information can then be used by the IT staff for optimizing their use of existing resources, improving their service level (through better performance and availability), and proactively managing their capacity planning activities.

On the other hand, users are facing some uncertainties to implement such solutions. Lack of skills to realize such virtualization concepts, or the inability to qualify the value, are the main inhibitors for effective implementation. The biggest problem for these services is to know the delivery mechanism – how it is used and how it is charged on the basis of usage. Automated processes for cost reallocation and analysis of security and misuse would result in a high level of cost savings.

IT services are viewed as critical to a business. Increase in the number of users, demand for new technologies, and complexities of client–server systems frequently cause IT service costs to grow faster than others. It is, therefore, common that enterprises are mostly not able to give business justification for service improvement investments which are then viewed as an expensive exercise.

The CPU, data store, and bandwidth usage based costing can be done by IT accounting. But it is not recommended to use it directly to charge the end-users as it loses its benefits. It is good for all to reduce the cost of the overall service rather than working on the IT accounting of the computer resources.

Current leading practice uses IT accounting to aid investment and renewal decisions, and to identify inefficiencies or poor value. A fixed amount is charged for a set capacity determined by the level of service detailed in the SLAs.

To provide cloud business with a clear understanding of the value they receive from IT, the cost model must be:

1. **Equitable:** The chargeback approach must allocate costs proportional to each unit's true consumption of IT services.
2. **Controllable:** Business units should have a degree of control over, and input into, IT spending decisions.
3. **Repeatable and predictable:** Charges for a given service should be consistent over a six- to twelve-month period enabling a business unit to forecast its IT costs over the period.
4. **Simple:** The chargeback algorithm should be easy to understand, implement, and administer to minimize confusion and overhead expenses.
5. **Comprehensive:** All IT costs must be associated with a service. There should be no 'tax' or overhead bucket to account for infrastructure.

A cost model works best when customers understand the pricing structures and their limitations, have some control or influence over the consumption of IT and thus, their cost for IT, and believe that the value is reasonable and equitable.

6.1.1 Service-Based Model

Recently, there has been a strong push for IT to invoice business units for services described in business terms instead of IT terms. This service-based approach has been driven in part by cost transparency and cost reduction requirements.

The success of a service-based model depends largely on business managers and IT managers working together to define the Service Portfolio, which includes the services the IT organization provides and the cost of these services to the business units. Making IT services understandable to business managers gives them a clear window into the infrastructure and application reinvestment. A business director may be persuaded to fund or support infrastructure changes that will drop or increase the consumption or price of services in order to meet business needs in a better fashion.

6.2 Resiliency

Resiliency is the capacity to rapidly adapt and respond to risks as well as opportunities. This maintains continuous business operations that support growth and operate in potentially adverse conditions. The reach and range step of the assessment process examines business-driven, data-driven, and event-driven risks. The objective here is to explore the risk situation for the company, processes, people, or whatever that affects the business of that organization. This can be divided further down after thorough investigation because risk in one section will not be same as risk in another section.

So we will be looking across different parts of the company. We like to focus on one specific area first – maybe a specific business process. By doing so, we usually arrive at the 80/20 rule which says that about 80% of issues are going to be common across all business processes, all business entities, and all buildings.

When you use the resilience framework to look at different parts of the company, you are trying to understand whether you have a risk that you can accept, or whether you have a risk that you want to avoid and mitigate. In other words, you may choose to do nothing about a risk, or you may improve your infrastructure to help ensure that you can handle events if they occur.

You may also decide that the risk is one that you would prefer to transfer to somebody else, such as business continuity and resiliency services. A lot of organizations feel more comfortable transferring risks associated with business continuity to cloud vendors rather than handling risks themselves, as recovery centers are designed to be robust and ensure resilience in the face of a disruption. Additionally, transferring the risk can be accomplished through managed security or resiliency services. This allows you to concentrate on strategic initiatives and leaves the day-to-day management and monitoring of your availability and security configurations to staff locations. So, what can we recommend to create a framework of resiliency? The resiliency blueprint includes different layers – facilities, technology, applications and data processes (both IT and business), organization, and finally, strategy and vision.

The framework enables us to examine the business, understand what areas of vulnerability you might have come across – business-driven, data-driven, and event-driven risks – and quickly pinpoint areas of concern and help you understand what actions you can take to reduce the risks associated with those areas.

6.2.1 Resiliency Capabilities

The strategy combines multiple parts to mitigate risks and improve business resilience in the following manner:

1. From a facilities perspective, you may want to implement power protection.
2. From a security perspective, that is, to protect your applications and data, you may want to implement a biometrics solution. You might want to implement mirroring, remote backup, identity management, e-mail filtering, or e-mail archiving.
3. From a process perspective, you may implement identification and documentation of your most critical business processes. You may split the functions of processes. You may also want to implement specific requirements confirming to government regulations and standards.
4. From an organizational perspective, you may want to take an approach that addresses the geographic diversity and backup of workstation data. You may want to implement a virtual workplace environment.
5. From a strategy and vision perspective, you would want to look at the kind of crisis-management process you should have in place. You may also want to examine how you can clearly articulate your security policies to everybody and how you implement change management.

Resilience tiers can be defined as a common set of infrastructure services that are delivered to meet a corresponding set of business availability expectations. The criteria describing resilience tiers were developed by the lines of business and include characteristics/attributes for business impact (e.g., revenue), risks (e.g., legal), application availability (e.g., 24 × 7), and agility (e.g., multiple physical instances).

6.3 Provisioning

The provisioning process is a service that uses a group of compliant processes called 'Solution Realization'. Environment provisioning roles separate the preparation tasks and assurance tasks from provisioning tasks. Provisioning design decouples provisioning build and integration activities from requirements, design, procurement, and hardware setup. The process formalizes Quality Assurance (QA) testing in preparation for turning over the provisioned product to the customer. Provisioning is a broad-based service that begins with a Request for Service (RfS) to build a fully provisioned environment for the purpose of hosting an application and database. Provisioning can also be invoked when a major modification must be made to the existing environment. Provisioned environments include development, test, QA, production, and DR. Provisioning defines and communicates the information that is required to begin provisioning. The output from provisioning is an environment configured and tested with an appropriate hardware platform, storage, network, operating system, middleware, other system software, backup capability, monitoring capability, and with the application installed per requirement. In this way

1. Provisioned products are servers built with all the software and infrastructure required to support a business application.
2. Standard solutions are defined so that standard workflows can be derived.
3. Design is completed with due diligence before the RfS is accepted, including documentation of all specifications.
4. Server hardware is assembled, cabled, and connected to the network and storage area network (SAN) before work orders are released to the provisioners.

6.3.1 Characteristics

There is an owner who provides technical oversight for the lifecycle of each project lifecycle defined from the initial request for comments (RfCs) through to the delivery to the customer. Specifications are reviewed for completeness and accuracy before the release of work orders to provisioners. Missing and incorrect information is resolved before provisioning begins.

Provisioner roles for each part of the stack perform build, installation, configuration, and interim verification activities (no change). A status of 'Hold' with a reason code indicates when work orders and the RfS itself are stopped, awaiting a response from an external process. The provisioned product is tested, assured for quality, and signed off by the technical owner before being turned over to the customer.

6.3.2 Approach

The environment provisioning process takes an assembly line approach to building a server and integrating its components. To prevent interruption of provisioning tasks due to unforeseen or redundant work, the process defines that upstream activities be completed and signed off before starting the downstream activities. Following are the activities discussed:

1. Planning precedes execution.
2. Validating build specifications precedes building.
3. Packaged software installation procedures, being tried and tested, precede the installation of the package on a server.
4. Having servers racked, stacked, cabled, and connected to storage and network precedes issuing work orders for provisioning the OS and base software image.

Measuring achievement is easier without having to account for stops and starts caused by handoffs. It becomes possible to automate building the stack and integrating more components with provisioning tools.

6.3.3 Benefits

This section discusses the benefits of provisioning.

1. **Ability to measure progress of all the work related to one RfC:** It supports the ability to deliver to service levels.
2. **Continuous improvement activities based on process measurements:** It enables eliminating delays and learning to continuously provision servers rapidly to shorten the time to deliver.
3. **Isolation of the build, install, configure, and customize tasks from requirements, design, and hardware setup activities:** It provides focus for leveraging provisioning automation tools.
4. **Role players performing a finite set of repeatable activities:** It enables the collection of intellectual capital necessary for beginning to automate their activities, and for planning full automation.
5. **An assembly line approach to provisioning:** It facilitates automation of piece parts of the process in an incremental approach to self-service.

Long-Term Goals

1. Achieve operational efficiencies by using a common set of processes and procedures to deliver provisioning services to the enterprise.
2. Achieve target environmental defect rate.
3. Establish and achieve service-level objectives for delivery of provisioned environments.
4. Reduce time to set up development and test environments.
5. Reduce hardware/software spending through optimization of all environments and reuse of assets.
6. Enforce enterprise provisioning standards.

Short-Term Goals

1. Reduce the defect rate for the setup of the development and test environments.
2. Improve and provide consistency in the provisioning of environments for all platforms.
3. Transfer skills and knowledge of new standard processes and procedures to the provisioning teams.

4. Gain stakeholder agreement before deployment of a provisioned product that all requirements have been met.
5. Reduce rework.
6. Improve quality of work experience for process participants.

6.4 Asset Management

Asset management and change management interact frequently. Several of the activities required to provision an environment rely on RfCs in order to get approval to change known configurations of infrastructure and software components. There are different factors that help to develop the asset management strategy:

1. **Software packaging:** Asset management relies on software packaging. The output from software packaging will be used on a daily basis during the installation and configuration of the various software packages requested by the customers. Asset management will only engage software packaging directly when there is an exception. It will pass information so that new or modified packages can be built to enable provisioning.
2. **Incident management (IM):** It is used to track any interruptions or issues to the asset management service. These are most likely to be encountered during the OS or application installation, or during the verification of other provisioned components. IM will also be used as an entry point to Problem Management, which will not be engaged by the Asset Management directly. IM's 'business as usual' escalation of recurring incidents as potential problems will contribute to resolve problems related to asset management.
3. **Pool management:** Pool management works with asset management to make sure that the products requested are available on the requested date and for the specified duration. Pool management serves as the intermediary process between asset management and the infrastructure-on-demand (IOD) process and activities.
4. **Release management (RelM):** It controls the scheduling and testing of additions and updates to environments.
5. **Configuration management:** It helps with its own repository for assets and inventory items in the absence of a process.
6. **Systems management (SysM):** It is both a process and a service. In order to interface with asset management, it provides all of the information on what attributes of OS, middleware, and business application components need to be monitored. A mature SysM process determines triggers, thresholds, event generation, severity, event correlation automated response, and the tools that will be used.
7. **Operational readiness (OPR) management:** Asset management interacts with OPR much as other projects and services do. To prepare for release into an environment, it is necessary that the documentation describing and supporting the provisioned product aligns with the enterprise standards.
8. **Backup management:** Enterprise performance management (EPM) links to backup management after the new server is added to the backup script, along with any customizations to the backup job.

6.5 Cloud Governance

One of the major components of any governance model is the proper definition of roles and responsibilities within an appropriate organizational structure. The domain owners within the organization own and are accountable for the business functionality within their proper business domain. These domain owners report to the head, but they also have direct reporting responsibilities within their business domain. These technical roles, along with the domain owners, strive to achieve a confluence between business and IT. One of the major aspects of cloud governance is to ensure that the lifecycle of services maximizes the value of service-oriented architecture (SOA) to the business. In order for governance to be effective, all aspects of the service lifecycle need to be properly handled.

The process transcends all phases of the service lifecycle: model, assemble, deploy and manage. Each task is numbered based on the phase it falls under. The cloud governance scenario should be broken down into realizations (see Fig. 6.1). They can be:

1. Regulation of new service creation.
2. Getting more reuse of services.
3. Enforcing standards and best practices.
4. Service management and version control.

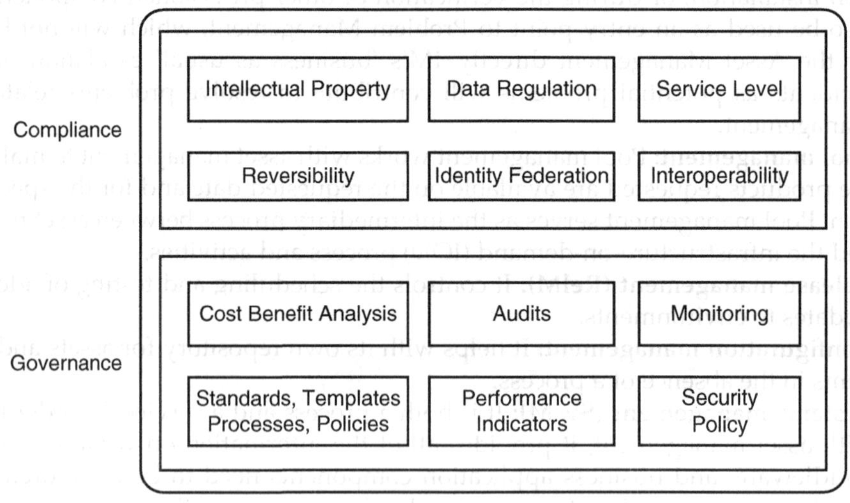

FIGURE 6.1 Compliance and governance.

6.6 High Availability and Disaster Recovery

High availability (HA) and disaster recovery (DR) are some of the important factors for cloud deployments. As the cloud is based on service models, different SLAs govern the service-based models to avail the service. HA and DR go together and define the factors for different SLAs between vendor and subscriber to ensure service availability and trust, and help develop credibility for the cloud vendor. Availability is not just a technology issue – it is a business issue as well. It is sometimes easy for executive management to take infrastructure availability for granted – by the business executives, not just the IT executives. The business must be able to make IT investment decisions based on business value. Achieving very high levels of availability usually requires substantial investment (and not just in technology). IT must manage the infrastructure to deliver the required and funded level of availability. But 'the business' must determine the level of availability required to support its business objectives and make the appropriate investments to support that level of availability.

HA and DR have often been treated as separate disciplines, but are converging. HA traditionally focused on avoiding/recovering from non-catastrophic disruptions – server failures, software failures, power failures, network disruptions, denial of service attacks, and viruses/worms – often relatively short in duration (minutes or hours). It may involve moving workload (dynamically) to another location, but typically does NOT involve moving people. DR traditionally focused on planning for and recovering business operations following catastrophic disruptions:

1. Site/facility destruction, hurricanes, tornadoes, floods, and fire.
2. Often long duration (days to weeks).
3. Often involves shifting work (and people) to alternate facilities for some period of time.

Similar disciplines are required for both HA and DR, but with different emphasis. This is the ability where the service or any component is required to execute its function at a state or desired time. It is based on the availability ratio such as the proportion of the service actually available with respect to the agreed service hours. There are various proportions to talk about, which are:

1. **Mean time between failures:** It is the average time for the failures occurring successively in a system.
2. **Mean time to recover:** It is the average time taken to recover from a system disaster.
3. **High availability (HA):** It is the functionality of the system that provides the agreed service levels to end-users during scheduled periods.
4. **Continuous operations:** This is the feature that gives continuous access to the end-user at any time, 24 × 7 × 365.
5. **Continuous availability:** This is the characteristic to deliver the agreed service level at any time, 24 × 7 × 365.
6. **Availability management:** This is the process of managing the resources such as people and technology to ensure the agreed service levels to meet the metrics and need of the organization.

Recovery capability is the process of planning for and implementing expanded operations to address less time-sensitive business operations immediately following an interruption or disaster. Recovery time objective (RTO) is the period of time within which tools and equipment, applications, or compute must be recovered after an outage (most of the time it is agreed time). It is the foundation for recovery strategies related to any development. It gives good points to think about how to implement the technology to meet the consequences of the disaster situation. It is that point in time where the system and data will be recovered after the disaster or outage. Recovery point objective (RPO) is the basis for strategizing the backup and determines how much data is to be recreated after the functions are recovered. DR is the process of creating, verifying, and maintaining an IT continuity plan that is to be executed to restore service in the event of a disaster. The objective of the DR plan is to provide for the resumption of all critical IT services within a stated period of time following the declaration of a disaster and perform the following activities:

1. Protect and maintain currency of vital records.
2. Select a site or vendor that is capable of supporting the requirements of the critical application workload.
3. Provide a provision for the restoration of all IT services when possible.

A DR plan includes procedures that will ensure the optimum availability of the critical business functions and the protection of vital records necessary to restore all services to normal. The DR plan is dependent upon and uses many of the same recovery procedures as those defined and developed by the recovery management process. The execution of the DR plan will use many of the same policies, procedures, and staff as defined in the crisis management process. The DR event is primarily a 'crisis' of greater magnitude and scope than the situations that are routinely managed on a day-to-day basis.

The true business need for HA of IT systems, including rapid recovery for disaster situations, must be determined and justified. The cost of down-time must be understood by business units to establish true business need for HA and rapid DR. An availability strategy is required to guide the organization in implementing HA and support rapid recovery from a disaster. An availability strategy should:

1. Support the IT strategy with the business policies and requirements.
2. Justify investment in HA and DR initiatives.
3. Ingrain HA in the IT culture.
4. Define a robust IT architecture and invest in building HA into the design of the infrastructure.

When DR plans fail, the failures primarily result from lack of HA planning, preparation, and maintenance prior to the occurrence of the disaster. Lack of an IT architecture employing hot back-up components and hot back-up sites inhibits the achievement of continuous availability across component failures or site failures resulting from disaster. Recovery severely delays when many back-up components have to be rebuilt from scratch. Change management processes fail to ensure backup components, and recovery documents are updated simultaneously with primary component upgrades.

The technology must fully exploit HA design techniques such as redundancy with hot back-up capabilities to support rapid recovery.

Application and data interdependencies are important considerations in determining business function priorities. Network connectivity must consider more than connectivity between the datacenter recovery site and the user site – it should consider connectivity to business users, system to system, customers, and outside agencies, and consider failure of multiple sites and setup for connectivity from one back-up site to another back-up site. Where critical business unit users must support the recovery effort, for example to prepare for end of day processing, immediate access to workstations is required. If the business processes are dependent on printing, printer recovery must be treated with appropriate priority.

The events of previous disasters confirm that effective and rapid recovery from any disaster is dependent on mature processes supporting HA. Service-level requirements and business requirements must be understood and objectives negotiated. An infrastructure supporting HA is essential for a rapid DR. The system and application designs must be built to support HA and rapid DR. Complete configuration information is necessary to reconstruct all system platforms following a disaster. Adequate testing must validate the capability of the plans and the ability to perform the procedures, whether for day-to-day HA or for disaster.

To prevent gaps in DR plans, recovery procedures, technology platforms, and DR vendors, contracts must be updated concurrently with changes. Fast and effective recovery from a component outage or from a disaster requires well thought out, pre-developed, tested, documented, and practiced recovery. Defects and shortcomings must be resolved quickly to ensure that the plan will work.

6.7 Charging Models, Usage Reporting, Billing, and Metering

Today, enterprise business units' budgets fund 60–70% of central ITs services. The other 30–40% is funded by other means, so it is clear that in general, organizations do not use a single charging mechanism, but a combination of mechanisms for different purposes to achieve an overall solution. Existing processes were institutionalized in many large organizations decades ago and the responsibility has been passed down from employee to employee over generations. The pitfalls of chargeback are well-documented; they include user architectural rebellion, IT investment vacillation, bureaucratic excess, and malicious obedience to IT standards. These pitfalls fall into an IT-centric view of providing service; these arguments and others like them seem shallow when presented with the business imperatives that are often at the root of maintaining a chargeback system.

6.7.1 Challenges

Many organizations do not implement sophisticated internal chargeback mechanisms due to their complexity. You should able to determine all the metrics, and in order to be able to break them out by the user, you have to keep track of what organizations the users are in, which is not a simple task. This creates a large volume of data for the items that you can directly tie to a user (e.g., CPU, memory, and disk that are associated with a particular transaction). While this is reasonably easy to do in a dedicated workload environment, enterprise environments add another layer of complexity.

Further, you have to make additions in the overhead (OS, program products, network, support, and processes such as space management). When you introduce the allocating of details, for example, the cost for SAN ports in a switch, you may have more of a political discussion than a technical one, as you may not be able to tie back specific items to transactions.

6.7.2 Benefits

The benefits from implementing a more effective system can be enormous. The following are the advantages for managers looking for the benefits of implementing a more comprehensive chargeback system. When forced to confront the issues of chargeback implementation or a chargeback system changes, managers should align their practices with the benefits of a chargeback system.

Charging for services will not solve all the problems of the IT department, nor will it be the source of all service problems when dealing with business managers. IT managers must leverage a chargeback system to harvest opportunities for improving and streamlining service delivery.

6.7.3 Cloud Chargeback Models

In consolidated environments, IT accounting service employs a cost recovery mechanism called chargeback. Chargeback is the system that is devised to put across the fee for the services provided in a cloud-based model. This allows the services in various bundles of value proposition to recover the cost for different offerings at different service levels.

In order to have the actual benefits of a chargeback model, organizations need to understand their own cost structures, and break down the components of the services and resources. The inner depth of devising an effective financial model requires functionalities such as the utility-based model to charge the various resources based on the billing costs (Fig. 6.2).

It is important to note that the chargeback models will not come with a silver lining and solve all the problems that are related to any organization's cloud commodity costing model. It comprises many proven, tested models in the industry, but each model is specifically based on

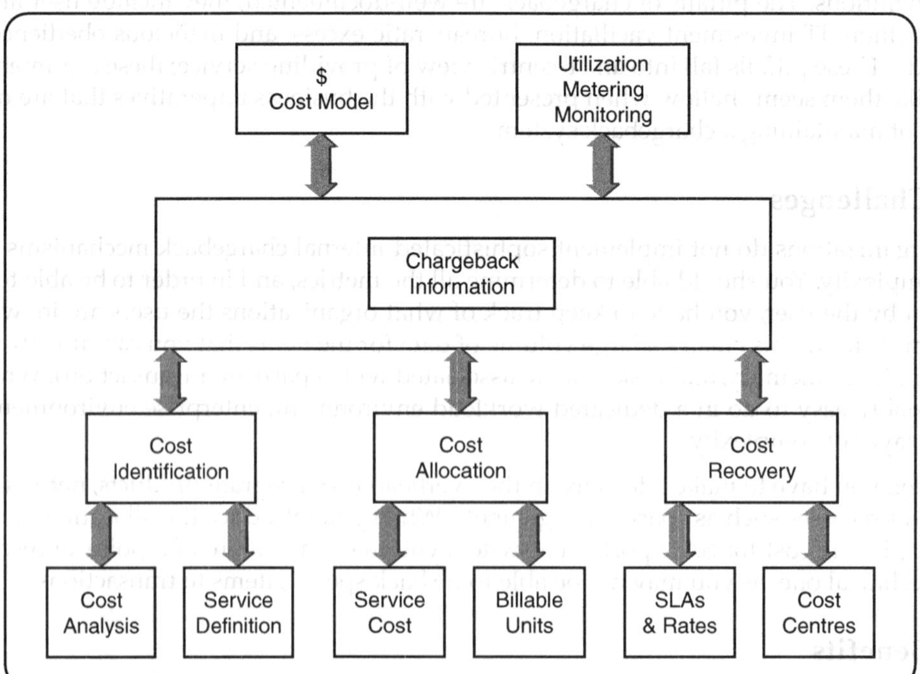

FIGURE 6.2 Chargeback model.

its situation and costing mechanism. It is advised to evaluate the various models and use them based on the culture, technology, financial or social boundaries. In the following subsections we will discuss some models of chargeback that can be adopted as stand-alone or as hybrid costing models.

Subscription Model

It is the simplest model. It is actually derived by dividing the total operational cost of the organization that runs IT and the total applications hosted in the environment. The cost mechanism is very simple and recovery is easier, because of which it is more convenient to adopt. Hence it is finding its way in many organizations. This type of model requires a constant addition in the costing model by adding the upgraded cost to the model with the subscriber. This is chargeback model, but at the same time it has a drawback that it provides subsidy and unbalanced allocation of resources. In other words, some applications that are not performing well are subsidized with the high performing application and infrastructure.

Pay-Per-Use Model

This chargeback model is good in an environment where the organization has multiple lines of businesses or tenants of different size and scale. The costing model is based on the actual application consumption based on agreed SLAs. The same application can be charged differently at different service levels. If the architecture of one application is not good and consumes more resources and time, it will be charged at the upper side. It can be a complicated model as it requires managing and monitoring the service levels and resource consumption. It is good from the recovery perspective, but it is difficult to get common levels with different teams to finalize the cost and financial models.

Premium Pricing Model

In this model service and availability is guaranteed for any critical service deployment. It is devised on the line of business priorities and preferential services rendered to specific tenants. This comes at a premium pricing and supports specific policies, resource reservations, and service levels. It is also dependent on the deployment model such as a dedicated or shared model. Therefore, based on isolation and separation, a shared service-costing model can be devised. It is always preferred by those units that are involved in mission-critical applications with a high revenue generation environment. It will never exist alone in any organization. It will come in combination with other models discussed above.

'Hybrid' Model

This chargeback model is an exercise to carry the best practices of all the models and create the best costing and chargeback model for any organization. This can combine two or more chargeback models, for example, a combination of a flat fee for registering for the applications services for the first time and then charge based on the resource usage. This way we can bring transparency in the system by showcasing the flat fees as the fixed price for hosting the service, and then actual charges based on the resource utilization and usage scenarios as a variable cost.

Similarly, if we combine the subscription and as pay-per-use model, it works like the utility services provided to any home by many agencies, such as water and electricity. In total, we can say that there is no one size that fits all situations. One model can be useful for one organization and the same will not work in other organizations. It is now customary to launch service catalogs for services offered, and any line of businesses (LOBs) can use any of the service pay back based on the agreed financial chargeback model. This gives freedom of choice to the LOBs to choose their services with their own flexibility. Cost will change from one LOB to the other if the volume, quality of service, policies, allocation, and service levels change. This freedom will help the LOBs to choose their model and add value to their services for end-users.

Aligning Chargeback with Business Perspective

In order to align the IT services with business objectives, chargeback tools become vital options. They bring together the IT systems and business users to realize the value of the infrastructure laid down to be shared by the community. The final goal viewed by the chargeback model is to provide the services at competitive prices with resiliency and robust value-added services. It is achieved by the optimized and efficient use of the computer resources, and enabling virtualized environment in the shared environment.

The chargeback models require good knowledge with respect to the organization. They require both technical and financial expertise to convert the service request into effective costing models. The other important point is the agreement between the IT and business community for values and services given by the chargeback models.

Therefore, it is very important to simplify the chargeback that can be understood by the business community, as well as it should be in agreement with the IT infrastructure managers. So, education of the models is very important to adopt and diffuse the characteristics to the indented users in the first step. Next, it is very important to divide the IT costs based on the organization's LOBs. This will help to understand the LOBs requirement and operating costs against the designated budgets to ensure transparency across the organization. The transparency characteristic motivates LOBs to work for the common objective of chargeback models across the organization. This can be the iterative process and will be reviewed by various participants from LOBs and finally agreeing to the common acceptable financial terms. It is common to use hybrid chargeback models to come to the agreement stage. Once all the models are reviewed and analyzed, the most suitable model will be opted and the most fair cost recovery model will be visualized. At the same time, organizational financial factors also play a vital role in the exercise with appropriate reporting practices. This will involve both operational and financial teams to work together and deploy mutually accepted chargeback models.

Governance is very important, especially in the shared infrastructure, as it is used by various business units, and requires policies and control to maintain the boundary conditions of any business units. The isolation of the infrastructure is also maintained for a dedicated set of requirements by the specific business units or application requirements. Under these situations, where shared, isolated, and dedicated environment is required, governance becomes supreme. It also helps to do the change management and RM to provide more satisfaction in the shared infrastructure

It is visualized that there exists flexibility in the virtualized environment with features like effective productivity and manageability. Governance helps to establish the following features:

1. Application enhancement.
2. Chargeback models.
3. Administration.

Also, it includes various features, such as responsibility and self-service controls. The best way to accomplish the governance is to categorize the policies and controls based on the services and chargeback models between the IT systems and the business community. This will help to adopt the model and any changes in the system can absorbed easily without any contention by the business community. Once established, other complex models can be introduced, such as chargeback, showbacks, transparency reports, and even penalties for operational and financial controls. This also follows the cyclic process and requires time for maturity under the supervision of the executive management.

6.7.4 Basic Requirements

The area of business unit contribution to IT funding can cause significant friction between business units and IT managers. For this reason the business units need a documented understanding of what they are getting (i.e., value) for their money. The chargeback metrics used in determining the individual business units' share of funding contribution should be directly tied to the SLA between central IT and the business unit and should reflect the following elements:

1. **Fairness:** The chargeback approach must be seen as allocating costs in proportions that reflect each unit's true consumption of information and communication services. One group should not be subsidizing IT usage at the expense of another.
2. **Control:** Business units should have a degree of control over, or input into, IT spending decisions.
3. **Repeatability and predictability:** Charges should be repeatable (there should be consistency in the application of data collection and charging methods so that charges are consistent) and predictable (a business unit should be able to create a reasonable forecast of its expected charges over a six- to twelve-month period).
4. **Simplicity:** The chargeback algorithm needs to be easy to understand, and simple and inexpensive to implement.

Chargeback works best when customers understand the pricing structures and their limitations, have some control or influence over costs, and believe that the policy is reasonably fair, given the limitations of a particular system and the underlying business rationale behind chargeback.

Chargeback Schemes

Possible chargeback approaches are listed below. It may well be that the best solution is to use a combination of these for different aspects of the IT infrastructure.

Allocation Based

In this model, IT service costs are buried in corporate overhead as a budget line item, usually determined one year at a time. The model has nothing to do with usage; instead, it charges business communities based on their position within the enterprise (e.g., the share of employees, unit shipment volume, or total revenue). This model is attractive as it is the simplest one and costs least to implement. However, the following are some weaknesses:

1. The difficulty of rebalancing the scale when the business measures change.
2. The lack of incentive for end-users to control their resource usage.
3. The frustration of business managers unable to control or influence their budget share–although, at least, it will be predictable.

Flat Fee

This model adds elements of negotiation and capacity planning. The IT organization determines what percentage of the IT service workload a business area represents, calculates a preliminary package rate for that area, then negotiates a rate with business managers. For example, if finance represents 8% of the IT workload, it might pay a proportional fee. Because the flat fee is tied to usage, it gives business managers a chance to understand what they are paying for. Flat fee is appropriate for environments in which third-party application packages are used heavily. Variations such as access fees and subscription fees can be relevant to certain components of the system, such as the network and specific end-user services.

Resource or Usage Based (Direct Cost Recovery)

Resource-based costing and its most common form of implementation, usage-based costing, focus on developing a standard unit cost for each major resource type or category that best represents the use of that resource. For example, the measure for CPU usage could be CPU seconds consumed by an application; for storage usage, it could be number of gigabytes of storage occupied by an application or business; for the network, it could be number of bytes transferred. The basic idea is that the costing unit represents some measure of the resource consumed that can be traced back to the user of that resource.

This method requires that all elements of the IT infrastructure and associated software specific to the application be identified and are directly charged to the end-user on a per-user basis. The cost per unit (whatever unit is chosen) needs to cover all IT-related costs – operations, support, buildings, and networks. There may be parts of the 'enabling infrastructure' that are chosen to be recovered through other methods, such as allocation, flat fee, or a per-user charge.

This cost-recovery model is still widely used as a traditional mainframe approach. However, bundling mainframe computing services into resource-based charges can create bloated CPU fees, which prompt users to purchase their own systems. This approach is not always effective in the complex PC-based and distributed computing environments where the mechanics and time involved in tracking usage may cost more than what the IT organization recovers. Moreover, the language in a resource-based chargeback scheme is so techno-centric that the bill mystifies business managers.

Product or Service Based

In the commercial environment, there has been a strong push for IT to invoice the lines of business or business units in business terms instead of IT terms. This means that instead of charging a business unit for CPU seconds consumed (or in the case of networks, the number of bytes transferred), this model defines IT costs in measurable events, transactions, and functions that are relevant to the business and outside the IT organization, for example, invoices produced, cheques written, e-mail messages sent, reports delivered, number of claims processed, number of policies written, or some other metric that represents the work performed. This method could be called a business product-based approach, whereas, the resource-based method is an IT product-based approach (e.g., bills are expressed in IT terms like CPU seconds).

In any case, the product-based approach requires all the data collection instrumentation and methods used in a usage-based approach to be in place, and then expanded to include the mapping of that usage data to the product and service categories in addition to department categories.

The success of the model depends on business managers and IT organizations together defining specific services that the IT organization agrees to provide and for which the business agrees to pay. Making IT services understandable to managers gives them a clear window into infrastructure and application reinvestment.

Activity Based

Activity-based costing (ABC) is the most difficult of all the methods to develop and implement. There are almost no large IT organizations that have a truly activity-based approach to IT costing. The IT organizations that claim to have ABC usually do not – they have product-based costing. Quite a few organizations started ABC efforts within IT, but stopped them before completion and settled them according to product-based costing.

ABC assigns costs to each activity that goes into delivering a product or service. ABC is a cost methodology which

1. Derives the costs of an organization's outputs (products and services).
2. Identifies the activities and tasks (processes) used in the production and delivery of the outputs.
3. Identifies the resources consumed in the performance of these processes and instruments these activities so that the cost per task can be rolled up into a charge per major activity by the department.

ABC takes resources (i.e., expenses from the general ledger accounting system), moves them to activities (i.e., moves those costs to activities), and then moves the costs from activities to cost objects (i.e., product and services).

Activity-based management (ABM) is the method or process of using the data produced by ABC. So ABC produces cost information, ABM takes that information and uses it to find ways to improve those costs and the overall operations of the organization.

While IT product-based costing produces a charge by product (e.g., claim or policy), IT ABC produces a charge by activity (e.g., printing a claim or handling a policy or printing a report). As can be seen by this example, the level of detail required and reported is significantly higher than product-based costing.

ABC is the 'premiere' approach of cost accounting options. Its strength is that costs can be managed very well since each activity has a cost driver that can be measured. So, a charge area such as 'handling a claim' may be broken down into 10 IT service activities. These activities can be ranked by their total contribution to the overall cost of 'handling a claim'. This allows cost managers to focus their time on the largest contributors to cost by activity.

Even though this information is extremely valuable to decision-makers, the cost of getting this information can be prohibitive for all but the most disciplined of institutions. It requires a major investment of time, people, and resources to build and maintain an ABC system, with an extended implementation period.

External Pricing Model/Market Based

This model is geared towards turning a profit. The model presumes that an IT organization operates in a fairly open market inside and outside the enterprise, and requires some 'market testing' for the cost of services. Pricing is determined by what is available in the outside market. Although a small percentage of midsize enterprises use this model, it has clear advantages; it may well become a hallmark of IT organizations recognized as value-generating service providers.

Determining the correct pricing can be expensive if a survey is required to support the scale of charges. However, basic comparison with contract, staff, and consulting rates and high-level assessment of IT spends against benchmarks is sufficient to support the cost model.

Very often, profit center cost models will lead to over recovery. This can be corrected with a simple adjustment within the accounting process. However, care must be taken not to under-recover costs. Year-end upwards corrections will often cause friction with the business units. Most organizations look to over-recover by a small percentage for cost center accounting.

6.8 Summary

Today IT delivers technology to the business units and assesses charges based on the number of devices provided. The business units do not have the ability to identify the elements of this cost and cannot manage their consumption of the technology.

This chapter addresses this problem by bundling the technology IT offers into services for the business units to purchase as needed. The cost model strategy detailed in this chapter provides recommendations about how to design and implement an equitable, accurate, and auditable method of charging for services that provide value to customers.

CHAPTER

7

Cloud Virtualization Technology

CONTENTS

7.1 Introduction

Today, Cloud is a buzz word in the IT industry. The advent of powerful virtualization technology in the infrastructure domain gives us options to reap benefits of various cloud deployments. A powerful line-up of servers, blended with advanced Web technologies, provide opportunities to exploit powerful features of virtualization combined with cloud concepts. Continuous improvement means leveraging technology and expertise to do the same things more efficiently. Continuous innovation is the fusion of new business designs and next-generation technologies to do things differently, not just once, but over and over again. While virtualization sounds like a very complex and technical thought, it is in reality a simple idea.

Virtualization is a fast-growing infrastructure in the IT industry, and new technologies are being introduced on a continuous basis. As a result, technology providers and user communities have introduced a new set of terms to describe these technologies and their features for virtualization. However, some of the terms may overlap in concept, while others may be ambiguous. For example, 'Hardware-Assisted Virtualization' and 'Hardware-Based Virtual Machine' refer to the same thing, while the term 'paravirtualization' may be something new for some users.

Virtualization represents the logical view of data representation – the power to compute in a virtualized environment, storing data at different geographies, and availing various computing resources. So, virtualization removes restrictions on computing such as difficult infrastructure deployments, collocated computing resources, physical movement, and packaging of resources.

This statement can be clarified by the following two points:

1. To virtualize systems, there is a need to separate the physical from the logical, and manage and utilize IT resources as a cohesive, holistic unit that is constantly adjusting, reallocating, and responding to changes in the business environment.
2. Virtualization is a liberating technology which implies to a having a better and more responsive access to the existing information. IT management can be further simplified by instituting a policy-based response that ultimately reduces the cost of operations.

For example, in the case of storage, we can say that we have a total 30 TB of disk space when put together rather than saying that we have three different types of storage systems, and thus we can manage the 30 TB of disk space as a single type of resource. So we can now focus on how to use the resource and not how to manage it.

Virtualization is a technique that is being used in large mainframe computers for the last 30 years – not to manage each computer or resource separately – but to manage them together or we can say virtually. This technique results in huge improvements in the utilization of resources. A typical mainframe today runs between 70% and 90% of its optimum utilization and the rest of the infrastructure is probably running at less than 15% of its utilization. Raising the level of utilization across the entire infrastructure usually means one needs to manage fewer things; fewer things require fewer people and cosequently need less infrastructure expenses.

By extracting some of the administrative cost out of the infrastructure, that is, by increasing the system and resource utilization and by improving the productivity, these 'virtualized' IT assets can help fuel the business growth we just talked about, control the cost in doing so, and increase staff productivity at the same time. Having simplified virtualization implementation as the first step, it is then easy to automate the system, which means reduced errors and streamlined business responsive systems.

7.2 Virtualization Defined

Virtualization is not a vague concept – you probably are already engaged in virtualization in some fashion – but it helps to understand virtualization as a process. So, how can a virtualized environment help an organization?

Virtualization is an abstraction layer (hypervisor) that decouples the physical hardware from the operating system (OS) to deliver greater IT resource utilization and flexibility.

The virtualization platform provides the isolation of platform and allows multiple businesses to run multiple virtual machines on the same physical machine.

How can virtualization help different lines of businesses is also a big question. Following are the benefits provided by virtualization:

1. **Money saving:** With virtualization technology, the number of physical servers can be reduced; therefore, the ongoing procurement, maintenance, and ongoing operational costs will also be reduced.
2. **Dramatic increase in control:** Virtualization provides a flexible foundation to provide capacity according to the demand for an organization. New servers can be quickly deployed; therefore, services can be provided within minutes. It is also easy to ship the infrastructure when it is deployed using virtualization techniques.
3. **Simplified disaster recovery:** More efficient and cost-effective disaster recovery solutions can be realized with virtualization technologies. Servers and business on-line can be transferred to an alternate site within minutes with the help of virtualization.
4. **Business readiness assessment:** Virtualization introduces a shared computing model to an enterprise and it is easy to understand infrastructure requirements in a virtualized environment as there is no need to implement them physically.

Depending on the organizational structure, virtualization change may either impede or enable the virtualization strategy.

7.2.1 Why Virtualization?

Let us now look at the need for virtualization in the infrastructure domain. Virtualization can help to:

1. Reduce the cost of the existing infrastructure by reducing operational and systems management cost while maintaining the needed capacity.
2. Reduce the complexity of adding to the infrastructure.
3. Gather information and collaboration across the organization to increase both the utilization of information and its effective use.

4. Deliver on-service-level agreement (SLA) response time during spikes in production and test scenarios.
5. Build a heterogeneous infrastructure across the organization that is more responsive to the organization's needs.

Implementation of solid information management solutions in an organization does not mean to change the entire IT environment in one major re-engineering project. There is a stepped approach that is followed by most of the successful companies. Some people may focus more on automation capabilities, others may focus more on virtualization; but it is the breadth of capabilities across the spectrum of information management that truly unlocks the value of the IT infrastructure.

Initial steps in the process are to simplify the environment by consolidating similar system platforms onto fewer, more manageable resources. In the last decade, this has been one of the primary ways in which companies seek to reduce costs and increase utilization of resources.

Once similar systems are brought together into a more efficient structure, the management of these resources can be automated by adding and moving the capacity as needed, thus allowing business needs to drive resource usage rather than resources dictating the performance of the business.

Automation of tasks, such as increasing or moving capacity, can lead to the progression of task automation that are associated with a given process or sub-process, such as application testing or release management of an updated production configuration. One may look up in the information technology infrastructure library (ITIL) for guidance on IT processes, which in turn, can lead to insights into the highest-priority tasks and processes to be considered for the automation.

Another key activity at this point is to start bringing together these consolidated resources across functions performed within the company. Begin breaking down the silos of technology and sharing resources across functions within the enterprise. By doing this, a company can use its resources that may sit idle at various times of the day to perform tasks of other resources that are overburdened at that time. The ability to share these resources in a seamless fashion gives companies the ability to quickly respond to changing business needs without over-investing in the technology.

To use these resources most effectively, companies cannot allow the standard process that may be in place today to slow down the adaptation of resources to new workloads. To facilitate a fluid environment, we need tools and processes that allow the automated orchestration of resources to respond to business challenges.

As virtualization and automation capabilities improve within an organization, companies will be able to move to the enterprise-wide virtualization that is enabled by a global virtualization fabric. This fabric utilizes advanced virtualization techniques available through grid technologies and more advanced mainframe virtualization platforms to allow seamless access to resources wherever they exist within an organization. Virtualization begins to eliminate boundaries between resources that have been created by organizational silos or management processes.

Finally, we see organizations using these advanced virtualization concepts not only to access resources within their organization, but also to see these resources in demand whether they are within the company or outside at partner or vendor locations. In this state, resources are available when needed, peak demands can be serviced without keeping unused capacity on the floor for extended periods of time, and information flows seamlessly between organizational functions, both within and outside the company.

One of the most essential ingredients for successful enterprise-wide and inter-enterprise resource sharing, application integration and business process collaboration is security management. Fundamentals of security such as authentication, authorization, and access must be in place across systems, networks, and applications. Establishing roles and using identity management will save time and money in the long run and immediately tighten the security. Having the right solution provider for security and verification between suppliers, partners, and customers will help a company to get to that 'always on' state.

All of these infrastructure management techniques are available today, but many companies find it difficult to implement them as rapidly as they would like to due to outdated IT governance and management processes. Therefore, companies must address those processes and cultures that hold them back from taking full advantage of technologies available today.

7.2.2 Infrastructure Virtualization Evolution

First of all, the objective is to take what is complex today and to try to consolidate it physically. Increasingly, physical consolidation is becoming easier to implement as processes deliver even greater virtualization capabilities and are more flexible. But ultimately, this is the farthest that one can go with physical consolidation. It is easy to claim that all Window servers can be moved to a mainframe Linux-based system, but it is not so easy to do so. There is a huge potential in consolidating processes, but it is more difficult to do and it also takes time. One of the key things in terms of what we are doing with virtualization is to treat things much more logically. What is desired is to develop an environment where resources that make up computer systems, local or remote, make one logical pool of resources that can be used as per needs of business applications. So, if one have got smaller servers that are capable of running additional work, it can be done automatically and dynamically rather than trying to get more value from them by physically removing them and transfering the workload onto a bigger system. However, two things are complementary: the ability to deliver logical consolidation and logical simplification, and the ability to deliver physical consolidation.

Virtualization of physical resources has been used in mainframes for production workloads for many years. Different virtual machines can run different OSs and multiple applications on the same physical computer. Each virtual machine is encapsulated and segregated, contains a complete system, including CPU, memory, and network devices to prevent conflicts, and allows a single physical machine to safely run several different OSs and applications on the same hardware.

7.3 Virtualization Benefits

Traditional benefits of virtualization include:

1. Server consolidation.
2. 'Greener' IT – reduced power and cooling.
3. Reduced hardware costs.

Virtualization benefits have expanded to include:

1. Increased availability, business continuity, and disaster recovery.
2. Maximized hardware resources.
3. Reduced administration and labor costs.
4. Efficient application and desktop software deployment and maintenance.
5. Reduced time for server provisioning.
6. Increased security at the client-level desktop.
7. Dynamic and extensible infrastructure to rapidly address new business requirements.

7.3.1 Current Virtualization Initiatives

We will now discuss new initiatives that are being used in the industry and how they help in the infrastructure domain:

1. **Virtual CPU and memory:** Physical CPUs and RAM can be dedicated or dynamically allocated to virtual machines. As there is no OS dependency on the physical hardware, with the CPU checking off, virtual machines can be seamlessly migrated to different hosts, with background changes to the physical CPU and memory resources being transparent to the guest OSs running on virtual machines.
2. **Virtual networking:** This creates a virtual 'network in a box' solution that allows the hypervisor to manage virtual machine network traffic through the physical network interface controller (NIC) and allows each of the virtual machines to have a unique identity on the network from the physical host.
3. **Virtual disk:** Storage area network (SAN)–based storage is presented as storage targets to the physical host, which in turn are then used to host virtual machines' vdisks (virtual disks).
4. **Consolidated management:** The performance and health of virtual machines and guest OSs can be monitored and 'console' access to all of the servers can be obtained via single console.
5. **Virtual motion:** Active virtual machines can be seamlessly and transparently transferred across physical hosts with no downtime and no loss of service availability or performance. The virtual machine's execution state, active memory, network identity, and active network connections are preserved across the source and destination hosts so that the guest OS and running applications are unaware of the migration.
6. **Storage virtual motion:** Vdisks of active virtual machines can be seamlessly and transparently transferred across data stores, while the execution state, active memory, and active network connections remain on the same physical host.
7. **Dynamic load balancing:** Dynamically load balances virtual machines across the most optimal physical hosts to ensure that pre-defined performance levels are met. Virtual machines can be automatically and seamlessly transferred to a less busy host if a particular host in a resource pool is in a high-utilization state. Different resource pools can be defined for different business needs. For instance, production pools can be defined with more stringent service-level requirements, while development pools can be used with more relaxed service-level requirements.

8. **Logical partitions (LPARs):** LPARs result in hardware layer logical partitioning to create two or more isolated computing domains, each with its own CPU, memory address space and I/O interface, with each domain capable of housing a separate OS environment on single physical server. LPARs can share CPUs or have dedicated physical CPUs. Likewise, an LPAR can be a dedicated physical memory address space or memory addresses can be dynamically allocated among LPARS as needed.
9. **Logical domains (LDOMs):** Operating systems running in each logical domain can be independently managed, that is, stopped, started, and rebooted without impacting other LDOMs running on the host. A Type 1 'bare-metal' hypervisor isolates computing environments from physical resources. For example, domains across distinct threads can be separated using the multi-threading technology, because the hypervisor is dynamically managing and encapsulating the allocation of physical resources.
10. **Zones:** Zone is an OS-level virtualization solution rather than a hardware-level hypervisor solution. Each zone is an encapsulated virtual server environment running within a single OS instance. As such, zones share a common kernel, through a global zone, although 'non-native' zones can emulate an OS environment other than that of the host's native OS. Zones allow virtualization across a single physical server platform, but some applications may still be limited in their ability to run within zones if they require direct manipulation of the kernel or its memory space (since the kernel is shared across zones), or if the application requires privileges that cannot be granted within a non-global zone.

7.3.2 Virtualization Technology

Advances in computing, especially in hardware technologies, are driving the adoption of virtualization and help in meeting the corporate demand for computing that has grown exponentially over the past decade. Success of virtualization concepts over a period of time has led to the genesis of better infrastructure optimization. Virtualization has several benefits such as live migration, hardware support, virtual machines, management of virtual datacenters, virtual networking performance, networking support, dynamic VM storage, broad OS support, and network load balancing. These benefits can be realized through a virtualization platform which allows automatic provisioning of environments and deployment of applications into those environments. In addition to setting up a virtualized infrastructure with self service capabilities for provisioning, scaling, monitoring, and de-provisioning, the solution will also address application environment issues through best practices and automation.

A virtualized environment should enable the dynamic and repeatable process to create environments that will result in cost saving in terms of infrastructure costs and manual interventions. This platform capability for allowing backup of VM images for subsequent environment setup requests should be used for eliminating application deployment and configuration issues. This platform reduces the time required to obtain and boot new server instances, allowing upgradation of scale capacity quickly, both up and down, as computing requirements change.

An enterprise' workload is not constant and can be more during peak hours and less during off-peak hours. Therefore, computing resources have to be allocated more frequently during peak hours than off-peak hours. Downtime for a datacenter infrastructure, whether planned or unplanned, brings considerable costs with it. Downtime for higher levels of availability that have traditionally been very costly, hard to implement, and difficult to manage.

As the datacenter is virtualized, it is capable of delivering uncompromised control over all IT resources with good utilization efficiency of available resources. Virtualization of any datacenter would help to gain high performance, scalability, and flexibility. These critical underlying factors lay the foundation for adopting a hypervisor for datacenter virtualization, and for accelerating the transition of this infrastructure to a virtualized computing model in the near future.

For the purpose of virtualization, following subsections explain how various features of virtualization can be used in a virtualized datacenter. Hypervisor also acts as the foundation for virtualized computing and supports various applications that help in virtualization of critical activities of the business.

Hypervisor

Unique features of bare-metal hypervisors enable the hardware to be used efficiently. There are various memory-optimizing techniques that will make the hardware over-commit with the available resources, and also give high availability of the resources efficiently to the virtual machines running on host servers. Power-saving features also enable datacenters to 'Go Green' and save energy by powering off servers. This is done automatically as per the load of the infrastructure environment. Servers would automatically run when there is a requirement for more computing resources due to the load on the infrastructure. A bare-metal hypervisor uses high-level resource management policies to compute a target memory allocation for each virtual machine based on the current infrastructure load and parameter settings for each of the virtual machines. The computed target allocation is used to guide the dynamic adjustment of the memory allocation for each virtual machine in the infrastructure. In case the host memory is over-committed, the target allocations are achieved by invoking several lower-level mechanisms to reclaim memory from virtual machines.

Administration

To administer virtualized datacenter activities, a single console application is required. Using a centralized management software, a virtual management server manages bare-metal hypervisor environments centrally and allows IT administrator's centralized control over the virtual environment. The provisioning of VMs can be done by administrators on the basis of existing standardized templates. This ensures compliance of various policies with required hypervisor configurations and patches with automation, if required.

Various tools and software continuously monitor the virtual datacenter running on multiple hosts. So, on the basis of utilization, policies, and compute availability, VMs can be provisioned and decommissioned also. In the case of load balancing, the administrator or the managing software can dynamically move VMs from a physical host to another host without impacting the business with respect to the respective server.

7.3.3 Virtualization Use Cases

The following subsections describe the virtualization functionalities that can be used for datacenter applications and how virtualization improves the functionality of any datacenter environment.

Availability of Machines

This feature makes machines in a virtualized datacenter as 'highly available'. This feature ensures that multiple datacenter activities are carried out even in the case of hardware failures. This feature should be configured and used for all virtual machines in a virtual environment, as during a hardware failure, running virtual machines are started on another host machine and the downtime is reduced to minimal. If a server fails, the affected virtual machines are re-started on other production servers that have spare capacity. In a datacenter, this feature would give high availability to virtual machines by starting them on other servers, thus minimizing the impact of failures.

It is very useful to use the bare-metal hypervisor as it is less expensive and provides an increased level of availability for critical applications. It helps to increase the target level of availability to all application servers in a simpler and economical fashion.

By implementing the high availability (HA) feature of any datacenter, it is possible to reduce both planned and unplanned downtime. HA, a feature of bare-metal hypervisors, specifically reduces unplanned downtime by leveraging multiple hypervisor servers configured as a cluster to provide rapid recovery from outages, as well as cost-effective HA feature for applications running on virtual machines.

The HA feature protects application availability against hardware failure by restarting the virtual machines on other hosts within the cluster. Protection against OS failure is obtained by continuously monitoring a virtual machine and resetting it when an OS failure is detected. Unlike other clustering solutions, the HA feature provides the infrastructure to protect all workloads within the cluster. There is no need to install additional software within the application or on the virtual machine. This feature protects all workloads that are in the infrastructure. Once the HA feature is implemented, there is no action required to save VMs as they are protected.

Compared with traditional failover solutions, following are the advantages when we configure the HA feature:

1. Minimal setup.
2. Reduced complexity (e.g., no need for quorum disks).
3. Reduced hardware cost and setup.
4. Application availability without the investment of idle physical servers and complex identical failover servers.

A datacenter can be supported with the load balance feature as it is virtualized with a bare-metal hypervisor. The action taken by the HA feature for virtual machines running on a host when the host has lost its ability to communicate with other hosts over the management network and cannot ping the isolation addresses is called *host isolation response*. The term 'host isolation' does not necessarily mean that the virtual machine network is down, but only that the management network, and possibly others, is down. If server monitoring is in a disabled mode, restart of virtual machines in that server is also disabled on other hosts following a host failure or isolation. Essentially, a server will always perform a programmed server isolation response when it detects that it is isolated. The server monitoring setting determines whether virtual machines will be restarted in other servers in the same cluster following this event.

Fault Tolerance

Fault tolerance feature of a virtualized datacenter leverages the well-known encapsulation property of virtualization by building the HA feature directly into the bare-metal hypervisor to deliver hardware style fault tolerance to virtual machines. This feature is to be used for all virtual machines that require 100% uptime.

Dynamic Movement

Dynamic movement of virtual machines in a virtualized datacenter could give more options for load balancing and hardware maintenance. Usage of this feature does not have any impact on services offered by the virtual machine. This functionality is used by the distributed resource scheduling algorithm. Live migration of VMs is enabled by virtual dynamic motion from one physical host to another without impacting the business, with continuous availability, and tight integrity throughout the transaction. Storage dynamic movement enables to send VM files from one data store to another data store without service interruption. It is highly customizable to choose the target server that may be available at a single location with a single server, or multiple locations with multiple servers, with the required VM configuration and associated data store file disks.

This could be achieved using the distributed power management algorithm, which will help to reduce energy consumption in the datacenter by optimizing workload placement for low power consumption with distributed power management. The algorithm consolidates workloads when distributed resource clusters need fewer resources and switches off powers of host servers to conserve energy. When resource requirements increase, the algorithm brings hosts back online to ensure that service levels are met.

In any datacenter, this feature would be effectively used while provisioning machines on demand. A distributed power management algorithm would also use this feature to save energy during off-peak hours. Migration with dynamic movement allows moving a virtual machine to a new host without any interruption in the availability of the virtual machine. However, migration with dynamic movement cannot be used to move virtual machines from one datacenter to another.

Dynamic Storage

Dynamic movement of virtual machines along with virtual hard disks in any datacenter machines could give more options to do load balancing and hardware maintenance of storage devices. This feature allows administrators to move virtual disks or configuration files of a powered-on virtual machine to a new data store. Migration of storage with dynamic movement allows moving a virtual machine's storage without any interruption in the availability of the virtual machine. Usage of this feature does not have any impact on the virtual machine.

Resource Scheduler

In a virtualized datacenter, the presence of a resource scheduler algorithm would improve resource allocation, efficiency, and power consumption in virtual infrastructures. The resource scheduler balances workloads according to the available resources in the pool, and administrators can optimize the environment on the basis of manual or automatic intervention. If workload spikes are changing very drastically, the resource scheduler can power-off some of the unused physical servers.

The resource scheduler works with virtual dynamic motion to provide automated resource optimization. This helps to migrate and place the virtual machines. The resource scheduling algorithm simplifies the job of handling new applications and adding new virtual machines, simplifies the task of extracting or removing hardware when it is no longer needed, and replacing older host machines with newer and larger-capacity hardware. Adding new resources is also straightforward as one can simply drag and drop new physical hosts into a cluster.

A resource scheduler cluster is a collection of physical bare-metal hypervisor–installed servers and associated virtual machines with shared resources. When the host is added to the cluster, it becomes a part of the pool. Thus, the resource scheduler aggregates the resources and supports all physical hosts at the cluster level. The scheduler also enforces the policies applicable to all servers available in the resource pool. This helps to provision servers dynamically to meet the compute resources demand as well as maintain service-level agreements (SLAs).

The resource scheduler algorithm places the virtual machine on available servers and can manage the automatic provisioning based on resource allocation policies and the decision-making process. It can be configured to take action based on manual intervention after reviewing the reports which are generated from monitoring or utilization tools. The concept of resource scheduler and dynamic movement provides an integrated way of achieving the redundancy and availability of compute resources to minimize the impact of a failure event.

Power Management

Usage of power management options in virtualized environment would significantly improve efficiency. Power management applications balance workloads according to the available resources, and users can configure this feature along with the resource scheduler. If a workload's needs decrease drastically, scheduling algorithms can temporarily power-down unnecessary physical servers using distributed power management algorithms. These servers are brought back online automatically when there is a requirement for more compute resources.

Provisioning and De-Provisioning

Any datacenter infrastructure can be virtualized, and the option of provisioning comes along with it for creating a virtual machine. The simplest reason for using virtual machine templates is efficiency. By using templates, many repetitive installation and configuration tasks can be avoided. It is to be noted that a datacenter can utilize the capabilities of a hypervisor and a virtual management server for the automatic provisioning and de-provisioning functionality by making the infrastructure virtualized. The outcome is a fully installed, ready-to-operate virtual machine in less time than that required for manual installation with same features and configurations as the source machine. On-demand provisioning of resources for de-duplication process and provisioning of more servers require resources on demand basis so the hypervisor should also be able to scale up and down the infrastructure as per the demand.

Moreover, the hypervisor should also be able to detect new hardware such as servers and storage that are being introduced into the existing infrastructure. It should also maintain the balance of resources in the cluster. The HA feature of machines that are hosted in the virtual infrastructure should also be guaranteed.

Dynamic Allocation and De-Allocation

A virtualized datacenter is scalable and capable of using existing resources in an efficient way. This is achieved with the bare-metal hypervisor installed on servers in the datacenter. This environment will not only be scalable but intelligent enough to understand the load on the datacenter and allocate the computing resources accordingly. Such environment would save a significant amount of energy and will also be able to use the existing computing resources in the datacenter effectively. During off-peak hours, lots of computing power would be in unusable state. The distributed power management algorithm, with the help of the distributed resource scheduler algorithm, would identify the servers with consumption of fewer resources. Using dynamic movement, virtual machines running in that server would be moved dynamically to other servers. The server is then moved to power-off state by communicating through a remote console. These servers are brought online as and when the requirement for the computing resources arises. This would save a significant amount of energy in terms of power and computing resource, thus enabling a 'Go Green' datacenter.

It is advised to balance the load based on the peak and non-peak hours. The hypervisor helps to achieve this functionality by using the bare metal. This requires creating templates as a standardization process. Administrators save time by using these templates for deploying, cloning and converting virtual machines. These templates work like a golden copy and are managed with different types of permissions and authentication. This works like a protected copy and can be used for creating new VMs. Therefore, templates are a perfect and original image of a particular VM.

By using the distributed power management algorithm along with the distributed resource scheduler, multiple datacenters could optimize power usage by moving unused physical machines to a standby mode. The challenge here could be to understand which physical machine needs to be turned off. The resource scheduler algorithm should have the ability to understand the free and used resource capacities in a cluster. Using the algorithm, the VMs running on one physical host will be moved to another to make one physical host completely offline. This is done automatically and dynamically by the resource scheduler algorithm as there is no service loss to the end user. This feature also allows an administrator to define rules and policies, according to priority, which decides how each VM should share resources and how available resources are prioritized among multiple virtual machines. It also sends a heartbeat signal to all hosts to ensure that it is up and running fine. So, this feature is capable to dynamically provision and relocate the resources that are free in the cluster quickly as and when needed.

7.4 Server Virtualization

Server virtualization covers different types of virtualization, such as client, storage, and network virtualization. In this section, different implementations of virtualization, management software, constituents of virtualization platforms support, and other related topics such as appliance and cloud computing are discussed.

Server virtualization works as a masking of the server compute that comprises the count and identity of resources with servers, storage, processors and OS from the end user. Administrators actually divide the physical server into multiple isolated VMs talking to same resource pools. Virtualization of servers provides an abstraction of the physical server/s by maintaining resource pools for server users (Fig. 7.1).

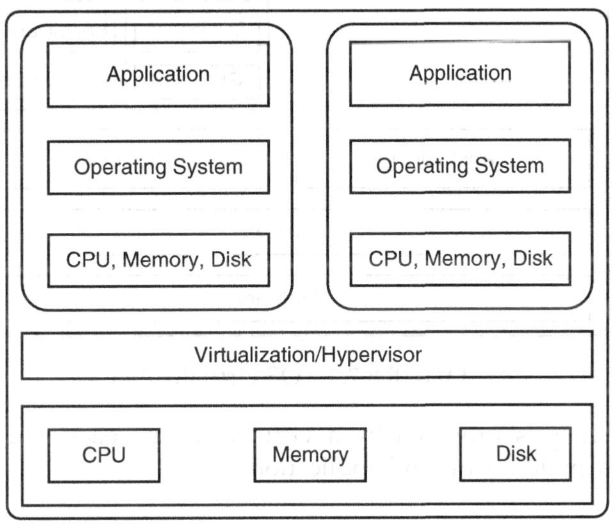

FIGURE 7.1 Server virtualization.

7.4.1 Virtual Machine

There are various terms to define a virtual machine. It can be termed as a virtual environment, partition, or container. In a server environment, a server that does not physically exist but is created on a different server is often called 'guest'.

The instance where a virtual machine runs is often termed as 'host'. These hosts can have multiple VMs running on the physical server. All VMs assigned to a pool of resources can be dynamically assigned to pool-based available resources.

When a user talks to this VM, he/she is privileged to use his/her VM as a physical server with all functionalities such as accessing the OSs, CPU, memory, and hard disk from the common pool. The hypervisor virtualizes multiple virtual servers based on supported architecture. Each virtual machine is bundled with an OS, CPU, hard disk, and memory.

7.4.2 Virtualization Technologies

Two major types of technologies are employed in server virtualization: hardware virtualization and OS virtualization. Hardware virtualization virtualizes the server hardware and OS virtualization virtualizes the application environment (e.g., file systems). These two technologies will be discussed in the following subsections.

Hardware Virtualization

Hardware virtualization is also known as hypervisor-based virtualization, bare-metal hypervisor, type 1 virtualization, or simply hypervisor. This virtualization technology has a virtualization layer running immediately on the hardware which divides the server machine into several virtual machines or partitions, with a guest OS running in each of these machines (Fig. 7.2).

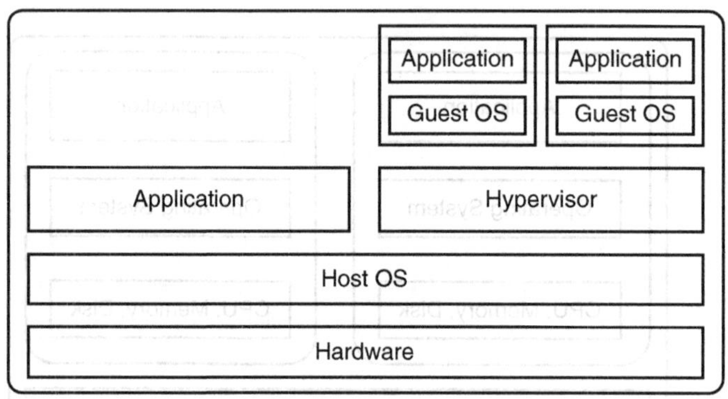

FIGURE 7.2 OS virtualization.

The binary transparency is provided by a virtualized approach and products enable the transparency for OSs, middleware, and applications.

OS Virtualization

This type of server virtualization is also known as OS-based virtualization, OS-level virtualization, or type 2 virtualization. OS virtualization creates virtualization environments within a single instance of an OS. Virtual environments created by OS virtualization are often called 'containers'.

Because all virtualization environments must share resources of a single OS while having a private virtual OS environment, a particular implementation of the technology may alter the file system orientation and often introduce access restrictions to global system configuration or settings.

7.5 Virtualization for x86 Architecture

Virtualization on processors encounters a set of challenges with reduced instruction set computing (RISC) processors. This is mainly because vendors or technology providers for processors, systems, virtualization technologies, and OSs are different and operate independently.

As a result, virtualization technologies and the rest of the system are available separately and on different timelines, rather than as a single integrated unit. Therefore, both forward and backward compatibilities must be considered when designing virtualization for x86. Most OSs, including those for x86, such as Windows and Linux, are designed to run directly on the bare-metal hardware, so they naturally assume that they fully 'own' the computer hardware.

7.5.1 Paravirtualization

Also known as OS-assisted virtualization, paravirtualization describes virtualization techniques that are used to overcome virtualization challenges on the older versions of processors. These techniques require modifying the guest OS kernel to improve the communication and performance between that kernel and the virtualization layer hypervisor. The newer versions of processors provide on-chip virtualization features called *hardware-based virtual machines* that make paravirtualization unnecessary.

Paravirtualization involves modifying the OS kernel to replace non-virtualizable instructions with hypercalls that communicate directly with the hypervisor. Paravirtualization also allows a set of kernel operations to be bypassed in favor of a hypervisor call that encapsulates the entire set. So, paravirtualization adds value beyond simple instruction emulation.

7.6 Hypervisor Management Software

For each hypervisor, there is a companion layer of hypervisor management software that provides a range of functions, such as create VM, delete VM and move VM as hypervisor management functions controlling the hypervisor. A unique set of application programming interface (APIs) and graphical user interface (GUIs) is available for each 'hypervisor/hypervisor management software' pair that is used by the client, IT staff and by independent software vendors (ISVs) to create management services or other applications.

7.6.1 Hypervisor

Hypervisor is the foundation for virtualization on servers as it enables the hardware to be divided into multiple logical partitions and ensures isolation among them. It also supports Ethernet transport mechanism and Ethernet switch, which are needed for virtual local area network (VLAN). VLAN allows secure communication between logical partitions without using any physical Ethernet adapter. The hypervisor uses a virtual small computer system interface (SCSI) to provide support for virtual storage.

Hypervisor is a global firmware image located outside the partition memory in the first physical memory block at physical address zero. It takes control as soon as the system is powered on and gathers information about the memory, CPU, I/O, and other resources that are available to the system. It owns and controls all the mentioned resources and other resources that are global to the system. It performs virtual memory management using a global partition page table and manages any attempt by a partition to access outside its allocated limit. The whole physical memory is divided into blocks called physical memory blocks (PMBs). The logical memory is divided into logical memory blocks (LMBs).

PMBs are mapped to LMBs. The hypervisor has access to the entire memory space and maintains memory allocation to partitions through a global partition page table. Service partition is a partition that is allowed to update the hypervisor, which is a processor-based firmware. The hypervisor is the nerve center of the virtualization engine. It handles micro-partitioning of the CPU and the memory pool.

7.7 Virtual Infrastructure Requirements

Virtualization products have strict requirements of back-end infrastructure components, including storage, network, backup, systems management, security, and time synchronization. Ensuring that these existing components are of a supported configuration is critical to the success of the implementation. During this engagement, an IT architect reviews and documents the current environment and, where applicable, recommends changes required to optimize the infrastructure.

Where applicable, enterprise tools are used to gain a clear understanding of the environment, and the configuration and utilization of various systems. A virtualization sizing tool is then used to accurately calculate the size of a potential virtualization platform.

7.7.1 Server Virtualization Suitability Assessment

One of the key advantages of virtualization is the greater utilization of physical server resources. However, achieving this advantage must not be at the cost of service to the business. It is imperative to ensure that the virtualization host server is sized such that it can deliver acceptable levels of service to all guests.

To ensure that existing servers operate in a shared environment, detailed hardware inventory and performance utilization information must be obtained, extrapolated, and analyzed for suitability and host server sizing.

At the completion of the collection phase, the architect evaluates results and provides documented recommendations on virtualization suitability across server candidates.

7.7.2 Detailed Design

Virtualization introduces many changes in the environment and ensures that the platform co-exists and interacts with the existing infrastructure, which is the key to a successful implementation.

The purpose of the design is to set naming and security standards, define the disk and network structure, document any required system-tuning elements, and produce a virtual infrastructure design capable of meeting specific requirements for a virtualized Intel server environment.

Detailed Design Document

Virtualization design document should include the following:

1. Security and administration model.
2. Backup methodology.

3. Host physical and virtual disk layout, specifically around file system structure, and dedication of disks to guests where applicable.
4. Virtual network topology structure/format and interconnection with the physical network.
5. Virtualization service console configuration.
6. Virtualization kernel device share factor configuration.
7. Host server hardware specifications.
8. Configuration of VM server with required database.
9. Virtual machine distribution among hosts.
10. Processes and procedures for ongoing management.
11. Implementation tables and configuration settings.

7.8 Summary

This chapter focuses on server virtualization but also covers other types of virtualization. Under server virtualization, we have discussed different implementations of virtualization, management software, what constitutes support for virtualization platforms, and other related topics.

CHAPTER

8 Cloud Infrastructure: Deep Dive

CONTENTS

8.1 Introduction

It is the need of the hour to reduce the risks and cost associated with business. At the same time, it is becoming vital to increase the agility and quality of the IT infrastructure. When we look at the compute business, it is more competitive to improve the utilization of the server and the flexibility by which hardware deployment can become an easier process and meet the changing requirements of the infrastructure market.

Virtualized IT environments and cloud computing will put new requirements on networks, both inside and to and from datacenters. Networks will require new levels of performance, availability, resiliency, security, and management while delivering cost-effectiveness and energy efficiencies expected from the rest of the infrastructure. Without the right networking infrastructure, businesses will not be able to realize the benefits of virtualization fully. These new services are designed to help networks adapt to the latest demands of virtualized infrastructure and condition the IT infrastructure for cloud computing.

What is happening in datacenters today is the adoption of virtualization. This helps businesses get better utilization out of the resources they have, makes them easier to manage, and saves money.

However, virtulization and its benefits are being adopted in multiple areas of the IT infrastructure, from different server platforms, such as x86, RISC, and mainframes, and different hypervisors, to storage and even the network. Businesses need help in understanding how the different virtualization techniques will affect their network and how they should plan and design their future network.

Multiple operating systems can run on a single physical server with the help of virtual machines (VMs) that enable various businesses to share the infrastructure. This results in effective utilization of the deployed hardware. The following varied scenarios can be deployed on the same server, where the developer and the administrator can bring in more optimization while working together:

1. Software testing and development.
2. Distributed servers and platforms testing.
3. Server consolidation.
4. Legacy application re-hosting.

The tremendous growth in data over the last decade needs lots of control mechanisms. But the IT business rule that works for an IT environment, in which computing is decentralized, does not control storage, processing, and networking requirements. This has made the system very complex, and the available data are fragmented over the legacy systems. This calls for complete lifecycle management of the cloud environment to help the cloud subscribers, which will make storage, archiving, and information dissemination easier for business operations.

Let us start with the following facts:

1. Data are growing rapidly, approximately by 50% every year.
2. Companies are running big amounts of storage, and some industries such as health and life sciences need 1 TB data per day.

3. Total IT budgets amount to around 15% because of storage.
4. Redundancies are higher.

Organizations are not able to handle the growth of the data, and this causes a lot of problems due to scarcity of efficient storage and information systems. Therefore, it adds more costs and gives rise to the problems of not meeting the service-level agreements. These problems lead to insignificant performance over legacy systems.

Indeed, there is requirement of information lifecycle management techniques to overcome these problems and meet the future high-volume data growth problems.

As company data loads continue to increase, so do the complexity and capacity of the storage environment. Storage area networks (SANs) can help overcome some of the storage challenges, but not all of them. The complexity remains. Multiple storage devices from multiple vendors can have inter-operability issues on the SAN. Storage management can be tedious and time-consuming. Also infrastructure changes can be difficult to implement.

By embracing storage virtualization, clients gain the ability to reduce storage network complexity by aggregating multiple storage devices into a common managed virtual storage pool. Storage optimization and integration services – storage virtualization service products – help businesses create an integrated, virtualized solution that aligns with their unique storage strategy, vendor choices, and environment. By gaining access to experienced, knowledgeable professionals who use proven methodologies, businesses can develop a storage virtualization solution that allows them to add storage solutions with live upgradation means, without effecting the actual servers and network. This will even help to develop a comprehensive approach to combine with varied speed-based drives according to size requirements of different vendors. It provides ease of access to storage devices across the enterprise.

8.1.1 Value Proposition

For organizations that need to reduce storage management complexity, increase storage capacity utilization, and enable non-disruptive hardware change, cloud vendors offer storage virtualization services. Designed to help clients reduce storage costs, centralize data management, and extend the life of their storage hardware, this service product provides experienced consultants a platform to design and build an integrated virtualization solution that aligns with clients' particular storage strategies and environments.

Unlike many of their competitors, cloud vendors are multi-vendor suppliers and integrators who use a comprehensive consulting approach and can provide the expertise, techniques, and broad product portfolio needed by clients to create an efficient virtualized storage environment.

8.2 Storage Virtualization

Storage utilization is improved by storage virtualization. It provides the common pool of storage in a self-service manner with access to and management of the resources among the various tenants of the organization, which may not be directly looking for physical location of storage (Fig. 8.1).

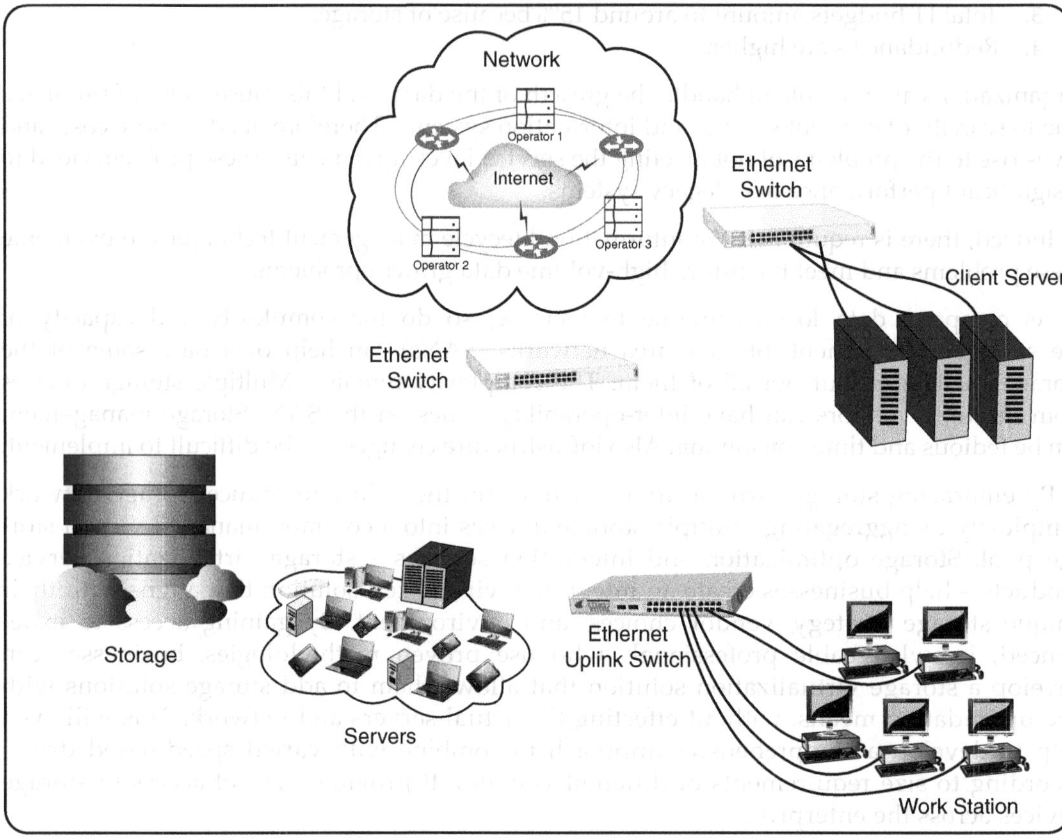

FIGURE 8.1 Storage cloud.

1. **Benefits:**
   - Make storage simpler.
   - Make storage more heterogeneous.
   - Make storage more manageable.
2. **Why the cloud?**
   - The cloud can assess, design, develop, optimize, and support on-demand infrastructure that is integrated, virtualized, autonomic, and built on open standards.
3. **The storage challenge:** Storage is a top priority for every business, mission-critical as well as challenging to manage. What makes it challenging?
   - Growth in storage demand and, therefore, growth in storage management costs due to digital content, e-mail, Internet-based applications, and emerging technology are one of the reasons.
   - Threats to business continuity posed by disaster or human errors as causes of 40% of outages are yet other reasons. Also, dealing with storage management strains your budget.
   - Pressure to retain data for compliance with regulations has increased worldwide.
   - Complexity of storage networks with devices from different manufacturers resulting in separate islands of storage is on the rise.

A single point of management over your entire storage network, using your storage and data resources to their full potential, among others, enables excellent productivity of storage administrators and increases the potential to reduce errors. Typical structural client savings of 30–70% on storage management costs are possible.

8.2.1 Storage Cost Drivers

Storage is growing rapidly. Although the cost of storage hardware is decreasing (halving every 12 months), the overall storage cost is increasing as a result of increased demand for storage (nearly doubling every 12 months) and complex storage management:

1. Only 14% of the total cost of ownership (TCO) is hardware cost.
2. Studies indicate that storage-related cost (hardware and software) will peak to 23% of the total IT budget.
3. Today storage administrations are islands of point solutions, which increases the management cost.
4. While the purchasing cost per GB goes down by 20%–40% yearly, the cost of managing storage may rise high with the growth in traditional storage environments.

8.3 Storage Area Networks

Storage area network (SAN) is a method of provisioning by locally attaching the device to the operating system, and to the servers. With the SAN architecture, we can connect different types of disk arrays, tapes, and other storage devices (Fig. 8.2).

Network-attached storage (NAS) is different from SAN as it uses file-based protocols such as Network File System (NFS). In this architecture, it is evident that the storage is available remotely and can be accessed as a file and not as the disk block.

SANs are becoming a pervasive technology. The following list shows their evolution through several stages:

1. **Direct-attach storage:** Hosts can only use storage that is directly attached through point to point small computer system interface (SCSI) connections. The disk storage is physically separate and cannot be configured to attach to multiple hosts.
2. **Centralized but still direct-attach storage:** The storage is physically centralized in one unit. The disk controller is connected to multiple hosts with point-to-point connections. Re-assigning storage to different hosts requires re-cabling.
3. **Shared storage:** A SAN enables point-to-point connections between any host and the disk controller. Disk volumes can be dynamically assigned to different hosts, without requiring re-cabling. SANs have enabled several benefits, including:
   - Better connectivity (avoidance of re-cabling).
   - Improved performance (through higher-bandwidth connections).
   - Distance flexibility (overcoming SCSI limitations).
   - Scalability (enabling storage capacity to be increased with less disruption).
   - More vendor/product choice (by separating the disk storage from the host server and using open-standard Fibre Channel connections).

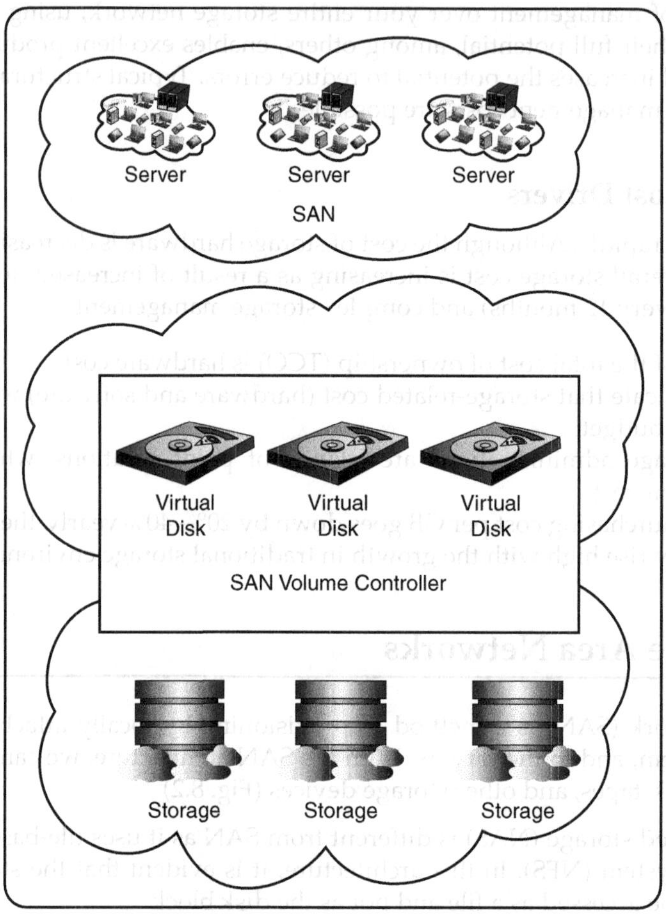

FIGURE 8.2 SAN.

However, these benefits have also resulted in new issues and increased complexity. Let us see what this means:

1. **Complexity case A:** Enterprises have a SAN with many UNIX/Windows servers attached.
2. **Complexity case B:** Within the SAN, there are many different types of storage. In some cases, customers made this choice to stay vendor-neutral; while in others, it was a result of mergers or consolidations. The storage administrator has to configure logical unit numbers (LUNs) to servers and keep track of which servers have what storage. Surprisingly, most customers admit that they are keeping track of all this with spreadsheets, as SAN managers are not as prevalent as we would have thought. You can imagine the complexity of reallocating LUNs to different servers as the need for storage shifts from one server to another.

3. **Complexity case C:** Complexity of different file systems. Now the storage administrator needs to know the different commands to be used depending on the file system being dealt with.
4. **Complexity case D:** On top of all of this, each of these storage devices has to be configured and installed. But because there are no common standards, each storage device has its own procedures and user interfaces for doing this. Now imagine that you are in production and the storage administrator is faced with the task of replicating all of these devices across all servers and managing the performance and capacity of each device. Again, they each have their own separate interfaces and procedures to do this.
5. **Complexity case E:** Last but not least, because the file systems are tied to each of the hundreds of servers, all of the storage management functions have to be run on these hundreds of servers. If you ask businesses what percentage of their storage is actually being utilized, most of them will not know the answer.

So, this is what businesses mean when they say they have inter-operability and manageability problems with their storage. No wonder, if you think about the many permutations and combinations of 'x' servers/operating systems times 'y' device types, you know that the complexity is daunting.

8.3.1 Storage Virtualization Benefits

Storage virtualization makes storage simpler, more heterogeneous and more manageable. It creates a logical view of storage that simplifies management and makes physical changes to the infrastructure transparent to the user (Fig. 8.3).

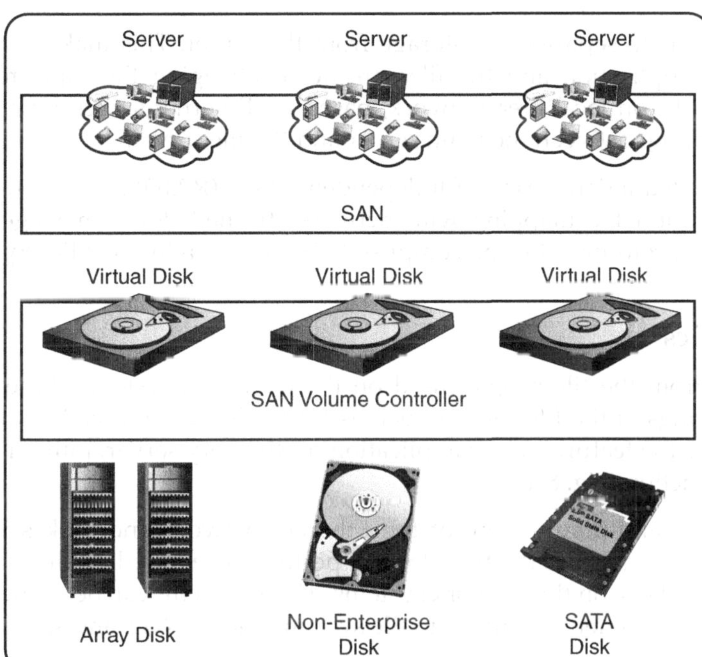

FIGURE 8.3 Virtual storage infrastructure.

1. **Make it simpler:**
   - Effective use of capacity.
   - Effective management of capacity.
   - Lower cost of ownership.
2. **Make it more heterogeneous:**
   - Any-to-any attachment.
   - Data migration.
   - Security.
   - Investment protection.
3. **Make it more manageable:**
   - Scalable.
   - Quality of service management.

This gives the options to control the storage volumes through a central point. It even reduces the server down-time for different predicted outages, maintenance, and support activities. This helps in effective resource utilization and sets the storage management tools in a cost-effective fashion.

8.4 Network-Attached Storage

Network-attached storage (NAS), based on its network address, is a hard drive storage. It is not directly connected to the server that actually serves the workstations connected to the network applications.

It is advantageous to separate the storage from the server. This makes the process faster because both the application and the files are not challenging the same resources on the network. NAS works on local area network, based on Ethernet switch with the IP address. There exists a mapping between the main server and the file server.

NAS comprises Redundant Array of Independent Disks (RAID) systems, hard disk storage and configuration, and file mapping with network-attached device management device. It works on file-based protocols. This can comprise NFS, Common Internet File System (CIFS), etc.

8.4.1 NAS Basics

NAS is different from the file server based on the operating system. These file servers are based on the offerings of the file servers such as UNIX, Novell, Linux, Windows, and OS/2. NAS does not have the features of the application or directory server; rather it is based on the specific Storage function (Fig. 8.4).

NAS uses a plug-and-play feature of the Ethernet network and makes it available in a fraction of a second. It delivers the fully loaded performance-based application environment to serve the files available on the network systems. These systems can be connected to the non-Windows–based environments to attach to file systems such as NFS and serve the large ports.

Implementation of NAS architecture is not difficult, but the administrator should know the gamut of its components such as the interconnection points and NAS protocols.

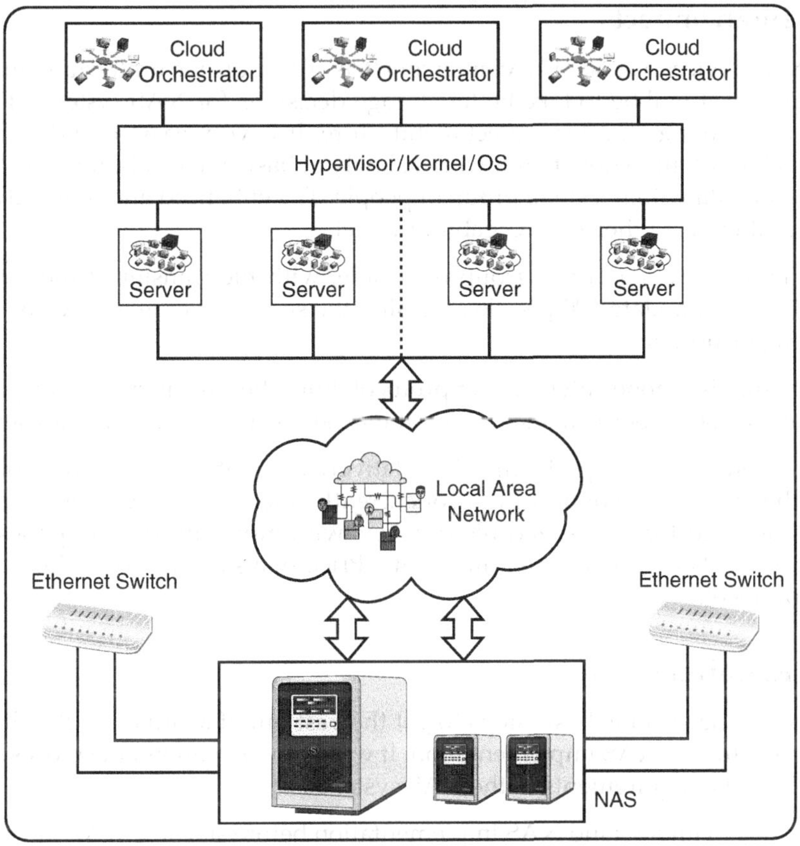

FIGURE 8.4 NAS.

8.4.2 NAS Protocols

We need a language to talk to the NAS interconnects. It is important to have knowledge of the protocol that is the key for NAS implementation. CIFS started as the project outcome of server messaging block protocol and was later renamed as CIFS. CIFS is the most common protocol for windows environment.

Another protocol for the NAS is NFS. The combined power of virtualization and performance gives an upper hand to use NFS as a preferred protocol among NAS vendors. This helps in storing the data at the file level, rather than at the block level.

Internet small computer system interface (iSCSI) is another protocol stack for NAS and gives the option to access the data at block level. This is an inexpensive protocol compared to the other two as it works without using expensive adapters and sophisticated software.

Fibre Channel over Ethernet (FCoE) is another NAS protocol. It is a combination of Fibre Channel and Ethernet, but it is difficult to determine its success as there are few Fibre Channel over Ethernet deployments.

8.4.3 NAS Interconnects

To integrate NAS devices, we need NAS interconnects. The more we understand the NAS interconnects, the easier it will be to take better storage decisions for NAS systems. Fast Ethernet is one of the best among all interconnect architecture. It is very easy to understand and not expensive. It is important to note that it works slowly at basic file levels. It is good for transfer of up to 10 MB of data within a small group of people. The enhanced and more advanced level of interconnect after Fast Ethernet is Gigabit Ethernet.

Gigabit Ethernet serves a larger group of people, with file transfer of more than 10 MB. This can easily accommodate 100 people accessing the same server at a very good speed and relatively good performance.

Gigabit Ethernet is a good interconnect protocol, but when we increase our group size, to say 500, we can face some performance issues. It may also cause issues for block-level accesses.

In order to overcome these problems, the relatively new interconnect protocol 10 GE is of help. This is the fastest interconnect protocol currently and provides very good performance when there is demand for huge-sized file transfers with more speed. Enterprises use hybrid interconnect protocols as per their requirements. Price plays a vital role while choosing the interconnect protocol.

8.4.4 NAS Requirements

NAS requirements need some basic steps to get the best out of a situation. It will help you to define the success for the NAS implementation. It will help to maintain the most suitable set of vendors based on the requirements of the NAS systems.

It is a good idea to understand NAS implementation before starting it. All the vendors have different devices available over different deployments, so having a clear idea of the same gives an edge to the best fit of the NAS system. It will be good to evaluate the different options available by distributing the requirements among the vendors and outlining the different extremities of the situation.

Listing of the requirements required for the device can be the easiest step. The primary requirements can be connecting to the multiple servers without any performance loss, the amount of the storage to handle the file use, etc. This will require little bit of research on the current offerings available to handle these requirements. The requirements that are technical necessity of the NAS systems can be maintained as a list to match up with real-world deployment and budget management to buy them.

8.4.5 High-Performance NAS

NAS works with file-based systems that help companies to work with distributed file systems such as NFS and CIFS. This consolidates the distributed file system into different, small file-based storage systems. There were some problems associated with NAS such as reliability, connectivity, and scalability with the enterprise storage. But now, the new-generation NAS systems have overcome it and promise higher value in the same file-based storage systems.

In order to differentiate the high-performance from regular NAS, there is no common single point of agreement. But we can have some distinction at least, such as high-performance NAS provides more ports on the interface level. Connectivity is an important factor for performance and more the number of ports, more reliable the NAS implementation.

High-performance NAS systems operate with the Serial Advanced Technology Attachment (SATA) or serial-attached SCSI. As a result, we get higher scalability with the disk controller engines available within the system. High-performance NAS systems work with various heads that can access various disks, and at the same time, improve performance. It is also possible to analyze the input/output operations per second (IOPS) to optimize the high-performance NAS system. We can have the concurrent file access in the high-performance NAS platform or access to multiple metadata points at the same time.

Clustering also plays an important role in increasing the throughput of NAS systems other than having a single pool of storage. It also offers resiliency as even if one of the cluster is not working, the other will not be affected and the workload of the failed one can be transferred to the working and free cluster.

The unique feature of high-performance NAS is Global File System (GFS). It is very helpful in the clustered environment where all the clusters share a single pool. GFS can be added with the operating system or as a separate layer on top of the high-performance NAS. GFS helps the cluster to work independently or as the same entity while sharing the same pool. High-performance NAS has an upper and helping edge over the deployment challenges. It helps to

1. Perform more work in less time.
2. Reduce the number of file servers.
3. Simplify NAS storage infrastructure.
4. Save energy.

Administrators should evaluate the prospective high-performance NAS system for

1. Underlying NAS systems management requirements.
2. Expectation of NAS systems management efficiency.
3. High-performance and -throughput issues.
4. Demand of special host software or drivers.
5. Expense of added software maintenance issues.
6. Tuning and load balancing.
7. Appropriate system for data workload.
8. Management and interoperation with storage vendors to ease compatibility concerns.

The most important step for better performance results is to optimize the workload and understand the data workload with the inner depth of application. We can find out what type of application it is and how it works sequentially, or by storing transactional data with the known IOPS. High-performance NAS systems require the following to accommodate high-performance systems:

1. New switching.
2. Network architecture changes.
3. Additional LAN bandwidth.

High-performance NAS is evolving fast, but still many features of traditional NAS are not available in it as yet, such as

1. Snapshots.
2. Replication.
3. Point-in-time (PIT) copies.
4. Finer management granularity.
5. Better load balancing and data migration.

High-performance NAS has also renewed interest in the following:

1. Storage virtualization.
2. VMs used throughout.
3. Storage virtualization aggregation.
4. Live storage mobility.
5. High-capacity storage systems.

8.4.6 Network Infrastructure

Network infrastructure helps organizations in understanding their networks and their network usage better, addressing specific networking issues or problems, and reducing networking costs. The service provides relevant recommendations based on the analysis of data from the client's network and networking environment, industry insights, and leading practices in networking. The service is composed of three activities from which the client may choose one or more activities to engage:

1. **Network infrastructure assessment:** It focuses on helping clients understand the components that are deployed in their networks and includes reviews of their network designs, devices, service-level agreements (SLAs), readiness reviews for deployments or refreshes with new technologies.
2. **Network performance analysis:** Network performance analysis and capacity planning focuses on helping businesses understand how the performance of their network is being affected by business critical applications and background traffic, and to determine or predict the network sizing requirements to optimize the usage by applications.
3. **Network diagnostic assessment:** Network diagnostic assessment focuses on helping businesses with problem determination, problem source identification, and root cause analysis of network performance problems.

Network infrastructure services can be appropriate any time your network is experiencing performance problems, you are under pressure to do more with fewer resources, or you have other networking issues to address. These services are also beneficial when you are planning to deploy important new business applications, bring in significant new traffic driven by organic growth or a merger or acquisition, introduce a new and network-dependent business model, or deploy a new technology such as voice or video over IP (VoIP), wireless communications, or radio frequency identification (RFID).

Network infrastructure assessments, network performance and capacity planning studies, and root cause analysis of infrastructure performance problems help to prepare for new initiatives or to repair the current networking environment.

8.5 Cloud Server Virtualization

This section provides an overview of the architecture, features, and benefits of server virtualization solutions that provide a cost-effective VM solution for OS platforms. VMs help to run various OS concurrently on the single server. This helps to cater various scenarios such as consolidation, automation, test and development environments, migrating from x86 to non-x86 env, workload management (Fig. 8.5)

8.5.1 Datacenter Virtualization

The primary requirements of the datacenter with respect to datacenter virtualization are as follows:

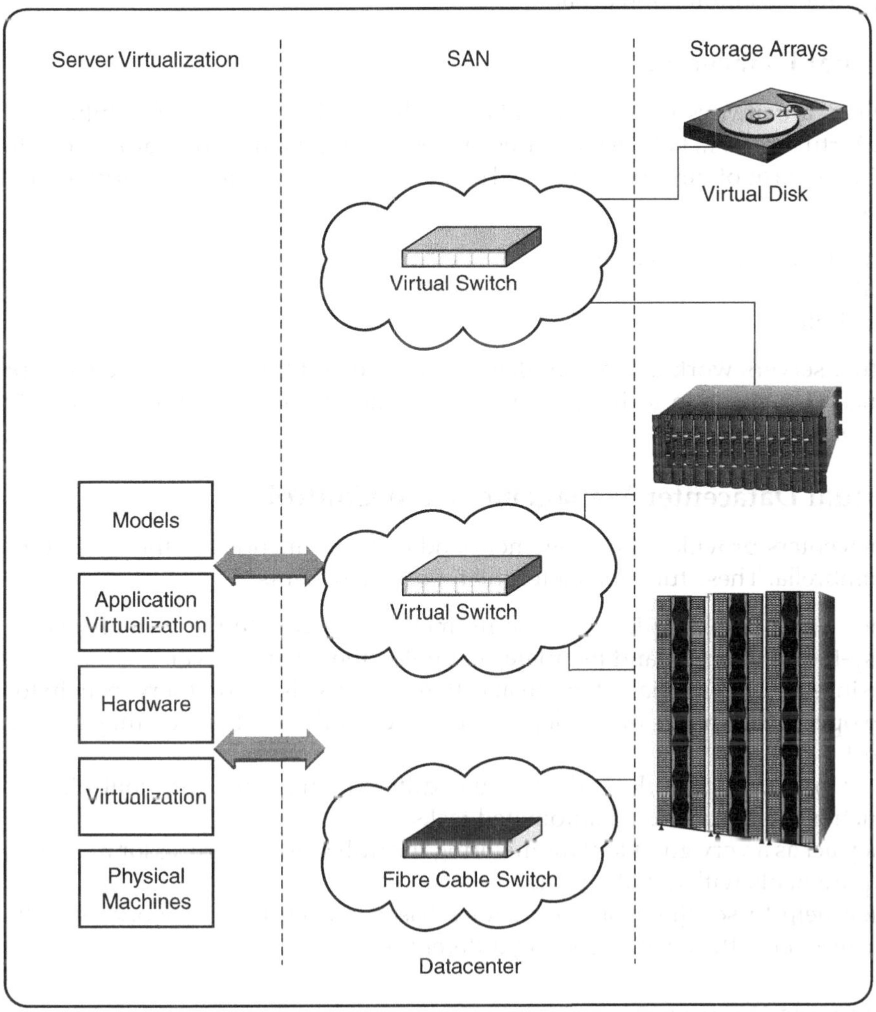

FIGURE 8.5 Server virtualization.

1. Virtual servers.
2. Storage.
3. Networking.
4. Unmodified operating systems.

These servers help to run independently the application on the VMs by sharing same pool of resources. They enable

1. Comprehensive virtualization.
2. Management.
3. SAN.
4. Resource optimization.
5. Application availability.
6. Operational automation capabilities.

8.5.2 Virtual Datacenter

Organizations are always in need of higher levels of utilization and flexibility of hardware resources. Virtual servers help achieve this by abstracting the memory, processor, storage, etc. available in the form of virtual resources. The most important feature of virtual servers is that it provides

1. High level of performance.
2. Scalability.
3. Flexibility.

These virtual servers work like a complete server and fulfill the requirements of processors. The advance virtualization techniques ensure availability of the resources when there is an acute need of resources.

8.5.3 Virtual Datacenter Management and Control

Virtual datacenters provide all management and control functions of the environment under the same umbrella. These functions offer the following benefits:

1. They use a very simple provisioning method to allocate the virtual servers with the easy-to-use interface and templates to deploy the virtual server.
2. Businesses need special attention at different intervals; virtual servers help to automate the operational needs of the deployment and set the alerts when they are required the most.
3. They help to schedule and alert the different management, control, and support functions with scheduled automated tasks.
4. They act as a very good tool for metering the utilization of processor memory and IOPS requirements with detail reports.
5. They help to set the customized roles based on the type of work as well as access permission to the resources using different tiers.

8.5.4 Dynamic Resource

In the virtual datacenter, resource requirements are not same every time. They have different spikes to meet the dynamic nature of the environment. Dynamic resources adhere to the requirements and allocate the computing resources dynamically to meet the business goals. This helps in

1. Monitoring utilization.
2. Common resource pool maintenance.
3. Matching the business needs and changing priorities.
4. Making additional capacity available.
5. Migrating live VMs.
6. Dynamically allocating IT resources.
7. Creating rules and policies to prioritize resource allocation.
8. Granting IT autonomy to business organizations.
9. Providing dedicated IT infrastructure to business unit by higher utilization achievement.
10. Having centralized IT control over hardware resources.

8.5.5 High Availability

A virtual datacenter requires the features of high availability to provide cost-effective failover options. It should not be based on related operating systems and virtualization technologies. The following features for high availability make a datacenter more robust and reliable:

1. Failover options to protect applications.
2. Consistent defense mechanism for IT infrastructure.
3. Live workload transfer in case of failover.
4. Alerting the administrator for stringent situation.
5. Zero down-time to meet SLAs.

8.5.6 Live Migration

Similar to the high availability option we have already discussed, live migration helps the environment to run and gives unparalleled availability and flexibility to meet the requirements of the business goals. It monitors the utilization of servers, storage, and networking and leverages the virtualization technology to move the VM from one server to another at unprecedented situations. This is maintained by a set of files managed by shared storage-based file systems to access the VM at different periods of intervals or simultaneously. Even the network is virtualized, which ensures smooth migration. The main features/benefits it has are that it

1. Balances the workloads by transferring the under-performing servers.
2. Ensures live migration within no time and not even traced by the end-user.
3. Maintains, manages, and supports the resource pools automatically.
4. Provides ease of hardware maintenance with failover alerts and scheduled maintenance activities.

8.6 Networking Essential to the Cloud

Network plays a vital role in infrastructure management to:

1. Reduce costs.
2. Improve service.
3. Manage risk.

It is important to focus on infrastructure initiatives essential for reaping benefits such as:

1. Server.
2. Storage hardware optimization.
3. Technology enhancements.
4. Service management improvement.
5. Security.
6. Resiliency.
7. Optimization of the network (hardware, software, management).

Highly virtualized infrastructure-based clouds meet with demanding network requirements that can restrict the growth of the infrastructure management activities. There is a need of the following features:

1. More stringent network performance.
2. Fast reliable access to virtualized resources.
3. Flexible and adaptable networks.
4. Application workload mobility.
5. Response to variable capacity requirements.
6. Security to support multi-tenancy.

8.6.1 Datacenter Network

To get the dynamic and self-service based environments, networking is very essential for initiatives such as datacenter consolidation and virtualization. Networking is very pivotal to the success of transforming the infrastructure to improve services and risk management. Though only server and storage are more in focus for virtualization and provisioning, network optimization is also essential to ensure the overall benefits of networking. To support these networking requirements, businesses will need the following:

1. Expertise to assess, plan, design, and implement networks with holistic consideration of servers, storage, application performance, and manageability.
2. Different options of cost and different ranges of performance to match their needs.
3. Technological expertise to design and deploy security policies.
4. Simple operational software to lower the cost and to integrate the network and manage it.

8.6.2 Market Opportunity

1. **Cost control, high availability and performance, and robust security are business imperatives:**
   - Businesses are looking for cost containment and reduction in the datacenter – while addressing challenges in responding quickly to rapidly changing business requirements.
2. **Datacenter networking technologies are changing fast and in-house staff does not always have adequate time and experience to take appropriate actions:**
   - Businesses need help, especially in new areas such as infrastructure virtualization, private optical networking, and converged data and storage networking.

3. **Datacenter consolidations as well as server and storage virtualization impact the network in terms of new requirements for flexibility, performance, and security:**
   - A near-capacity and often difficult-to-manage datacenter networking infrastructure resulting from years of ad hoc changes and updates that can impede plans for server and storage virtualization.

First, especially in today's economic environment, cost control, and cost savings are key considerations. Cloud vendors can help businesses save money by optimizing their current network through consolidation and virtualization of network devices, while helping them plan for the future. With the rapid changes occurring in IT infrastructure technologies, many businesses do not have the time or experience to understand how the network will be impacted. Most of the focus is on consolidating and virtualizing servers and storage without thinking long term about the supporting network.

8.6.3 Datacenter Network Services

Network services help to model, design, and architect solution for the organization to:

1. Develop the network infrastructure to work for the initiatives such as compute, storage, network consolidation, and energy optimization.
2. Integrate services of infrastructure.
3. Improve facility management for energy, cooling, and space optimization by adopting new and transformed networking devices.
4. Prepare for new technologies while maintaining security and resiliency.
5. Provide greater freedom to focus internal resources on critical operational concerns.
6. Help reduce datacenter sprawl.
7. Help build differentiating advantage through improved efficiency and business innovation.

8.6.4 Data and Storage Network Convergence

The convergence of the data network and storage network into a single physical infrastructure will be attractive to businesses that want to lower costs and complexity in their datacenters without forfeiting high availability and performance. Data and storage network convergence eliminates duplicate infrastructure, reducing the required hardware components – adapters, cables, and switches – and resulting in savings on hardware expenditures, power, cooling, and space. At the same time, with a single physical infrastructure, deployment, upgrades, and management will be simplified, contributing to lower total cost of ownership.

The services include the following:

1. Developing the network design.
2. Selecting vendors and preparing a detailed design.
3. Creating a roadmap for migration.
4. Carrying procurement, logistics site preparation.
5. Deployment, testing the network.
6. Providing on-going maintenance support.

Comprehensive network infrastructure solutions are designed to meet the changing requirements driven by consolidation and virtualization in support of dynamic infrastructures and cloud computing. The service product consists of the following components:

1. **Consolidation and virtualization:** These help to consolidate the datacenter by designing and deploying the virtualized IT environments. Convergence of data and storage networking helps to design and deploy a converged data and storage infrastructure that allows quick achievement of the financial benefits of Fibre Channel over Ethernet technology.
2. **Private networking:** This helps in establishing the private network and design and deploy the connectivity between the resources of different datacenters.
3. **Security/firewalls:** This helps to design and deploy network firewall technology to support the security requirements in today's datacenter network.

8.6.5 Network Infrastructure

Network infrastructure engagements are assessments that look at the performance, availability, resiliency, and cost of the network. A major target audience for these services is clients who are facing pressure to do more with less or who are or experiencing network performance or availability problems. Another important target audience is clients who are planning changes such as the deployment of a new application that may require network redesign, anticipation of increased network traffic from organic growth or acquisitions or new network traffic flows driven by datacenter consolidation, green datacenter migrations, and server relocations.

Network infrastructure optimization includes four components: network infrastructure assessment, network performance analysis and capacity planning, network infrastructure for consolidation and virtualization, and network diagnostic assessment.

Network infrastructure assessments are designed to help organizations provide an in-depth view of an existing network infrastructure and identify gaps between the client's current and desired capabilities. These assessments are designed to determine if there are resources that are underutilized or untapped and if more value can be extracted from the investments a client has already made. They can also include reviews of network designs, devices, configurations, and service level agreements (including service level objectives) as well as an assessment of the readiness to deploy a new technology or upgrade the infrastructure.

Network performance analysis and capacity planning helps clients understand how overall network performance is affected by applications and background traffic, whether current or new. It also demonstrates how the network may react to failures or changes in configurations. It captures the traffic flows across the infrastructure to establish baselines and trends, including usage patterns to provide inputs for simulation modeling or virtual testing of proposed changes in the infrastructure. Outputs of network performance and capacity planning can be used as inputs to make immediate changes to improve performance and capacity as well as determine network sizing requirements for a planned environment change or for setting appropriate SLAs with carriers.

Network infrastructure for consolidation and virtualization is a service component that helps clients address the increasingly complex networking aspects of a virtualized IT environment by identifying cost savings and delivering an optimized networking infrastructure. The service can also help to plan, design, and build a networking infrastructure that contributes fully to a dynamic infrastructure – one that adapts quickly and effectively to business opportunities and rapidly changing demands.

A network diagnostic assessment helps clients identify problems, pinpoint sources, and analyze root causes of specific performance issues. This type of assessment can uncover problems such as traffic congestion, latency, suboptimal configurations, or the impact of application behavior on the performance of the network. For converged networking environments, network diagnostic can determine the issues around VoIP and video real-time protocol issues so that additional drill down can be identified. The objective is to recommend approaches and corrective actions that help the client maintain business-critical application performance at levels that support their business goals.

All engagements result in actionable recommendations for optimizing the networking infrastructure like given below:

1. **Main points:**
   - Rising costs and challenges in responding quickly to rapidly changing business opportunities.
   - Critical business processes jeopardized by down-time, security breaches, or the poor performance of the networking infrastructure.
   - Determining the networking alternatives that address immediate challenges and protect future flexibility.
2. **Network infrastructure provides the following benefits:**
   - Identifying areas to cut costs through consolidation and virtualization.
   - Planning a network that fully contributes to a responsive IT environment.
   - Removing network as a bottleneck to meeting availability, security, and performance requirements.
   - Leveraging expertise to plan and justify a dynamic networking infrastructure tied directly to business needs.
   - Achieving the optimal balance of business needs, network enhancements, and cost savings using a proven, structured, and robust approach.
3. **Business impact:**
   - Increasing costs for a proliferation of hardware.
   - Business constrained by IT infrastructure.
   - Lost returns because of customer displeasure and reduced employee productivity.
   - Poor business image, fines, and investigations due to security breaches.
   - Risk of inexperienced staff making poor long-term, strategic decisions.
   - Inability to achieve the right balance of business, cost, and network benefits.

The technique provides a structured approach for deploying business applications integrated with IT capabilities.

8.6.6 Datacenter Networking Services Enhancements

There are three service products under networking strategy and optimization services:

1. Organization network strategy and planning.
2. Network application optimization.
3. Network infrastructure.

The following are four service components available under network integration services datacenter networks:

1. Consolidation and virtualization.
2. Data and storage network convergence.
3. Private optical networking.
4. Security and firewalls.

8.6.7 Network Integration – Consolidation and Virtualization

The consolidation and virtualization component helps clients understand, plan for, and meet the new demands of virtualized servers and storage while also addressing consolidation and virtualization of the network itself to further reduce infrastructure costs. It is designed to

1. Address the new demands that virtualized servers and storage devices place on the network *and* the benefits of consolidating and virtualizing the network itself.
2. Deliver cost-effective, optimized networking infrastructures that support and fully contribute to a responsive, consolidated, and virtualized IT environment.

Cloud vendors can help businesses migrate from a traditional, isolated, static network design for the datacenter to one that is integrated with other IT resources to provide dynamic, scalable network resources. Regardless of the brands of technology in their environment, network consolidation and virtualization services are designed to offer guidance throughout the process – from developing the strategy and assessing the current infrastructure to designing and implementing a networking infrastructure that comprehensively supports a dynamic infrastructure.

In the big picture, IT infrastructure is moving left to right – servers, storage, and networking are becoming more and more interdependent, leading ultimately to a set of resources that are provisioned together to deliver services:

1. **Legacy environment:** Static, endpoint agnostic, strict, limited change windows, proliferation of special-purpose devices (firewalls, load balancers, IPS).
2. **Device virtualization:** Physical consolidation and optimization, basic virtualization of servers, storage, and network, simply network management.
3. **System virtualization:** Connecting virtualized servers and storage, support platform–specific network requirements and multiple layers of network virtualization.
4. **Cloud computing:** Architect responsive, secure network; support automated provisioning of servers, storage, and network; increase operational savings.

8.6.8 Datacenter Network Thinking has to Change

Static, secure datacenter networks that meet their non-functional requirements through limited, controlled changes are no longer adequate. Datacenter networks must become significantly more flexible and responsive, capable of dynamic change. The datacenter network is a critical success factor for storage and server virtualization initiatives – ignore it at your peril. Consolidation and virtualization in the datacenter is increasing demands on the network in terms of throughput and traffic patterns, upending traditional performance and capacity 'rules of thumb'. VM mobility and mixed-platform environments will require the network to be much more dynamic in terms of scaling and services provided, to transfer workloads without disruption to end-users and business processes. The network must be integrated into the overall IT systems management environment to provide dynamic services in response to automated provisioning.

8.7 Summary

This chapter provides an overview of the architectures, features, and benefits of cloud infrastructure solutions which provide a cost-effective solution for any datacenter cloud implementation.

CHAPTER

9

Cloud and SOA

CONTENTS

9.1 Introduction

Any enterprise-wide transformation has significant challenges for people, processes, and technology. Therefore, identifying challenges ahead of the time and defining a mitigated approach can help in making such a transformation successful. Some of the challenges include resistance to change by people and organizations. The transformation factors include roles and responsibilities, management, skills development and discipline, and cultural shifts. This also includes creating awareness in the organization for the need to drive such a transformation in the best interests of the business. It is very difficult to deal with infrastructure complexity, including hardware, software, and applications, across disparate environments ('line of business' stakeholders, partners, and customers). Well-planned assessments are needed to understand where to start from and how to progress in a staged way.

Service management is one of the similarities between the cloud infrastructure and Service-Oriented Architecture (SOA) approaches. Developing an integrated service management approach for both application and infrastructure services will drive efficiency in IT operations by improving resource utilization and service levels. Such an integrated service management can move IT toward an end-to-end service-oriented environment. Such an environment enables business agility by aligning IT with the business in a better way.

9.1.1 Enterprise Infrastructure and SOA

Design and provisioning of an enterprise infrastructure must be focused on the needs of enterprise organizations. Through comprehensive capabilities of products, services, and integrated solutions, IT organizations are delivering increasingly complex solutions driven by SOA and related methodologies. To achieve their ambitious growth goals, leading IT organizations require continuing investments in IT and taking the advantage of emerging capabilities. A future technology platform will need to support agile business organizations through the simplification of information systems and reduce the complexity of the IT ecosystem through consolidation and rationalization.

We need a governance model for the heterogeneous environment owned by many parties and providing an end-to-end IT infrastructure. This governance model will define the IT infrastructure service requirements in support of an integrated service offering for business systems.

As the SOA projects are deployed, development of an effective design of the supporting infrastructure becomes critical. SOA introduces the requirements for availability, service continuity, monitoring, scalability, and geographic dispersion that are different than those of the past architectures.

SOA converts IT applications into composite applications. Instead of traditional monolithic applications, composite applications are created, which are composed of many services often developed and deployed independently by separate development teams on different schedules. By adhering to common standards and interfaces, the development of new composite applications and the extension of existing applications are made easier through the reuse of existing services and the rapid integration of new services.

Similar concepts to SOA drive the cloud infrastructure, an approach that makes an IT infrastructure a collection of service components with common standards and interfaces. The cloud infrastructure makes the deployment of new infrastructure using repeatable and existing processes.

Cloud infrastructure service components include the physical infrastructure (such as processors, memory, storage, and I/O networks), system software (firmware and OS), and management software (monitoring, provisioning, and workload management). While the cloud infrastructure is particularly suited to support SOA applications, Service-Oriented Infrastructure (SOI) is well-suited to legacy application support. The service components of cloud infrastructure are independent of application architecture and capable to provide flexible support to any application.

Cloud infrastructure strongly leverages virtualization technologies, which enable rapid deployment and redeployment of service components.

9.2 SOA Journey to Infrastructure

The path to transformation consists of a long journey with a staged approach, leading to the ultimate goal of a service-oriented enterprise. Multiple islands of disparate infrastructures in today's environment need to be consolidated to gain control, reduce costs, and become operationally efficient. The next step is to introduce virtualized infrastructure to improve the utilization levels, allow dynamic flexibility to move resources, and the capacity to meet fluctuating workload demands. It is important to note how service orientation (SO) can be achieved by building capabilities on the top of virtualized and automated infrastructure. Service orientation is a state where the infrastructure is provided and utilized as a service rather than in piecemeal. Latest innovations, such as cloud computing, will help to further expand the service-oriented paradigm to meet the scaling demands of future state of businesses.

9.3 SOA and the Cloud

SOA binds both the deliver and leverage cloud-based services. Cloud computing relies on service orientation (virtualization at the application layer) to loosely couple the applications with the underlying infrastructure model for using Web services – such as service requestors, service registry, and service providers. Web services are required to compose the complex distributed legacy applications that can be customized later. This helps to integrate bespoke applications and provide the service for extensibility, encapsulations, and interoperability. SOA works as a foundation for the stepping stones to the cloud journey. It embraces all the characteristics of the cloud – such as self-service, shared and dynamic infrastructure, and virtualization (Fig. 9.1).

Cloud computing is an infrastructure management and services deployment method with virtualized resources and it is managed as a single large resource. Clouds share and leverage the characteristics of SO with flexibility and agility. Applications and services are reused in new and dynamic ways and so rapid deployment happens in SOA-based cloud implementation.

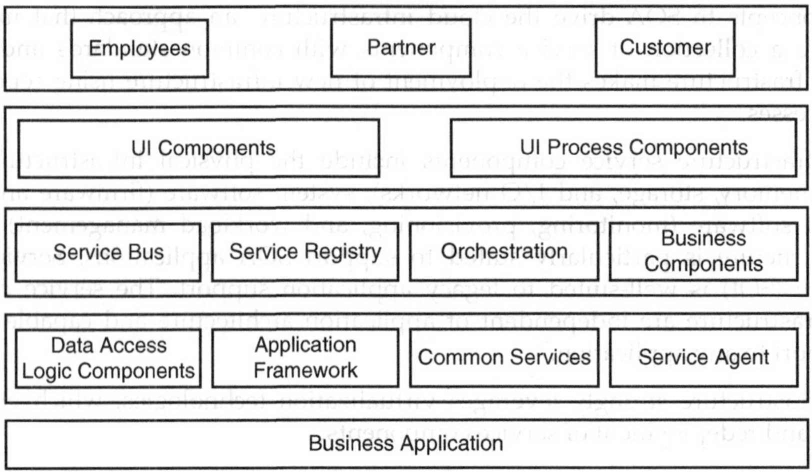

FIGURE 9.1 SOA model.

The SOA infrastructure is required in order to effectively apply SO to an enterprise or large-scale software component development. Basically, the SOA infrastructure consists of middleware, physical infrastructure, and management – collectively covering the non-functional requirements.

SOA is an application framework for building better applications. Web services and SOA do not replace applications as they are today; they complement their functionality and allow for better reuse and business flexibility. SOA helps to break an application framework into discrete service components (i.e., mini-applications) so they can be reused as common services between different applications. An IT infrastructure must continue to evolve and mature to support the new demands in the industry on a distributed and virtualized application framework. SOA applications require the same end-to-end performance, security, and management.

The key to an effective SOA infrastructure is to understand the changes that will take place and which tools are available for infrastructure architecture and design. The best SOA infrastructures have been designed keeping both application and infrastructure perspective in mind.

A well-designed SOA infrastructure is a mix of current processes and SOA infrastructure technologies. SOA and traditional applications do not exist outside of one another. All applications are a part of a shared services environment and use common infrastructure components. Traditional system designs need to be updated to support the new application requirements.

Clouds enable the deployment of cloud services, and SOA is the most sophisticated architectural approach for building and delivery of services. SOA is a design pattern that is composed of loosely coupled, discoverable, reusable, and interoperable platform-neutral services. Each of these services follows a well-defined standard and can be bound or unbound at any time as needed. The value of SOA comes from having an architecture that readily accommodates change.

Clouds are about infrastructure and deployment technology. The concept of service delivery is independent of deployment scale and may operate via a connection between two or three computers only; whereas, cloud computing represents a much larger-scale implementation. SOA is the way an enterprise builds, maintains, governs, and orchestrates the services to be delivered; cloud computing is an instance of SOA. Software-as-a-Service (SaaS) is a term used by a group of companies or individuals when they host a set of software services over the Web. SaaS focuses on the software hosted as a service, and may be considered as a consumption model in which a user is involved. Whereas, SOA focuses on the software designed as a service, and is a design model in which there is no restriction on the consumer.

Private clouds can simply be seen as SOAs with the added characteristics of virtualization and self-provisioning. Those who use private clouds, or virtualization, typically break down new and old applications as services, processes, and data, and address each as an architectural component that may be freely distributed in private clouds.

SOA is important to cloud computing and the use of SOA will promote the adoption of cloud computing. Enabling SOA is important for enabling an infrastructure for cloud service delivery. Most experts agree that without SOA, a move to clouds will be tough to justify financially, because re-engineering legacy systems that are not built to be exposed outside of the usual user community may end up being too costly. Enterprise cloud initiatives require decoupled data systems working together, without the need for personnel and other resources to set up and maintain them. To achieve this objective, integration is the key. The loosely coupled aspect of SOA is very important.

Loosely coupled application, processes, and data give the best option to move to the cloud for migration services. If SOA is not practiced in an organization, the migration to the cloud will be a difficult option as all applications, processes, and data will be tightly coupled. Subsequently, it will really be difficult to change, transform, rewrite, or migrate them.

If a service is initiated by a cloud user, there is a requirement to provide the application programing interface (APIs) for the legacy functionalities in the service model. In order to accomplish this, it calls the integration services to form firewalls for the technology and architecture barriers. This gap is bridged by the service bus and it is the pivotal point for the IT infrastructure and cloud services. SOA helps to identify service portfolios or part of the services, and decides to transfer certain services which are cloud ready to the cloud. If one thinks for the cloud services without SOA proposition, it becomes the cause of failure of the infrastructure.

A 'service communications backbone' is needed to run between the different clouds being used, allowing users to utilize remote services from any cloud without dealing with connectivity and interoperability issues. It is a simple concept, but without it, cloud-to-cloud interoperability issues may limit the growth of cloud computing. This is really going to require state-of-the-science SOA, with the ability to access thousands of services that could be hosted anywhere and to abstract them from interoperability issues. As is always the case with such industry efforts, the standards process takes time. The trick is to develop service architectures that will not require an overhaul in the future based on specifications that are yet to be defined.

9.3.1 Infrastructure Technologies

Cloud infrastructure is based on virtualization that is composed of dynamic systems that enable the definition and delivery of resources on demand. Current server technology can deliver hundreds of virtual servers on small clusters of physical servers, enabling flexibility and high availability.

In a virtual environment, workloads can be moved dynamically between components, allowing minimal unplanned downtime and no planned downtime. Each server contains a pool of processors, memory, and I/O resources that can be dynamically assigned and reassigned to meet needs. Surplus capacity cannot be pre-provisioned until activated.

9.4 SOA Defined

SOA is defined as a methodology for architecting the solution that looks for flexibility based on loose coupling and encapsulation. The functionalities of SOA are exposed as services, and there exists an instance for each service and its implementation. The deployment of these services requires less deployment time as they are built once and can be redeployed at multiple instances, and can be invoked at remote or onsite locations.

SOA is about an evolving living organism and not about building a house. This is an ongoing journey and not a project that finishes with a concrete result. Agility of the business is an important factor for business continuity as it helps to find faster solutions to changing business priorities and leverages the competitive effectiveness of business change requirements. SOA is defined by what a service is. Services are defined by the following characteristics:

1. Explicit, implementation-independent interfaces.
2. Loosely bound.
3. Invoked through communication protocols.
4. Stress location transparency and interoperability.
5. Summarized reusable business task and assets.

Conceptually, SOA can be visualized by the roles of individuals in any organization. The architect sees SOA from the perspective of the entire business and uses SOA implementation to bridge the gaps of the business.

SOA is very flexible; therefore, it facilitates the different elements of business. The most important characteristic of SOA is the flexibility to treat the following elements of business:

1. Business processes.
2. Underlying the IT infrastructure.
3. Secure standardized components (services).
4. Changing business priorities.

So when we look at the SOA vision, we need to look at the following three aspects:

1. The business view of a service – what is needed to support the business process?
2. The architecture view of a service – how do we define and design these services?
3. The implementation view of a service – how do we implement the service through the component deployed on the technical infrastructure?

In order to run the business in a smooth manner, we should bundle the business requirements in a simplistic and standard way. This creates the service offerings and helps to get the right information from the right source, particularly the information about when the service is needed. This enables us to reuse and combine different other services being offered to answer the requirements of winning against competition.

9.4.1 SOA Lifecycle

The SOA lifecycle is not so different from the traditional application lifecycles. It provides a new methodology. The lifecycle starts with the gathering of an organization's requirements, and information for designing the processes and architecture in the SOA model. After the optimization phase is over, SOA is implemented with the help of integrating new and existing services. Once SOA is deployed, the end customers administrate and monitor the services from the business and IT perspective. The information gathered in the steady-state operations is fed back into the lifecycle to improvise the services. Assembling all the stages of the lifecycle gives governance and becomes the torch bearer for the guidance and supervision of the SOA project.

9.4.2 Service-Oriented Computing

Service orientation is a design paradigm comprising a specific set of design principles. Its most important feature is its reliance on the 'separation of concerns' design philosophy. Separation of concern is based on the simple fact that a problem becomes easier to approach if it is divided and each part is handled separately.

The first question that should come into the mind is what a service is. Service is not only limited to software or IT; it is actually a culture of the organization and how it performs its operations on a day-to-day basis. We can divide all these tasks into small processes and investigate the processes that can be repeated and can be used as a business continuity process. This also implements the agility factor for the business. Now, if we talk about SO, it is based on the integration of all the business processes as related processes to get the achievable outcomes intended from the business.

The next question that arises is regarding the technology associated with SOA. This visualizes the architectural aspects of service orientation to make the process simple and gives the option of composite application. The composite application ties the running process and business requirements in such a way that it helps to achieve the business goals.

9.5 SOA and Infrastructure as a Service

Major industry analysts view cloud infrastructure as a key IT ingredient for business agility. With a predicted 60% of the IT spending being applied to infrastructure, analysts recommend an IT infrastructure that is:

1. Shared across customers, departments, and applications.
2. Dynamically driven by business policies and service-level requirements.

The analysts view IT virtualization and IT automation as two major elements in realizing the infrastructure as a service. One of the technological aspects of the cloud infrastructure is IT virtualization that helps to create pools of compute in shared models. This masks the physical topologies, boundaries, and restrictions from the users, and powers the user with unconditional infrastructure. In other words, virtualized resources are viewed as fluid-utility services for the consumers to consume as needed (Fig. 9.2).

At the same time, automation provides the option to govern and optimize the utility and self-service based model to enable infrastructure, policies, dynamic management, and service orientation. This works as a strategic and optimized return on investment (ROI) option rather than looking for a short-term, unpredictable, and quick fix alternatives.

9.5.1 Architecture

Cloud infrastructure has many service components. However, they all need not be implemented concurrently. Services can be divided into four domains: application services, information services, common IT services, and infrastructure services. Within each domain, SOA can be measured and charted across a continuum of increasing dynamism and partner involvement.

Application services provide application frameworks to enhance the execution of business services through software engineering. Adopting new technologies and techniques can accelerate the delivery of new services through the use of consistent, repeatable SOAs.

Information services provide a common, repeatable method for cataloging, accessing, and managing information. Innovative technologies can streamline information access and data management, making it easier to integrate packages and new acquisitions. Common IT services create enterprise pools of commonly used IT services. Simplifying the environment can enhance the management and cost, and increase responsiveness.

Infrastructure services provide pools of processing and networking resources for applications and business functions. Today, these resources may be isolated into business silos, but with virtualization, they can evolve into virtual pools that are dynamically allocated based on business needs.

Continuous improvement is mapped within the maturity levels of the company itself and can be measured in each domain of the service. SOA plays a fruitful exercise to decide on how to implement the infrastructure design based on SOA principles to attain the targeted goals. It offers a number of business values.

Business Agility

This helps in defining the right time to launch or rapidly scale the deployment efforts needed to implement the new solutions.

Lower Cost of Operations

1. This helps in utilizing the virtual pools efficiently which decreases the chance of procuring new systems.
2. It helps in increasing the overall effectiveness while working in an automated environment.

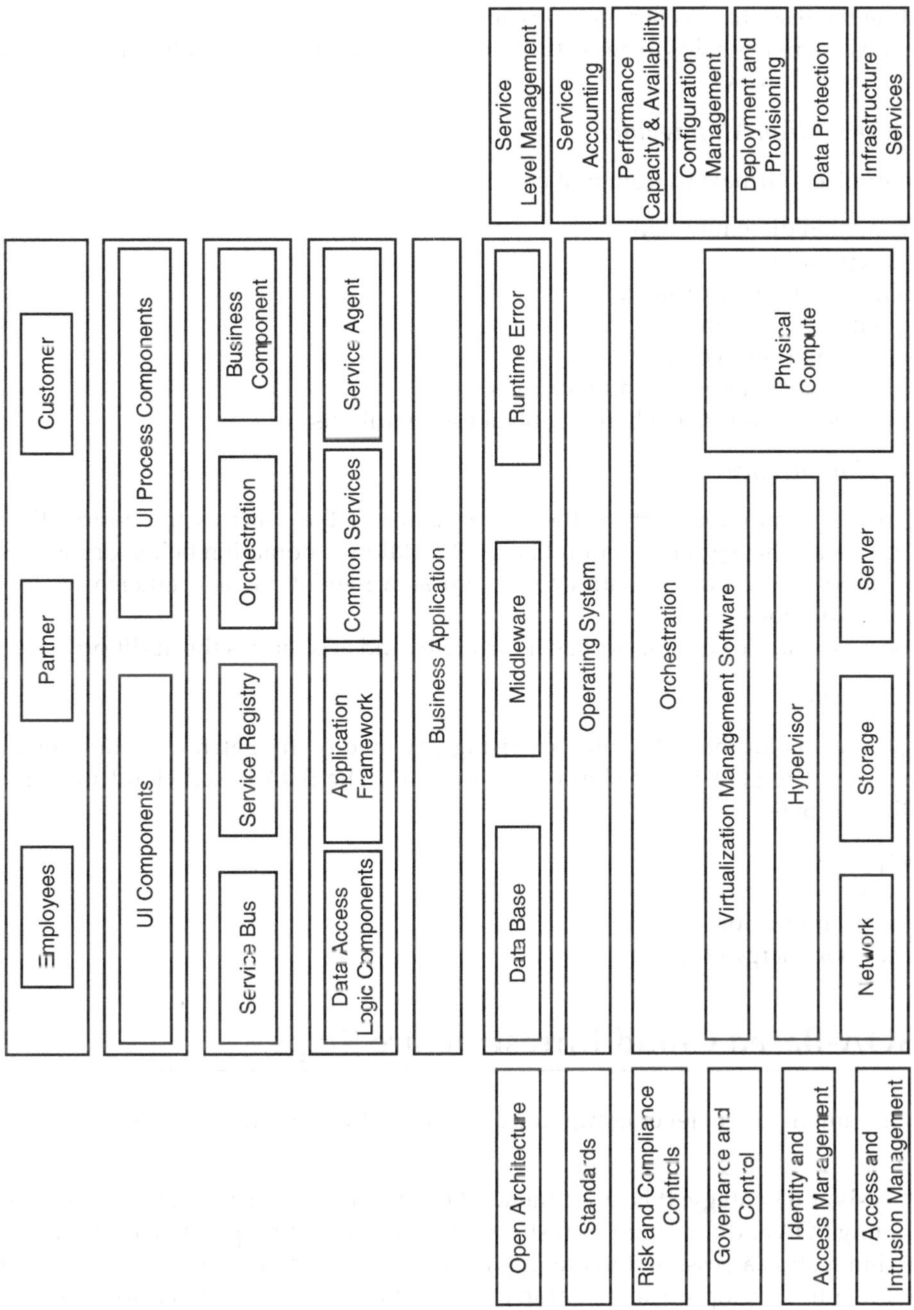

FIGURE 9.2 Cloud IT service management.

Improved Service Levels

1. SOA-based infrastructure helps to adhere to the SLAs efficiently and helps in orchestrating the resources as per the rules and policies.
2. Business analytics helps to decide different predictive, proactive, alternative approaches when we follow SOA.

Efficient Information Management

Efficient centralized virtual environment enables:

1. Information dissemination.
2. Data replication.
3. Business continuity protection.
4. Regulatory compliance.
5. Maximizing resource utilization.
6. Rapid deployment of new applications.
7. More timely response to changing business conditions.

Regulatory Compliance

1. We need monitoring to track the performance of the services to confirm that they comply with the regulatory compliances. Workflow automation helps for the same.
2. It is important to adhere with energy emission regulations and efficiencies to adopt greener solutions.
3. If there is centralized data storage it facilitates and accelerates the audit process.

Energy Efficiency

Energy requirements for the datacenter are rising day by day. To match the requirements, we have the answer: The SOA-based cloud infrastructure. The SOA-based cloud infrastructure substantially improves

1. Computing.
2. Storage.
3. Network utilization.
4. Datacenter energy efficiency.

9.6 SOA-Based Cloud Infrastructure Steps

Organizations intent upon leveraging cloud infrastructure should consider the following steps:

1. **Analysis and strategy:** It is recommended to have an incremental, phased approach for adopting SOA and the cloud infrastructure. A good starting point is to conduct a business innovation assessment to identify the business needs and key areas of impact, and use them to develop business value cases for SOA adoption. It is also recommended to conduct an enterprise IT architecture assessment to determine the IT readiness, including the applications and integration capabilities to support the business needs

and the current gaps. Furthermore, an IT infrastructure assessment should be conducted to determine the capabilities and entry points for (SOI).

2. **Planning:** Once the business needs and IT gaps are identified, a strategic and tactical planning effort can be launched to develop an IT value case and roadmap for incremental IT transformation to enable business innovation/agility leveraging SOA. Through a careful portfolio analysis and change management process, the current IT efforts can be aligned and adjusted, and tactical/focused projects can be selected based on the strategy and roadmap. At the same time, organizational impacts should be analyzed and a SOA governance model, standards, and guiding principles should be developed to accelerate and manage the pace of the transformation.
3. **Implementation:** It is an excellent idea to establish an enterprise-level SOA, as well as the development and run-time environment standards before the first set of SOA projects are launched. It is best to couple the virtualization projects with SOA so that the benefits of the virtualization can be realized at the lower level (service-level versus server-level). SOA and cloud infrastructure governance should be incorporated into the existing IT governance bodies, and performance and SLAs' impacts should be monitored and managed under the same set of business rules.
4. **Value-driven:** It is important to note that the purposes of SOA and cloud infrastructure are to improve the business performance, flexibility, and agility so that IT can support business at the right speed. All SOA projects should be driven on the basis of business values rather than technical merits alone. Technical merits can only be realized when they match the business needs.

9.6.1 SOA and Cloud Infrastructure

SOA is an approach to decompose business processes and applications into loosely coupled components of service providers and consumers, and then connecting them through an enterprise service bus. It enables enterprises to reuse existing business and IT components quickly to develop new capabilities and software solutions. SOA provides an enabling foundation for enhancing business and IT flexibility and agility. The approach is gaining significant momentum not only in designing new solutions, but also in transforming monolithically defined legacy applications.

We can bank on the traditional IT model that has been successful for the deployments. These models can be based on processing of historical data and transactions. As these are established models, they gel well with the high-structured environment. But they break down when you try to extend them into applications or processes that are not so highly structured. They either feel too complex and static [e.g., long-term enterprise resource planning (ERP) projects] or are plain impossible.

With the advent of Web and Internet, we got the new wave itself for the new paradigm of models. It is based on open standards and linked easily for different requirements and components, which can be used for relatively simple activities like communication, browsing, searching, and sending e-mail. It works incredibly well. But it soon became clear that the Internet standards and mechanisms were needed to be extended to handle more sophisticated applications.

The SOA-based cloud computing model builds on IT and Internet models. It is based on what we call a service-oriented architecture, which essentially provides us with a set of modular components to be defined and manipulated (Web services), and a set of XML-based standards for doing so. Since the characteristics of the components can now be expressed in XML, we can define applications that work and manipulate these modular components. It enables a much more flexible and real-time way of implementing business policies than was possible with more structured computing models.

SOA-based cloud computing is not about technology for the sake of technology – it is about enabling new ways of doing business. It is about helping a company to reach new levels of maturity while continuing to deliver the best in class services with productivity; these are necessary to improve the bottom line.

As the processes are integrated in the SOA environment, it gives an option to the enterprise to deal with any type of situation and answer any type of customer demand with the help of partners, suppliers, and customers.

One should follow the most important approach for SOA to consider not only the technical foundation of the business but also the business' underlying principle as it will help to determine the cost of investment. Now we are in the era where models are evolving and changes are very dynamic; therefore, all the technological steps should have business backup to support it. We can consider different types of capabilities related to the organization, strategic values, and market factors that are driving the business.

SOA means that a company finds a pragmatic balance between technical rigor and time-to-market. IT organizations realize that perfect technology stacks cost far more than they deliver, but they also recognize that delivering key functions and reliability of service make it easy for the employees and customers to use the software, and drive the desired business results.

When we adopt SOA, ROI is also required to understand the value of the investment model. A simplistic approach will be to calculate the cost of change and see that it should not be more than the actual cost of implementation, and highlight the important point to adopt the changed approach.

Diversity in the portfolio gives an alternative to face the risks, it is better to work for a different set of applications and not on a single application. Therefore, it is recommended to give space to a larger range of future prospects and create value to improve the business.

It is important to integrate and control the business functions across all the units of business with the help of partners and customers. So, automation in the process delivery should be valued as it increases transparency in the system and also reduces the manual intervention. Sometimes it alerts the organization about the available opportunities and gets unexpected results out of them.

Competitive advantage and system-based performance are the levers to progress for the business. But the balance between the two is very important. SOA helps to balance both. It helps to consider the risks and overcome with spikes in standards and product deployments. This ensures security, and companies can leverage the power of software application in a more efficient way.

9.7 SOA Business and IT Services

We need different management tools for the comprehensive integration of SOA. These tools help to leverage the benefits of infrastructure services. They also help to measure the performance of business functions, and manage the run-time application and system across the portfolio of business functions. These development tools aid to get the specific outcome based on the skills and roles possessed by the people in any organization.

There is a requirement of various modeling tools to depict and simulate the processes by the analysts when they are working on business process management (BPM) projects. These tools help to model information and data flows, and system communications and functionalities. Integration architects are required to model the interconnections and integration existing in the solution. When we follow the SOA implementation, it is evident that the people in the organization will use the systems based on their roles in the organization. The tool environment and deployment framework allows working in an integrated way and using the development tools in a joint manner that ensures collaboration and asset management. So the activities, for example using tools such as version control and project management tools, are provided in the SOA framework under the banner of unified development platform. Generating metrics to measure the performance is pivotal in the progress of the business. SOA services incorporate functions to generate the metrics to control the system and processes. This requires special competencies to deal with the IT operations with the skill sets of experienced business analysts and professionals of an enterprise These capabilities are delivered through a set of comprehensive services that collect and display IT and process-level data, so that business dashboards, administrative dashboards, and other IT level displays can manage system resources and business processes. These tools make it possible for the line of business (LOB) and IT personnel to determine business process paths that may be existing as the inefficient tasks in specific processes or in the relationship of system performance to business process performance, so that IT personnel and assets are tied more directly to the business success of the enterprise.

9.8 Summary

This chapter shows the integration of SOA with the cloud technology. SOA is essentially the idea that displays that companies can treat their applications and processes as defined components that can be mixed and matched at will. SOA is much more than the architecture flavor of the day – in fact, it is a new way of thinking about enabling cloud technology.

CHAPTER

10

Cloud Mobility

CONTENTS

10.1 Introduction

The rising utilization of consumer applications, technologies, and the utilization paradigm is continuously shaping user expectations about the workstyle milieu. Many workers are interested in carrying their own devices to their offices. Workers want to be able to perform their jobs using the software, platforms, system, tools, processes, and offerings they choose. 'Bring your own device' (BYOD) enables workers to choose the platforms and devices that best fit their needs, providing them with greater flexibility and ultimately making them more productive. IT consumerization, especially the desire for BYOD, is a significant trend that both offers benefits and incurs expenses. The benefits include the following:

1. Enhanced employee productivity and job satisfaction.
2. Reduced cost to the company compared to the cost of providing the devices.
3. Greater business agility gained by the use of a wider array of usage models, many of which offer a greater degree of mobility.

The expenses associated with BYODs include those related to developing new infrastructure and implementing the controls required to bolster back-end device support because of potential information security risks. However, the benefits far outweigh the costs.

Companies are using mobile applications in greater-than-ever numbers to get better business dexterity and deliver greater customer values. Information seized and distributed at the boundary of companies broadens the accomplishment of enterprise applications to major decision support systems. Previously, mobile communications for an enterprise tended to be isolated and all over the place. To productively distribute on the idea of mobility and expand the reach of mobility, enterprises require a structural design and approach that allow a comprehensive view and integrate mobility as a fundamental fraction of the enterprise architecture.

With the amplified espousal of mobility as a premeditated plan, these next-generation strategic architectural advancements for mobility will enable companies to solve their mobility requirements for diverse business problems across a multi-tenant environment in an enterprise.

10.2 The Business Problem

Organizations choose and work on the best platforms to optimize their tools, application, and software business processes and systems for support. These elements range from huge ERP implementation to legacy application and business intelligence systems. A lot of attempt has also been made to put together various applications that often have diverse data formats and semantic dissimilarities.

Enterprises have come to comprehend that the next step in the fruition of their business progression is to mobilize key business elements that will provide both domestic and peripheral interactions via mobile devices. These devices are not just mobile phones; they include various tablet phones, iPads, ipods, notes, etc., and any prospective devices that can communicate with the existing applications.

To move toward a mobilized world, enterprises will have to struggle with several issues, which are discussed in the following subsections.

10.2.1 Segregate Systems/Data and Intangible Business Processes

Every enterprise has multi-tenants who have their own applications, processes, and data. It is essential to be able to segregate the processes from each other so that transformations in department-specific processes do not affect the whole enterprise. This can be enabled only if a general service level is defined for all the business processes that offer a basic edge and a conceptual layer to incorporate in every persona-based process. Any mobility response needs to present a methodology where any business process that one can wish to mobilize is understood first and the interfaces are definite with an understandable generalization. The service levels thus developed will facilitate external devices and applications deployment safely, and any internal transform will not influence or split the integration. The other key benefit of this methodology is that only the smallest amount of requisite functionality is provided to outside applications to enable them to be incorporated into a precise business process. Conception and segregation are two foundation stones of good design, and allow wider usability of any organization's applications in the center of varying business requirements which austerely affect the general amalgamation.

10.2.2 Security and Access Controls

The most important and dominant factor of any mobile solution is data security, which needs emphasis where encryption methodologies, authentication, and authorization are involved. It is imperative for the solution to clearly endow with controls for authorized access not only to dissimilar applications, but also at a coarser level, that is, data within an application.

10.2.3 Amalgamation

No application can exist in segregation – enterprise-level systems are not only interconnected but also amalgamate through data. As data flow from one system to another to help complete business processes, data reliability and validation become significant to business compliancy. As a consequence, the solution should be able to represent the methodology that allows standards-based amalgamation and integrations to enterprise resource systems, and even custom applications through standard and open amalgamation methodologies.

10.2.4 Elasticity

The number of mobile devices is increasing day by day, and enterprises have come to recognize that with time, an ever-increasing number of their accessible processes will have to be available on mobile devices. The mobility solution should be elastic to cater to increasing devices; this will need to be made accessible over time.

10.2.5 Support

Mobile devices come with different functionalities, form factors, abilities, and in different types. And it is not just about a mobile phone anymore – there are tablets and various other interconnected devices that will need to put together into the solution. All well-liked mobile device operating systems (OS) should be supported. The mobility solution should be able to allow the right of entry or amalgamation by various mobile devices via an open standards service level. This service level should be idyllically written once to accommodate manifold applications from numerous devices.

10.2.6 Infrastructure

Enterprises need a spotlight on their business functionalities relatively more than on their infrastructure services, as it is the second step. The mobility solution should be able to make available various infrastructure services such as Service Management, Monitoring, Scheduling Engine, Allocation Engine, Notification Engine, Resource Integration Engines, Integration Adapters, Identity and Access Management, etc.

10.3 Mobile Enterprise Application Platforms

Mobile Enterprise Application Platforms speed up and make the development, use, and administration of smart mobile devices simpler. They are endowed with a set of toolkits and a coupled run-time infrastructure to connect mobile task workers to a variety of data foundries in a device and a network without any problem.

Mobile Enterprise Application Platforms promote 'any mobile application to any device' model strategy which brings together five key elements – mobile devices, middleware, management toolkits, application development environment, and resource integration framework. Together, these elements work with each other and with the on-premise infrastructure for uninterrupted mobile connections and networks. By bringing these advantages to mobile application development and implementation, Mobile Enterprise Application Platforms allow companies to fruitfully address many of the challenges faced today by mobile developers.

10.3.1 Freedom of Choice

With a distributed development methodology that supports diverse device types and platforms, Mobile Enterprise Application Platforms can get rid of the recurring, resource-intensive activities involved in developing and implementing mobile applications. This enables enterprises to lucratively flick the application development proportion so that they can spend less time on familiarizing applications for devices and instead use the effort in developing mobile applications that bring value to the customer business and a pertinent, appealing experience to end-users.

Developers can also contemplate on building powerful business layers and content-rich interfaces that acclimatize to different user needs. That is where the added value to users comes in. This gives developers the litheness to support different workflows within the application life cycle.

10.3.2 Agility

Mobile Enterprise Application Platforms' solutions provide an end-to-end development platform for developing, designing, testing, and building mobile applications across heterogeneous devices and OS platforms. This gives developers the litheness to support different workflows within the application life cycle environment that uses popular open source IDEs.

This elastic platform is vital for enterprises that want to accelerate development while lowering costs because it permits developers to utilize existing expertise and experience.

To make development simpler, Mobile Enterprise Application Platforms also comprise templates and baseline application stacks, and tools to develop, test, and debug, and also simulate an application on a device emulator, which considerably speeds up development and testing of devices.

10.3.3 Feature Rich

Applications developed in a Mobile Enterprise Application Platforms permit users to take advantage of the unique capabilities of their selected mobile devices as well as consumables, such as barcode scanners and printers.

10.3.4 Robust Connectivity

Mobile middleware is at the focal point of the Mobile Enterprise Application Platforms architecture. Acting as a controller for bi-directional communication between back-end infrastructure and development systems and mobile devices, this is where the wireless message change takes place, as well as transaction routing functions.

Mobile Enterprise Application Platforms connect with data sources to mine, change, and assimilate data. They then encrypt the data and propel back in real-time to the mobile middleware.

A Mobile Enterprise Application Platform integration methodology can comprise a range of pre-built application integrators for adaptors with bundled and home-grown applications running on enterprise management systems. This decreases the need to build up integrators from the beginning or to modify existing integrators.

10.3.5 Offline On-Premise Integration to Business Processes with the Clients

In Mobile Enterprise Application Platforms, applications can work separately of a master server connection so that users can keep on working offline. Applications run in the vicinity on mobile devices for better response time, and updates are pushed without human intervention when the devices reconnect to the network.

10.4 Mobile Application Architecture Overview

Most mobility systems widen an existing business system or edge with an existing system. There are typically three major parts to a mobile architecture: An enterprise system, a middleware, and a handheld application (Fig. 10.1).

The rationale for using a middleware that is generally desirable is to grant data changes, apply business intelligence, and be a focal point of messaging for the devices. If a new business system is being built or customized, then no middleware may be essential; the appropriate flow can be built into the system to converse with the devices from the beginning. Most business systems are not written from scratch very often, and it is expensive and impractical to rewrite them just to provide mobility to the application. Mobile system developments frequently engage various technologies due to environment limitations.

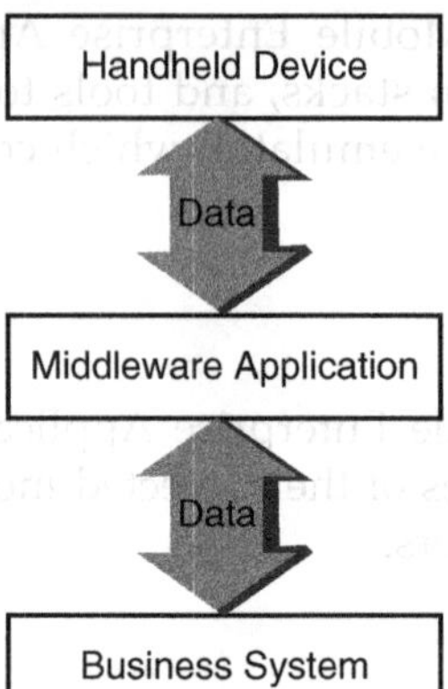

FIGURE 10.1 Mobility application model.

10.4.1 Device Application Installations

If the application is being installed on new mobile devices, there is a good probability that some arrangement will be required. After a device is started, the installed application must be loaded. Various companies use IP-based mechanism for installing applications and configurations.

10.4.2 Upgrades

There are software updates that administer device configurations. Such management packages work on a client that sits on the device. Manufacturers' IP-based packages must classically be written for the administration which identify the software and upgrade files to be downloaded and installed.

10.4.3 User Interface

It is extremely difficult to design graphical user interfaces on mobility-based devices as there is usually very little screen space and a very small keypad for data entry. If the application or data is multi-faceted, the user will be required to act together, that is application and data, with many screen items. Intricate screens will need to be separated and divided into sub-screens or tabbed icons.

10.4.4 Performance

Servers and desktops have improved considerably, and now their performance is characteristically not a matter of discussion. Mobile-based computing devices, however, require a different treatment as these devices are very slow. Intricate user interfaces, CPU exhaustive algorithms, and data processing can straight forwardly make an application user aggressive. It is important to take corrective measures to evade performance drawbacks.

10.4.5 Memory Management

Most mobile computing devices come with limited memory even though memory is becoming cheaper with each passing day. It is really difficult to push configuration changes and upgrade patches. Data storage is also a critical factor as it is very limited in handheld devices.

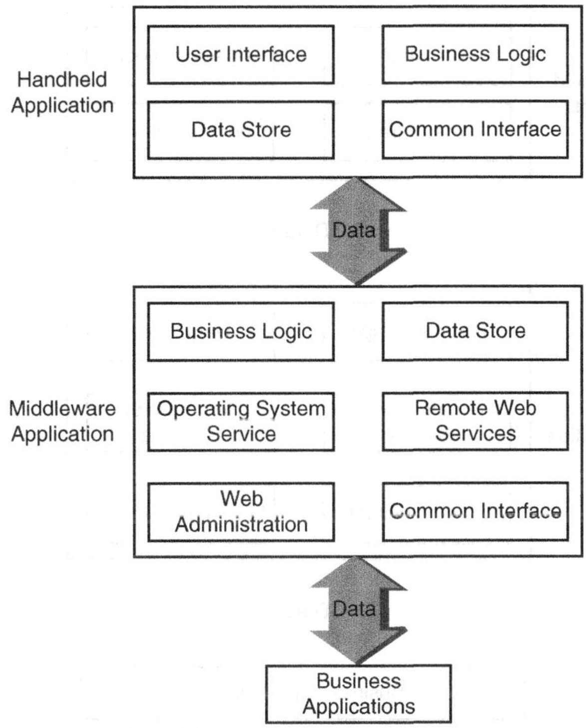

FIGURE 10.2 Mobility application architecture.

10.4.6 Security

As mobile devices are becoming computing devices, security is of prime concern, for example, security of desktops and servers. If the device is lost, there should be provision to encrypt the data so that it cannot be used by the one who has stolen it. Some devices come with various methods of authentication such as biometrics, voice recognition, and login credentials (Fig. 10.2).

10.4.7 Business System

The business system can be the platform for running an enterprise management system. The only crossing point is the import or export interface already available on the enterprise server. Data from handheld mobility devices must be imported by hand manually or automatically in the business system.

10.4.8 Middleware Application

The middleware application can be included in an OS service, a Web service, and a multi-threaded socket server. It is accountable for downloading business data from the server and changing these data into smaller files that are better organized for handheld mobile computing devices. It also provides data files to mobile-based applications of handheld devices through the server. Also, it retrieves data from the handheld mobile system through the services from the server. It applies various business rules to the on-premise internal handheld mobility data, sends the data to the server, and provide with administration capabilities with a Web-based application.

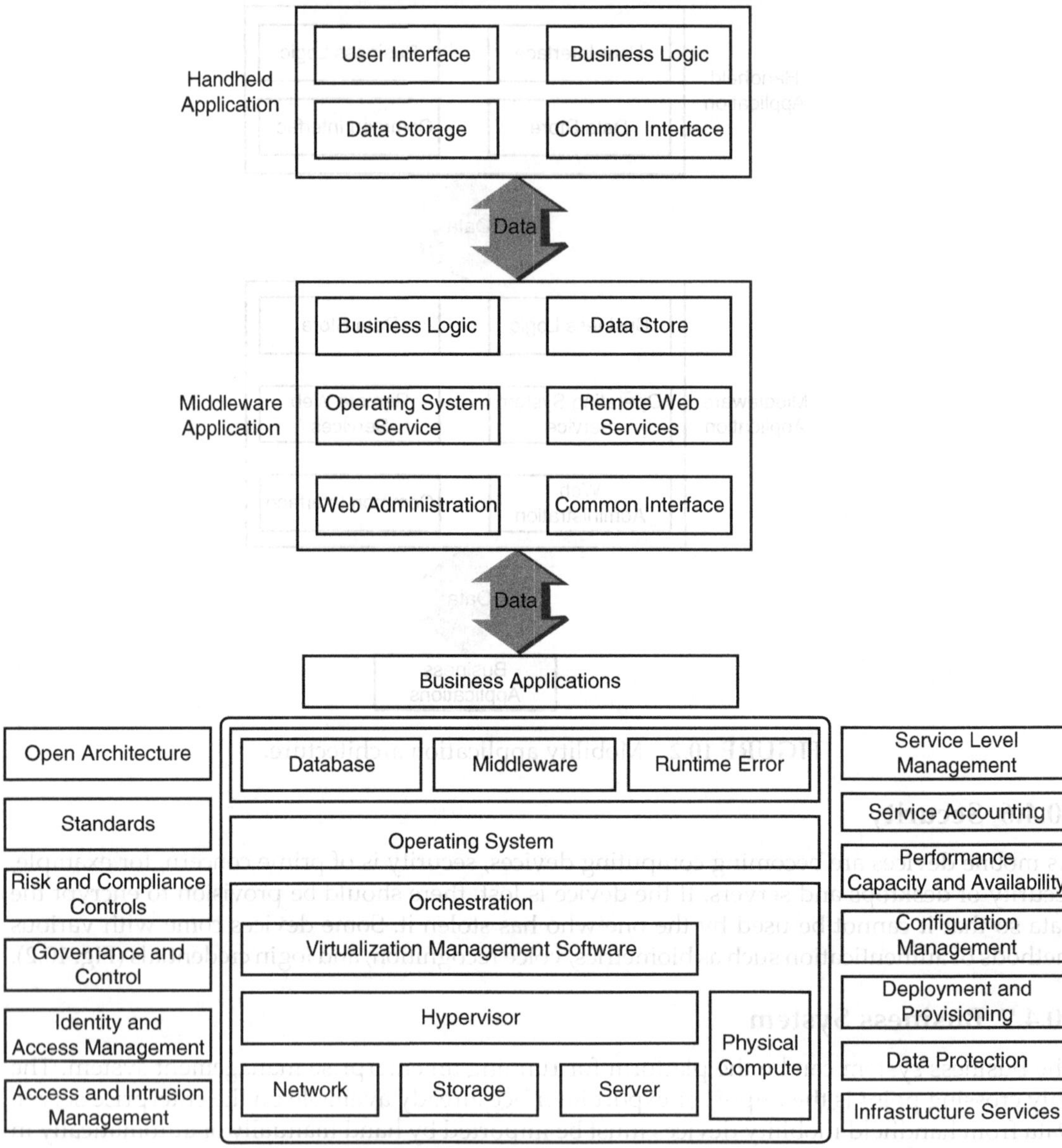

FIGURE 10. 3 Mobility cloud model.

10.4.9 Handheld Application

The handheld application comprises multiple screens. Users should log on to the application by inputting username and password. The data authentication logic is part of the business data from the system. The applications are self-configurable; they download and install new software via the server from the middleware (Fig. 10.3).

10.5 Summary

The force of mobility on the industry is apparent. In growing numbers, business users are expected to handle serious tasks and decision-making in real time, no matter where they work from. An enterprise that endows with field service support is expected to have real-time transparency in inventory positions, enabling it to accept fresh deals on the fly with real-time changes from the field. These quick and well-organized operations are quickly becoming the important way to do business in order to maximize not only internal business requirements, but also external customer-facing units.

The propagation of network connectivity, standards, and handy devices has made all of this possible. By adopting mobility, companies today are transforming the supply chain – from inventory to tracking to field offerings such as scheduling, delivery, and navigation. In the case of financial sector enterprises, it is becoming necessary that at least some vital information and some dealings are available on mobile devices, whether the users are internal field users or the customers.

CHAPTER

11

Cloud Governance

CONTENTS

11.1 Introduction

If the operation of an IT organization is running behind the firewalls, the environment will be isolated at network, compute, and organizational levels; but the case will be different in a cloud service provider's environment. In a cloud environment, the cloud service provider segments IT organizational workloads on the basis of isolation from one customer to another by segmenting the network on the basis of regulations and compliances.

We have till now covered learned and appreciated all the characteristics delivered by this unique computing model. Still there is a need of service models to drive the datacenter innovations such as dynamic workload management, resource scheduling, automation, and orchestration. But there are never-ending concerns about security, compliances, risk, governance, legal issues, interoperability, and information management. First, we will discuss the compliances in detail that are related to a cloud environment.

Today almost all the enterprises in some way or other adhere to various compliances. Like European Union (EU) Data Protection Directive emphasizes to place the data based on geography within the borders of EU region or with the provider which gives protection at adequate level in third-party country. In other words, it emphasizes to place personal data within the EU borders.

As far as the cloud service providers are concerned, they offer their services from global datacenters and the data is archived and processed at various locations. Most of the reputed players are already aware of the problems and are compliant with the situations. They are giving the flexibility in their portals to choose location-based provisioning of services.

The most important thing is to keep a record, in writing, of where the data are stored and where the archival copies of data are available. It should also keep an eye on who is accessing the data in what format and how it is getting used at a third-party partner or organization.

One more point is also very important that it may be possible that the service provider is following the regulations but it does not make a consumer compliant with them. So it is mandatory for the consumer to be compliant at the same time. Also from time to time, a review of the compliance status of the service provider should also be done on an ongoing basis.

11.2 Service-Level Agreement and Compliance

Service-level agreements (SLAs) are made mutually between the parties on the basis of availability, support, and uptime. On the basis of SLAs, penalties and rewards can also be discussed between the service provider and the consumer. SLAs go hand in hand with compliances and there are serious penalties when the regulations are breached; therefore, it is meaningful to ensure that the compliances are followed by the cloud service provider. The most effective way to implement this is to write the SLA and spell out the type of services with regulations and controls.

Writing the terms and conditions is not the guarantee that the service provider will comply with all the requirements. Therefore, the consumer's responsibility is to ensure it by putting pressure and conducting reviews and audits on the cloud service provider.

We have seen advances in cloud computing in the last few years, but security is still the most talked and concerning area when the cloud is discussed in any arena. This gets compounded when it is bundled with compliances, risk, governance, regulations, etc.

Now there are a lot of advancements in the areas of security, risk, governance, certificates, and regulations. It is important to know the technologies in the cloud and virtualization that are creating robust platform. In addition to this, mobility is also strengthening the model with the help of new paradigms.

11.2.1 Security Innovations

Now cloud is inevitable and will be staying as a robust technology. Organizations are trying, as much as possible, to move their IT operations and services to the cloud. As a security solution, firewalls are not competent enough to face the threats of attacks in a service-based model. Now firewalls are getting integrated at application, data, and user levels. Now the whole application can be masked behind intelligent and learned systems to monitor anomalous actions and attacks. These systems monitor the threats internally as well as externally on the basis of signatures available in public information. The systems are also equipped with IPS/IDS-based [Intrusion Prevention Systems (IPS) and Intrusion Detection Systems (IDS)] solutions for the prevention of data loss.

Mobility, collaboration, and data sharing are the new platforms that demand new security models. These platforms require security solutions to share files where the data can be housed on both on-premise and cloud-based platform. These platforms also require that the administrator owns the encryption keys for the entire process to make the sharing more strong in terms of security. Following are the options that are available now to solve these problems:

1. **Certificates and control:** Certificates are crucial for the cloud. It is important to monitor the SSL and security certificates because one expired service will affect not only the system but also the dependent services.
2. **Alerts:** It is very important to know when the certificates are getting expired and keep an eye on the expired certificates using the alert system. Alerts can also be generated while working in communications using certificates.

11.3 Data Privacy and Protection Risks

The risks related to data privacy and the processing of personal data can arise because of controls and transparency issues over the data and information.

While moving the personal data to the systems that are managed by third-party providers, consumers are not in the condition to implement technical- and enterprise-level measures to achieve isolation, transparency, intelligence, availability, and confidentiality.

1. The first shift required is in the field of interoperability where the cloud service provider should rely on open standards rather than locking into the proprietary technology and making the system closed. Open standards adoptions will give an option to the consumer to play with multiple tools available on-premise or in a Software-as-Service (SaaS) model.

2. Cloud uses shared resource pools. This sharing calls for the requirement of the integrity of data on the shared platform to resolve the conflict of interests and requirements.
3. Various compliances enforce confidentiality for citizen data to regulate data protection law within the boundaries of the union or state.
4. No standard is adopted by the current service provider. Ideally services should be launched in such a manner that the services from one provider can be bundled with the services of the other cloud service provider dynamically.

11.4 Enterprise Governance

Governance in an enterprise is the factor of effective security policies in overall governance structure. If all the processes in the security model are strongly implemented with repeatable cycles and continuous improvement, governance in the cloud will be easier. The measures in the security model should be identifiable, repeatable, and cost effective. Governance is related to the robust organization structure, processes, and policies with information security while working through the third-party integration services in any cloud deployment model.

It is good to enjoy the benefits and economies of scale of the cloud, but at the same time consumer and provider should also invest to make scrutiny, audit, and control mechanism stronger.

1. Both service provider and service consumer should establish a robust governance platform irrespective of the cloud deployment or the service model.
2. There should be agreed goals between consumer, provider, or partners, preferably in writing, to avoid conflict of interests with proper RACI (Responsible, Accountable, Consulted, Informed).
3. Consumer should also understand all governance and compliances enforced by the local agencies and bodies even when the service provider is compliant with all the required regulations. This will help the consumer to review, audit, and access the maturity of the service provider's security, compliance, and governance models.
4. The design of the structure, policies, and processes should be taken collaboratively between the consumer and the service provider. It should include risk management policies, delivery mechanism, transition, and executive protocols.
5. All security stakeholders should be engaged while designing the service model.
6. There should be agreements, rewards, and penalties attached with security obligations to enforce the service model with greater effects.
7. Service accounting should be in place to capture all the metrics, standards, and maturity of the governance, security, policies, and processes in a documented fashion.
8. It should also be tried to make all the security metrics and standards a part of SLAs and contracts, if possible.

11.5 Risk Management

Risk management capabilities are also required to be factored for any enterprise adopting the cloud-based services. Some of the accepted choices that act as a best practice are as follows:

1. SLA and service-provider-published documents play a vital role when the infrastructure is not owned by the parent consumer company but leased from the provider organization.

2. The cloud provides multi-tenancy, resource pooling, and self-service based provisioning. Due to this, some providers do not provide audits logs, assessment reports, and monitoring results in an in-depth fashion. Therefore, consumer organization should think for other mediums to overcome these problems.
3. Risk management process should be in place related to the identification, valuations, threats, potential impact, acceptance levels, and how to control or transfer, or accept or avoid it.
4. Risk scenarios should be jointly developed between the consumer and the provider. They should also include the likelihood and impact analysis of the risk management.

11.6 Third-Party Management

1. The services in the cloud management should be viewed as supply chain management.
2. Third-party management refers to auditing, reviewing, and assessing the provider relationships, partner ecosystem, and dependencies before signing the contract.
3. It is also required to check the service management, support capabilities for availability, backup archival, and disaster recovery capabilities.
4. One of the most important assessment and evaluation is business continuity plan. It should mention the loss and recovery of consumer service in the advent of any natural or manmade calamity.

11.7 Information Management

Cloud-based architectures, such as multi-tenancy, resource pooling, and self-service, are challenging the traditional methods of information management. Now the data are managed not only on the on-premise infrastructure but also on the external clouds. There are various challenges developed because of this new disrupting model. Some of the key challenges include the following:

1. **Geography and location:** This comes with the service assurance from the service provider that all the formats of the data at different locations are maintained as per the agreed terms and agreements.
2. **Persistence:** There should be a foolproof method for the removal and finally 'destroying` the data as per the rules of data removal and relocation of the data from one place to another.
3. **Shared platforms:** Sensitive data must not be shared on a common resource pool–based data platform. It should be practiced with different cycles of information while data in transit, use, or storage.
4. **Backup and recovery:** All the latest techniques related to the backup must be available in the cloud environment and also for data availability in case of any loss, overwrite, or destruction of the data.
5. **Aggregation:** In a shared environment, cloud aggregation and composite data models are required to maintain the integrity of the data. Hence, best practices and technologies are required to assure that no data breach is developed between the owners and the stakeholders of data.

11.8 National Institute of Standards and Technology (NIST) Cloud Computing ModeL

NSIT Cloud Computing Model enables compute to have ubiquitous, on-demand access to the shared resource pool of servers, network, storage, and services. This shared resource pool facilitates provisioning and commissioning of services with minimal efforts or with the help of any provider. This model comes with characteristics, service, and deployments models.

11.8.1 Model Characteristics

1. **On-demand self-service:** As cloud consumers, users are privileged to request and provision computing capabilities bundled with services with or without an approval process powered by the automation and workflows.
2. **Broad network access:** This is the characteristic by which the end-user and server computing devices can be accessed over the network even by using next generation heterogeneous devices such as smart phone, tablets, phablets, thin, and thick clients.
3. **Resource pooling:** This characteristic refers to the pooling of resources across multiple datacenters. These pooled virtual datacenters are then divided into multiple pools to cater their services to various consumers in a multi-tenant model. These pools can have both physical and virtual resources. Also the devices provided by these pools give the notion of location-independent compute [storage, servers, processing, network bandwidth, virtual machines (VMs), etc.], where the consumer does not have any control or visibility about the service location and its geography.
4. **Rapid elasticity:** This characteristic makes the provisioning rapid and elastic. This provisioning can be automatic, and can flex-up and flex-down on the basis of the spikes of utilization. The consumer can view the infinite capacity available as a service, which can be bought at any point of time.
5. **Measured service:** The cloud environment is optimized by an effective workload management. This management requires measured service, monitoring, metering, and chargeback capability with the required abstraction and optimization at the user level. The usage of resources can be controlled, reported, monitored, charged, billed, and invoiced on actual from provider to consumers.

11.8.2 Service Models

1. **Software-as-a-Service (SaaS):** This refers to provisioning a purpose-built software over the Internet that uses underlying hardware, operating system (OS), and distribution capabilities.
2. **Platform-as-a-Service (PaaS):** This refers to provisioning the platform of the developer who writes custom application using the hardware, OS, database, and middleware. There are some software policies using which developers write and balance the scalability for the application development.
3. **Infrastructure-as-a-Service (IaaS):** This refers to the provisioning of hardware or virtual computers when the organization has control over the OS, thereby allowing the execution of an arbitrary software.

11.8.3 Deployment Models

1. **Private cloud:** A private cloud is a deployment made inside the company's firewall (on-premise datacenters) and traditionally run by on-site servers. Private cloud offers some of the benefits of a public cloud computing environment such as elastic capacity on-demand, self-service provisioning, and service-based access. The private cloud is suitable when the traditional requirements, such as control, security, and resiliency, are more emphasized by an organization with the restricted and designated user access and authorization.
2. **Community cloud:** A community cloud is managed by groups of people, communities, and agencies (especially government) that have common interests – such as maintaining the compliance, regulation, and security parameters – and are working on the same mission.
3. **Public cloud:** A public cloud is offered by a third-party datacenter provider to end-users over the Internet. Public cloud offers resource pooling, self-service, service accounting, elasticity, multi-tenancy to manage solutions, deployment, and securing the resources and applications. Companies can use the public cloud on demand and with pay-as-you-use option, which is much like utility consumption. Enterprises are able to offload commodity applications to third-party service providers (hosters).
4. **Hybrid cloud:** A hybrid cloud is a combination of interoperating public and private clouds. This is the model where the consumer takes the non-critical application or information and compute requirements to the public cloud while keeping all the critical information and application data in control. The hybrid model is used by both public and private clouds simultaneously. It is an intermediate step in the evolution process, providing businesses as on-ramp from their current IT environment into the cloud.

11.9 Compliances in the Cloud

Migration to the cloud can be an easier task technically or economically but maintaining the compliances is difficult. In the cloud, when workloads are moved from an on-premise environment to a third-party cloud, controls and federation are handled by the service provider. It is difficult to follow regulatory policies when data is not in our control. Now the question arises, what are the important compliances (but not limited) required in a cloud? The straight answer is: Whatever is required in the current IT, same will be required in a cloud-based approach also. Most commonly and widely accepted compliances applicable for the cloud are as follows:

1. Health Insurance Portability and Accountability Act (HIPAA).
2. Payment Card Industry Data Security Standard (PCI-DSS).
3. Sarbanes–Oxley Act (SOX).
4. European Union Data Protection Directive.
5. Federal Information Security Management Act (FISMA).

These compliances will be discussed in the following subsections.

11.9.1 Health Insurance Portability and Accountability Act

HIPAA is the abbreviated form of Health Insurance Portability and Accessibility Act and HITECH is the abbreviated form of Health Information Technology for Economic and Clinical Health. Both the acts work for the protection of health-related information of an individual. This information consists of medical history, current and future health state, health care provision, and payment details of the individual. These acts are applicable not only to the service provider but also to all the agencies working with the service provider. These agencies can be insurance providers, HR companies, etc.

It is important to understand the act by the service provide before giving the offerings to the end-users. It is also important for the end-users to check the compliance of the service provider at the first level only before adopting the cloud computing.

11.9.2 Payment Card Industry Data Security Standard

Payment Card Industry Data Security (PCI-DSS) is related to the financial institutions which work with merchants, retailers who work online, and ecosystem player-based agencies working in the environment. In simpler terms, these financial institutions need to protect the information of the individual such as credit card details, expiry dates, etc. Hence, they are responsible to create an infrastructure to protect this information. So all the companies involved in an online transaction of any financial details in one form or another need to be compliant with the PCI. Also their client and financial partners are also required to be compliant with the PCI, regardless of whether they are using the individual card details or data for any transactions.

11.9.3 Sarbanes–Oxley Act

Sarbanes–Oxley (SOX) act states that an institution is responsible for any unlawful accounting or financial activity even if it may be because of any third-party engagement or agency, or even by the cloud service provider activity transactions. If the company is adhered by the law to abide the processes of SOX, then the service provider must follow the SOX compliance. It also requires the audit standards to comply with the controls of SOX. This audit standard is called SSAE 16 that is actually a report for the controls and processes for the data and information and impact in form of financial terms or other forms. Audit standards can even come from infrastructure such as power redundancy, high availability, fault tolerance, and disaster recovery.

Like the previous data protection compliances, in order to ensure SOX, it is good to check whether the service provider itself is SOX compliant at the first level. It is also required to check whether the provider has SSAE16 audits in place if the service consumer is looking for SOX provisions. It is good to consume the services of the providers that are already SOX compliant as it will help in the long run.

11.9.4 EU Data Protection Directive

EU Data Protection Directive is designed as a directive to protect the data privacy of all the European Union citizens. The directive protects the interests of all EU citizens regarding personal data collection, processing, or exchange. It encompasses the entire requirements related to the rights of protecting the privacy of personal and family life even when corresponding in the home and personal level. The principles to adhere to the policies are as follows:

1. Information to be given from where the data is collected to individual or agency.
2. Reason why the data are collected.
3. Permission required to share the data with third parties.
4. Protection of the data from potential theft.
5. No disclosure of the individual for whom the data is collected.
6. Proper access to be provided to modify or add the personal data with proper authentication.

Data collectors are accountable to adhere to the principles. In the directive, personal data of an individual refers to any type of information related to a natural person. A natural person can be identified with the help of an identification number directly or indirectly with the factors related to mental, physiological, social, or cultural aspects. A personal data can be considered as personal when it can be linked to any specific person. This data can be address, credit card details, bank information, etc. Processing of the data can take various forms such as organization, collection, storage, de-duplication, recording, archival, distribution, transmission, retrieval, or even publication. These directives are applicable not only when the parties are executing the data in the European Union but also when the controller or service provider or third party is utilizing the equipment within the European Union to process the data. Also the outside controllers, who process the data inside the European Union, should comply with the directives.

11.9.5 The Federal Information Security Management Act

The Federal government established a comprehensive framework called The Federal Information Security Management Act (FISMA) to secure IT. FISMA provides a guideline-based help to the federal agencies when they are looking for services for budgeting, implementing, planning, and designing the security systems.

All the agencies are required to create the requirement and development document to establish the security for the IT and data systems operations and asset maintenance. This should also be complied by the agency, or third-party contractors, or service providers supporting the overall program. It is important to plan, establish security authority, review controls, and process authentication before the operation phase. A grade is assigned to each agency and is published on the website. The higher the grade, the more secure the agency; hence, more data is locked.

There is a concept of responsibility sharing among various agencies to ensure the security of the data in the federal government. It is required for each agency's head to conduct review for information security for risk management to manage the acceptable levels in a cost-effective fashion. NIST has given the directives for compliance to FISMA with the help of following steps:

1. Information categorization as per the scope of security.
2. Baseline controls selection.
3. Control refinement using assessment.

4. Security control plan documentation.
5. Information systems security implementation.
6. Implemented security control assessments.
7. Risk assessment for each agency based on the business case.
8. Authorization of the information system.
9. Continuous security control monitoring.

11.9.6 Geographical Aspect

One very important concern for the cloud adopters is the geographical location of the service provider. The location becomes more critical when it is judged for a software-as-a-service provider. In this case, software services can be given to the whole world over the Web-based Internet and the data can be stored on a single shared platform. As a service provider, one should know the customer's location and geographical-location-based state or union laws while storing the data in a compliant fashion. It should be based on the country's data protection laws and data privacy legislations with the correct authentication and access requirements. The multi-country based geographical spread can become a problem due to compliances while it is used by service providers to reduce costs and improve the datacenter reliability.

The concerns related to various compliances, regulations, risks, geographical locations, legislations, and protection laws can easily disrupt the chances of adopting the cloud. All providers and consumers should be well versed with the implications and requirements of data migrations and processing of the same externally outside the firewalls. Within the same organization, same service compliance can change when the identical service is consumed in a different state or geographical location. It is also dependent on the business type, data regulations, or when a vertical service is provided.

11.10 Summary

An enterprise must reach a cloud service provider as an agent of change. The cloud service provider should also help the enterprise to understand the cloud features, its portability and interoperability with respect to the governance, policies, regulations, risk management, and compliance maturity and requirement.

CHAPTER

12

Cloud Readiness and Migration Assessment

CONTENTS

12.1 Introduction

Nowadays organization's data centers have various applications that are getting deployed on current infrastructure with identified resiliency and scalability issues. Though the movement of an application to a cloud will not unravel all inherent application resiliency and scalability issues, organizations will have the power to be able to develop real monetary and operational paybacks in migrating an application from legacy infrastructure to a cloud environment.

Application migration is the method of reorganizing and implementing an application, classically on a novel and upgraded infrastructure platforms. The practice encompasses the staging of this novel environment before the actual cutover and needs synchronization of IT teams at the cutover time. If the movement is on a well-matched platform, a compilation of the application is not required.

In a cloud scenario, the application can be moved from an existing on-premise/third party/hosting compute environment to the target cloud. The target environment can come in any form: public/private/hybrid cloud; that is, an infrastructure that evidently cartels several clouds, either private or public. Moreover, the movement can comprise a physical-to-virtual (P2V) movement if the existing application portfolio of services is not deployed on a virtual infrastructure.

To categorize applications for cloud migration, it is essential to recognize and assess the business and technical aspects for the movement. Typical factors that influence cloud migration are business agility and cost reduction. Cloud computing can deliver substantial cost savings as a result of the better infrastructure utilization optimized by resource pooling and cloud service standardization and automation.

Performance, scalability, and management for the operational activities are the distinctive reasons why businesses cogitate cloud computing. By outsourcing infrastructure management and software development platforms to a cloud provider, enterprises can unburden operational accountabilities to cloud-managed service providers.

12.2 Need for Migration of Applications to the Cloud

12.2.1 Business Needs

1. Large enterprises, Telcos, and SMBs with good application portfolio that is scattered and heterogeneous
2. Cost of infrastructure and maintenance for application centralization is too high

12.2.2 Technology Need

1. Still running obsolete hardware, sunset tools, and technologies
2. Maintain control of how various IT services are purchased and used for enterprise governance policies and standards that need to be managed and enforced
3. Central IT infrastructure is not conducive to "continuous innovation"

12.2.3 Key Business Drivers

1. Cost and Monetization
2. Scalability and Elasticity
3. Standardization
4. Speed to Market
5. Innovation
6. Collaboration

Cloud assessment and migration team will help the customer to take the leap of faith for cloud deployment by leveraging specialized tools and accelerators for evaluating cloud fitness, readiness, requirement, assess individual application readiness for the cloud, as well as by developing guidelines to target virtualization benefits, migration to the cloud, integration and testing services to enable the deployment in a cloud aggregated or hybrid model. Application criticality, business benefits, risks and feasibility for test and Dev cloud are the key factors that are taken into consideration for prioritizing for cloud adoption.

The purpose of cloud assessment and migration service is to demonstrate how cloud orchestration will deliver measurable business benefits to customer projects. A successful assessment requires a structured approach to implementation and the right application candidates. It also requires personnel with the right expertise and skill sets. The assessment service is a proven approach to understand the benefits of cloud computing in customer data centers, leased, third-party, public cloud, or hybrid cloud scenarios.

Cloud assessment and migration service enable customers to demonstrate the feasibility, business impact, and value for adopting this next-gen-technology. By providing project management, infrastructure and application architecture expertise, technical guidance and knowledge transfer by proven methodology, cloud assessment and migration service deliver the results that the customer needs — quickly and cost-effectively.

Generating confidence in the technology and business model of cloud computing, cloud assessment provides the following benefits:

1. A means of presenting the Business case and ROI of cloud
2. A way of involving users, at an early stage and establishing realistic expectations and gathering their 'buy-in'
3. Reduce project risk by identifying issues early, providing insurance for production rollout
4. Opportunity to build quality metrics into project
5. Gathering a clear understanding of overall project scope, cost and 'time to production'

12.3 Cloud Adoption Approach

Cloud assessment and migration service propose the following approach for cloud adoption process:

1. **Application portfolio analysis:** Cloud assessment and migration service team will work with customer application owners and infrastructure teams to identify the list of applications that can be considered for Porting to customer cloud ecosystem

2. **Identify applications:** The applications are further analyzed based on their data security and regulatory needs as well as system interface testing requirements to filter apps that can be moved to the private cloud.
3. **Migration planning:** Cloud assessment and migration service recognize the infrastructure and software requirements for all the applications needs to migrate. This data will be utilized to classify applications that can be deployed on cloud service provider-based platforms, based on application readiness and fitness requirement on the target platform.
4. **Setup cloud infrastructure:** Manage service provider, cloud provider, or the customer will procure the resources on the cloud platform and the necessary infrastructure to deploy the applications.
5. **Configure application:** Cloud assessment and migration service configure the application and the testing tools needed for the application. The test data required for testing will be migrated to the cloud platform. Also, necessary security features are enabled.
6. **Perform Testing:** The test tools and test data initiate application testing on the cloud. The test results collected are provided to the customer application teams using the web interfaces exposed by the application as well as sharing physical files Competency and Tools.

12.3.1 Assessment Process

Scoping and Planning: Cloud assessment and migration service consultant/s work with customer staff to analyze application and infrastructure environment, identify suitable use cases and applications, establish key performance indicators (KPIs), and define success criteria for the Assessment.

Representative KPIs include:

1. Increase in utilization
2. Potential server reduction
3. Potential reduction in admin time
4. Speed-up of application infrastructure provisioning

The consultant will also work with Customer team to identify any potential issues and risks.

Off-Site Preparation: Cloud assessment and migration service make all necessary preparations with remote involvement from Customer team to gather the required equipment and tools for the Assessment and prepare a thorough test plan to measure KPIs.

Results Review: Upon completion of the cloud assessment execution, cloud assessment and migration service team conduct a summary demo and present test results and recommendations to key stakeholders. KPI results are compared against industry best practices, and success criteria are jointly discussed. This review highlights both the opportunities presented and issues which need to be addressed to deliver the eventual solution. Every cloud Assessment ends with an agreed set of next steps.

By understanding scaling characteristics and the level of effort involved in adapting infrastructure and processes to cloud computing, IT and business unit managers can optimize their planning activities, ensuring a maximum return on investment. And with greater insight into how applications will run in production, we can avoid errors that often result in costly project delays.

12.3.2 Key Deliverables

1. **Results report:** test results and recommendations, measured against KPIs with industry comparisons
2. **Accelerated skills transfer:** administrators, developers, and IT staff gain valuable, hands-on experience in their environment
3. An itemized list of issues, opportunities, and the way forward
4. Confidence that the tools are appropriate for project and that chosen assessment team is the right partner

Cloud assessment and migration service enable organizations to demonstrate the feasibility, business impact and value before making a more significant technology investment. By providing project management, infrastructure and application architecture expertise, technical guidance and knowledge transfer by our proven methodology, cloud assessment and migration will deliver the results that customer needs quickly and cost-effectively.

The customer prototype provides many benefits by generating confidence in the technology and business model of private cloud computing, including the following:

1. A means of presenting the ROI of private cloud to senior management for approval.
2. A way of involving users, at an early stage and establishing realistic expectations and gathering their 'buy-in'.
3. Reduce project risk by identifying issues early, providing insurance for production rollout.
4. Opportunity to build quality metrics into project.
5. Gathering a clear understanding of overall project scope, cost and 'time to production'.

In simple terms, it can be a five-step process framework that helps the enterprise to take this journey (**Fig. 12.1**).

1. Discovery
2. Use Cases
3. Business Case
4. Pilot PoC
5. Production

By understanding scaling characteristics and the level of effort involved in adapting infrastructure and processes to cloud computing, IT and business unit managers can optimize their planning activities, ensuring a maximum return on investment. And with greater insight into how applications run in production, we can avoid errors that often result in costly project delays.

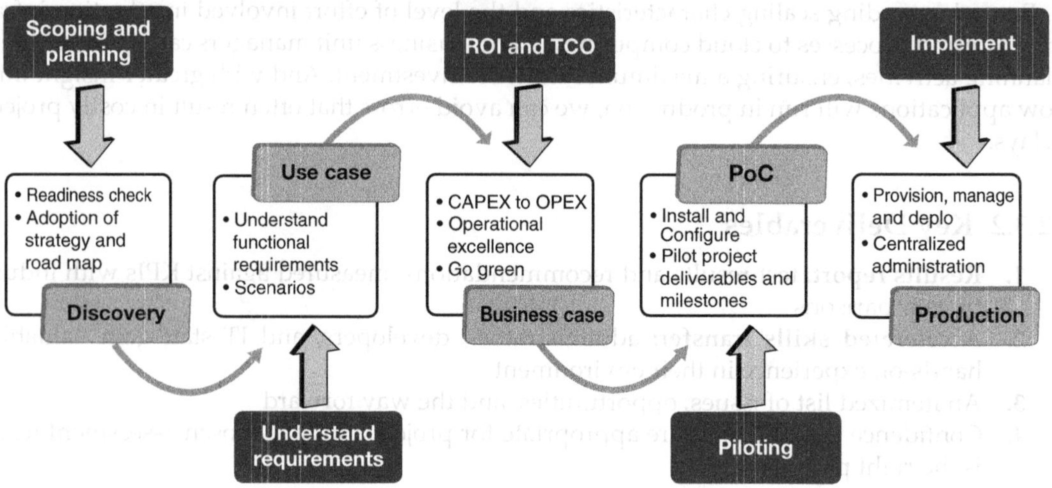

FIGURE 12.1 Journey to cloud.

Cloud assessment and migration requires dedicated teams to build competency in cloud services, including platform-based competency teams for commercial cloud platform vendors. Cloud assessment and migration should have competency units that build cloud services for middleware, BI and Reporting, Testing and SaaS services such as CRM, office productivity application.

Some of the internal tools that can be developed for the cloud computing practice are: TCO analysis tools, cloud suitability assessment models, migration checklists and cloud computing best practices.

Assessment and migration services for cloud can be categorized into the following three categories:

1. **Cloud development services:** These services are for new applications that are being developed for deployment on the cloud. Cloud assessment and migration team take into consideration the customer technology preferences and the application profile to determine the appropriate cloud platform.
2. **Cloud migration services:** Cloud assessment and migration provide customers assessment service to analyze the readiness of existing applications for cloud migration as part of its cloud migration services.
3. **Cloud integration services:** Cloud assessment and migration recognizes that most of the applications deployed on the cloud will require integration with other applications in the cloud as well as applications hosted on-premise on customer location. Cloud assessment and migration should have an active integration services practice that can help customers in building integrated cloud and on-premise solutions.

Cloud assessment service delivers:

1. **Results report:** Test results and recommendations, measured against KPIs with industry comparisons
2. **Accelerated skills transfer:** Administrators, developers, and IT staff to gain valuable, hands-on experience in their environment

3. An itemized list of issues, opportunities, and the way forward
4. Confidence that the tools are appropriate for the project for which the cloud provider is the right partner

12.4 ROI Calculation

The ROI calculation typically focuses on the business values of using cloud computing — public, private, or hybrid. It requires a complex and dynamic analysis that is unique to the problem domain an enterprise is trying to address. The value of cloud computing depends directly on the type of business, the core business processes, and the specific problems an enterprise is looking to solve. The values expected from the increased agility and scalability are the core benefits of cloud-based platforms.

Cloud assessment and migration would do a cost/benefit analysis for an enterprise by calculating various criteria of Direct and Indirect cost (Managed Services).

1. Direct cost criteria would include:
   - Capex: Hardware (servers, peripheral, and network components)
   - Opex: Software (license, software maintenance, SW development, and SW management)
   - Cloud management (architecture/administration, system hosting, and reporting)
   - Cloud support (support staff)
   - Cloud implementation (SaaS development/customization/implementation)
2. Indirect cost (managed service cost):
   - Cloud programme management
   - Account management
   - Cost of business operations
   - Cost of marketing/promotions for cloud pre- and post-adoption initiatives

The ROI calculation can be done by taking into account information as per **Table 12.1:**

Table 12.1 | Cloud assessment ROI calculator sample questionnaire

Type	Sub-Type	Questions	Notes
Direct cost	Hardware	Approximate # servers an enterprise intends to use?	These are number of services required to support an enterprise business, hardware capacity planning
Direct cost	Hardware	Storage amount?	Size of storage an enterprise need to buy or rent
Direct cost	Management	Nature of DC? Own or are time-bound on the lease?	Whether an enterprise is going to use existing data center space
Direct cost	Management	Will enterprise use existing racks and utilities?	Same as above

(Continued)

Table 12.1 | (Continued)

Type	Sub-Type	Questions	Notes
Direct cost	Hardware	Will enterprise use consolidate and free some existing servers, storage, and network devices?	Are enterprise re-provisioning something enterprise already use?
Direct cost	Hardware	If yes to previous question, how many servers?	This determines how many new servers enterprise will need to provision
Direct cost	Hardware	Amount that enterprise can expect to pay for data center costs associated with allocation of new hardware (on-premise or off-premise data center space)	This is the new space needed-on premise (rent, utilities, etc.)
Direct cost	Hardware	Amount that enterprise can expect to pay for New Racks	This is the NEW racks, cables, etc., if on premise
Direct cost	Hardware	How many servers, storage devices, and network devices will enterprise procure just for the private cloud?	This is the new hardware needed
Direct cost	Hardware	How much to enterprise intend on spending for these new servers, storage, and network devices will enterprise procure just for the private cloud?	This is how much it will cost to buy new hardware
Direct cost	Hardware/ software	How much will enterprise pay per server for Windows OS licensing?	Check Pricing online for OS of choice
Direct cost	Software	How much will enterprise pay per server for Linux OS licensing?	Check pricing for OS of choice
Direct cost	Management	How much will enterprise pay per server for IaaS solution?	Industry Average ranges from $$ - $$$ per server
Direct cost	Management	How much will enterprise pay per server for PaaS solution?	Computing's Top Stack licenses
Direct cost	Software	What is the estimated cost of the OS software?	Check price of OS Software
Indirect cost	Business operations	What is the estimated cost of the IaaS software per year?	Check price of Infra as a Service
Indirect cost	Business operations	What is the estimated cost of the PaaS software per year?	Check price of Platform as a Service

(Continued)

Table 12.1 | (Continued)

Type	Sub-Type	Questions	Notes
Indirect cost	Programme management	What would be the change in FTE headcount be if enterprise moved to a public cloud provider?	Include Network, OS, and System Admins
Indirect cost	Programme management	What would be the change in FTE headcount be if enterprise created a private cloud?	Include Network, OS, and System Admins
Indirect cost	Programme management	What is the average yearly cost of these FTEs?	Average Admin salary plus benefits and taxes
Indirect cost	Account management	Public cloud FTE resource	
Indirect cost	Account management	Private cloud FTE resource	

12.4.1 Environment Gathering and Apps Workload Pattern Gathering

Environment gathering and Apps workload pattern gathering comprises the following three steps carried out in-depth after workshop:

1. Due diligence
2. H/W, N/W readiness assessment
3. Security and migration assessment

The detail activities and the relationship are depicted in **Fig. 12.2:**

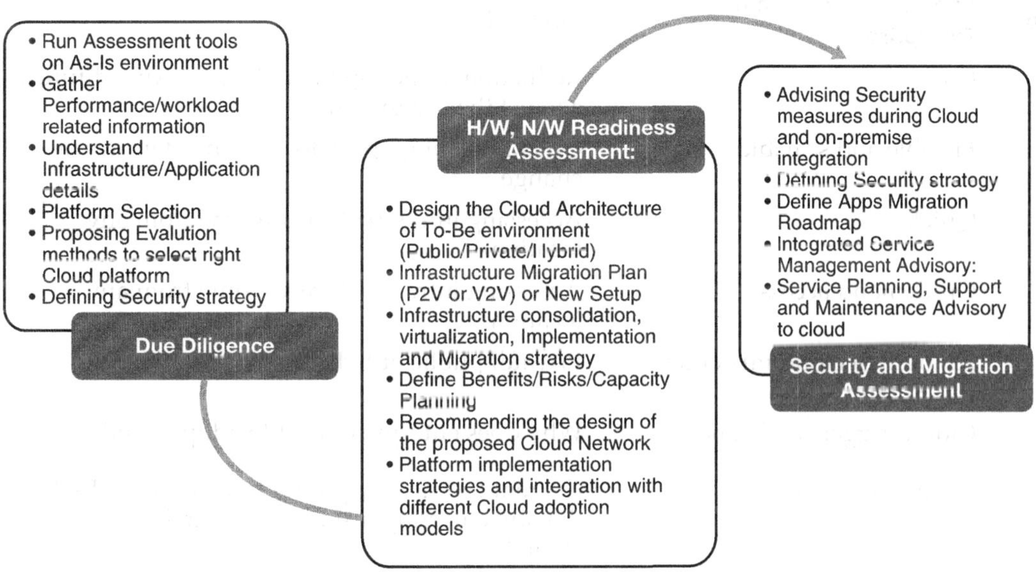

FIGURE 12.2 Environment gathering and Apps workload pattern gathering.

Table 12.2 shows the inputs of assessment. Modelling is used to prepare a project plan. Execution, handhold phase, and feedbacks refine the capabilities.

Table 12.2 | Inputs of assessment

1	Solution design and right mix of cloud	This is a critical phase of solutions
2	Developed detail project plan	This is generating a detailed project plan once the assessment is done, the actionable plan is prepared. Solutions are identified.
3	Project deployment	Project execution, controlling monitoring as per agreed scope with the enterprise.
4	Stabilize and handhold	This is a reverse and forward shadowing phase for setting up the cloud support.
5	Transition to operations	This is 'Acceptance-into-service" for cloud solutions has been implemented by enterprise or managed service provider
6	Refine capabilities	This is a feedback loop to improve the capabilities and embrace the lessons learnt in various phases.

12.4.2 Aspects to Consider

Managed service provider recommends enterprises to consider the following significant aspects of introducing IaaS/PaaS to enterprise (**Table 12.3**):

Table 12.3 | Significant aspects of introducing IaaS/PaaS in enterprises

No.	Conditions for Attribute Enterprise	Description
1	Cost	Reduction in the capital and Opex expenditure as against the investment.
2	Flexible and scalable	Quickly scaling up or down as need grows or change
3	Quick	Accessing infrastructure anytime from any location
4	On-demand access	Accessing infrastructure anytime from any location
5	Amount of cloud mix enterprise requires	Private/public or hybrid
6	Cloud triggers and concerns	Why does enterprise want to adopt cloud?
7	Technology landscape	Current technology products, landscape, Tools that are currently installed and can be migrated to cloud? Processes for IaaS , PaaS maintenance, SLA, KPIs

Cloud assessment and migration team provide methodical support in introducing IaaS/PaaS by collecting relevant information, such as enterprise business drivers, current pain areas, current setup, cloud roadmap, etc.

Cloud assessment and migration team work on this information and use tools to identify critical areas, and later conduct a workshop with enterprise executives and conclude on the aspects of introducing IaaS/PaaS.

We believe that cloud computing offers high-impact opportunities for enterprise business units in leveraging IaaS and PaaS while factoring in:

1. Effective monitoring and managing of enterprise exposures, risk governance, and control,
2. Tightening regulations and its compliance,
3. Modernization of legacy application landscape, and
4. Effective analytics for enhanced decision support.

12.5 Migration – Service Path

12.5.1 Migration Steps

The migration framework put in place ensures the efficient utilization of time and resources during the migration process (**Fig. 12.3**).

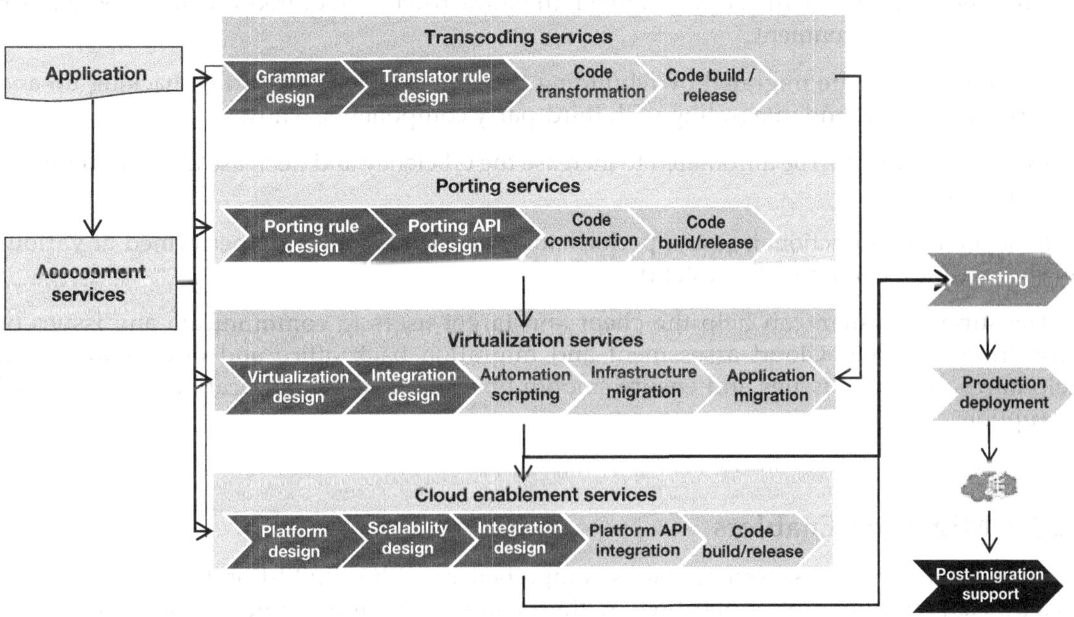

FIGURE 12.3 Migration service path.

Pre-migration step identifies the challenges, timeline, and changes required in the existing system through different techniques.

In **architecture assessment**, the infrastructure needs of the migration like effort required, resources like hardware, software and licenses are analyzed and planned.

As part of **solution modeling**, the virtualization environments are setup within the cloud environment in porting the application.

In **execution** phase, the source code would be rebuilt, and databases would be configured. The different software modules would be integrated, and test cases are created. The deployment process would be automated, and release management process would be defined.

Testing of functional and nonfunctional aspects of the application based on the test cases ensures that the application can be used in real-time.

In addition to migration, **post-migration support** should be provided where the issues can be reported and we engage the appropriate support personnel.

Migration and assessment team uses appropriate tools and artifacts at every stage of the migration process. The starting point is to understand the need and the current system through questionnaire session with the product owners. It is mandatory to find if an application can be migrated through our custom cloudification assessment process.

With the help of in-house expert team, the application architecture and the migration outcomes are analyzed, and possible solutions are explored. The recommended solutions are ranked considering the various factors in the migration process.

Once the proposed architecture is agreed, the infrastructure required is configured and set up in the cloud environment.

The applications are migrated by rebuilding the source code, configuring, backing up and restoring databases, and integrating with third-party components, if any.

Deployment can also be automated to increase the efficiency and decrease the time of migration process.

Functional, nonfunctional, stress, performance, and load testing are performed at various levels (modules/components/system).

The support system can help the client and target users to communicate any issues or raise trouble tickets. Cloud assessment and migration back office and development can help in resolving the issues and ensure smooth operations of the application with minimal disruption.

12.5.2 Migration Enablers

Cloud migration and assessment team's comprehensive BRO (Build-Run-Optimize) process enables easy migration of applications within a short time and optimizes the resources by automation and tool integration. It allows customers to centralize the migration process and operate the software infrastructure efficiently (**Fig. 12.4**).

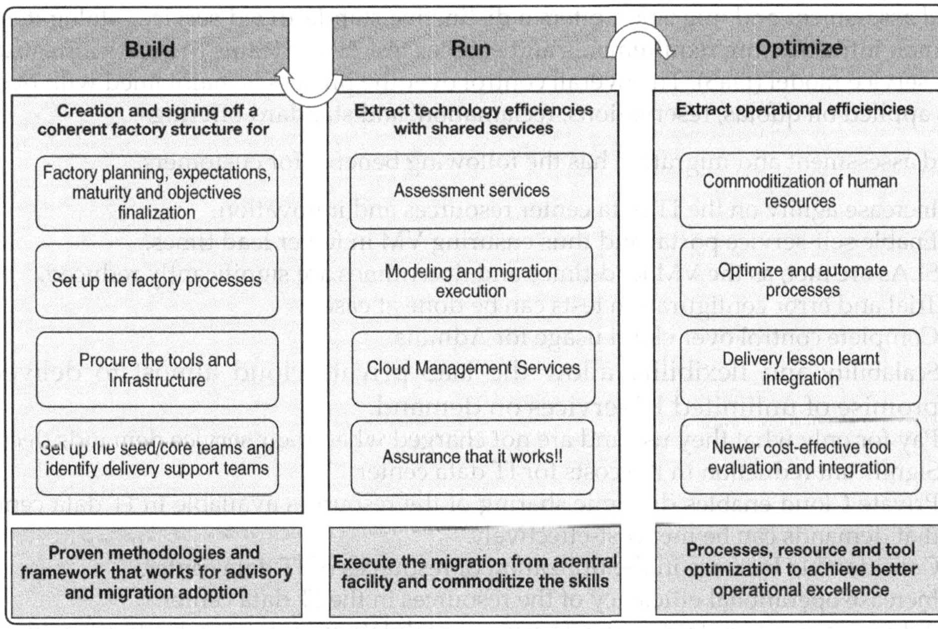

FIGURE 12.4 Migration enablers.

Relevant methodologies and framework are adopted during the various stages of migration. Resource utilization is optimized at different stages of the process that helps in achieving one of the important goals of the migration. Feedback on the performance of the system is analyzed in every possible detail to ensure the migration process is effective.

Operational challenges are captured and necessary remedial actions are taken. The lessons learned in the earlier migration projects can be helpful in seamless delivery of the project.

Availability of required tools in the different stages of the migration process improves the efficiency of the migration process and reduces the overall time.

The tools are classified as reusable assets, and they are required at every stage of the migration process. In-house tools are constantly developed and used across different projects. All repeatable processes and activities are automated using the tools. Appropriate external tools are used wherever required.

The reports and data generated by the tools are used in analyzing the complexity of the system during the assessment phase.

12.5.3 Benefits

Cloud migration services integrate state-of-the-art next-generation cloud management solutions to transform internal enterprise IT data centers into an agile and cost-effective cloud solution. Cloud assessment and migration team's unique ability to transform IT into a service organization with self-service, chargeback, service catalogs, and physical resources, complete application provisioning, reservations approach automates the self-service assembly and infrastructure management.

Cloud assessment and migration offers a distinctive standardized service catalog items for all common infrastructure requirements and enables test & dev teams to access infrastructure in a self-service model (IaaS). The overall control over the process is maintained with business policies applied on quotas, reservations, reclamation, and standard offerings.

Cloud assessment and migration has the following benefits for customers.

1. Increase agility on the IT data center resources and innovation.
2. Enable self-service portal and thus ensuring VM in fewer lead times.
3. SLAs are met, as the VM lead-times and downtimes are significantly reduced.
4. Trial and error configuration tests can be done at ease.
5. Complete control over cloud usage for Admins.
6. Scalability and flexibility allow the IaaS private cloud almost to deliver the promise of unlimited IT services on demand.
7. Pay for only what they use and are not charged when their service demands decrease.
8. Significant reduction in the costs for IT data center.
9. Private Cloud enables dynamic sharing of the resources available in IT data center so that demands can be met cost-effectively.
10. Considerable Increase in the utilization of resources of IT data center.
11. Increase operational efficiency of the resources in the IT data center.
12. Achieve a greener data center (server consolidation and virtualization enables over committed machines).
13. Support for heterogeneous hardware vendors. Avoids vendor locking.

Following should be the characteristic features while executing the cloud assessment and migration project:

Proven framework and execution approach for maximum ROI:

1. Uniquely specialized expertise for Repeatable process and tools
2. Robust migration framework supported by robust implementation model

Enable standardization and sustainability:

1. By leveraging various framework, artifacts or partner Services enterprise should immensely benefit by the best migration practices.

Deliver the benefits of economies of scale and end-to-end comprehensive services:

1. Enterprise should benefit from continual input, and asset growth as the customer base expands
2. Cloud migration should address BOTH operational and business transformation requirements to ensure a migration success.
3. Managed service provider should provide customer experience center which serves as a digital playground for partners and customers

Accelerate time to value and ROI realization, reduce cost, risk, and complexity and faster time-to-value:

1. Cloud migration and assessment team significantly collapse the time for an enterprise to implement a migration factory-type solution.

12.6 Summary

Cloud assessment and migration services pave way for organizations to dramatically reduce capital and operational expenses as more applications can be run without the cost of adding new resources. These cost reductions can be achieved by optimizing overall resource utilization of the compute resources available in IT data center. Significant improvement in service levels, as resources, can be dynamically added to higher priority applications when needed.

CHAPTER

13

Data Center Transformation and Workload Migration

CONTENTS

13.1 Overview

Data center transformation and workload migration to cloud require a phased approach for migration of an enterprise's IT infrastructure. Each phase addresses several layers: business, application, and Infrastructure. At the intersection of each phase and layer are key project functions and deliverables. Enterprise should follow a top-down approach during plan and design phases.

The migration approach used by data center transformation and migration to cloud is illustrated in **Fig. 13.1 (a, b)**.

Data center transformation and migration require years of combined industry experience, risk-reducing strategies, and cost-saving solutions in developing its migration/transformation techniques and frameworks. The data center (DC) migration techniques are delivered in discrete phases to ensure the programme is accurately scoped, consistently designed, and executed over time and across locations.

Organizations achieve higher productivity, enhance agility, and support business expansion by taking a holistic approach. Data center transformation and migration techniques include:

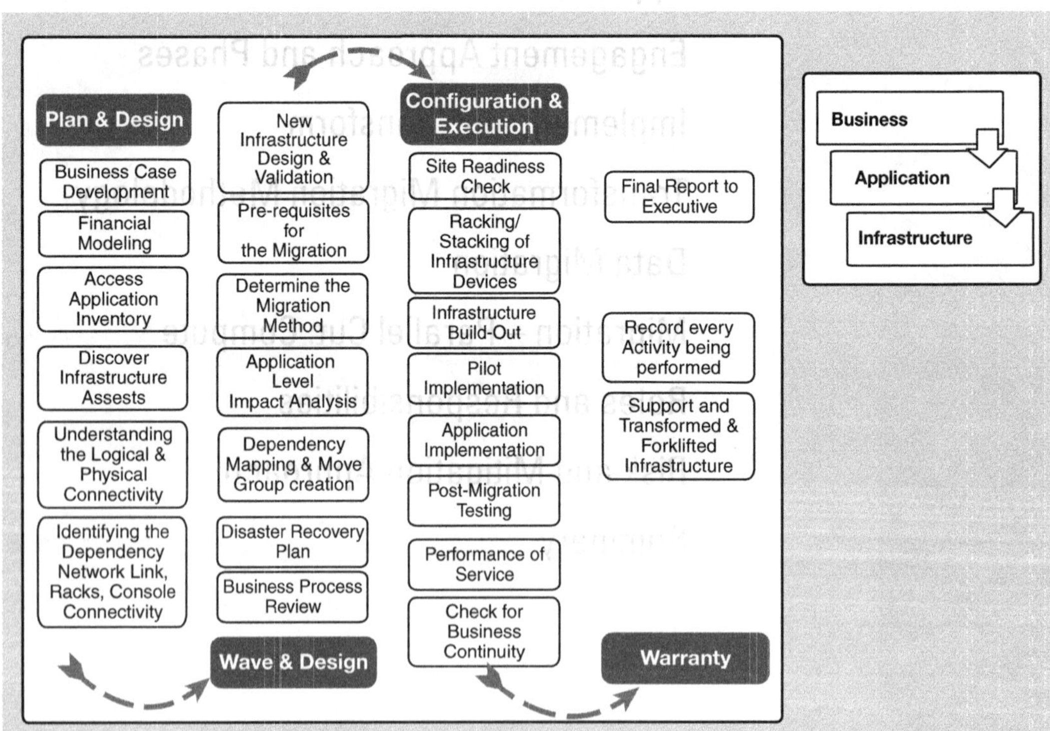

(a)

FIGURE 13.1 (a, b) Migration approach used by data center transformation and migration to cloud.

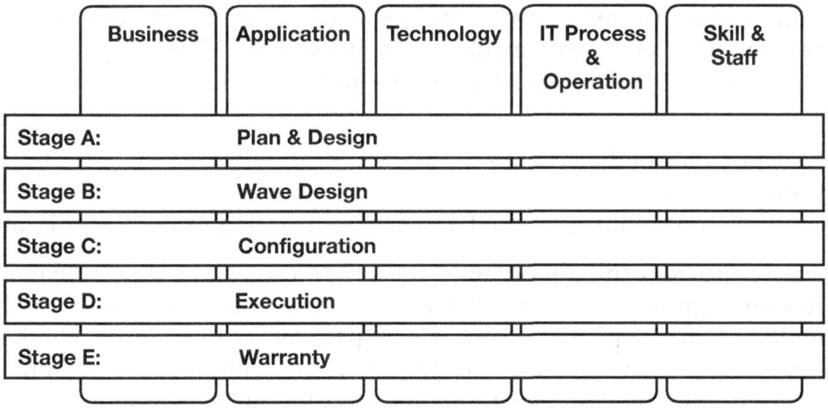

(b)

FIGURE 13.1 (a, b) (Continued).

1. Robust execution capabilities with profound industry insights and business process expertise.
2. Use of latest technology solutions to execute the migration while enabling the integrity of the application and minimizing end-user impact.
3. Broad skills in data center technologies help execute seamless transition, meet service level agreements, and exceed performance objectives.
4. Deliver rapid migration results that mitigate risks and achieve high performance.

13.2 Approach

The entire migration and transformation project is divided into phases and then further broken down into sub-phases and move groups.

The output of the Due Diligence and Assessment and Analysis phases will be an architectural blueprint for the transformed environment and a detailed project plan for the Implementation and Transformation phase.

The Implement and Transform Phase is further detailed in **Fig. 13.2**. This phase has additional multiple sub-phases; each of these sub-phases would address specific data centers and move groups.

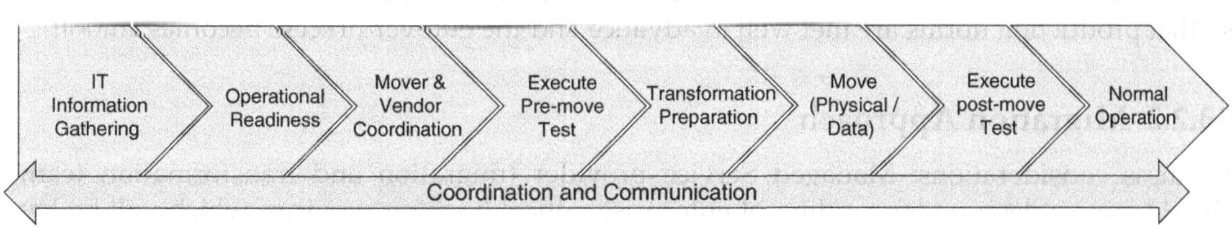

FIGURE 13.2 Implement and transform phase.

As an example, the first sub-phase addresses source data center. Accurate determination of sub-phases can occur post-assessment and analysis phase. The sub-phases and the move groups, which are part of that sub-phase, are prioritized in time based on a combination of the following:

1. Lease expiry date of data centers
2. End-of-life assets
3. Business processes and associated applications needing prioritized migration

Managed Service provider (migration and transformation team) executes two sub-phases in parallel to reduce migration times. A detailed assessment and analysis is conducted to determine if more than two sub-phases can be run in parallel, or to what degree the sub-phases should be staggered to arrive at a realistic migration plan. Within each sub-phase, Managed Service provider (migration and transformation team) establishes elaborate quality gates to determine the readiness to move to the next step.

Before the migration commences, infrastructure for the first sub-phase is installed and tested in the new primary data center. Simultaneously, the secondary data center infrastructure is also set up. The actual migration is based on a combination of lift-and-shift for reusable assets and parallel cuts wherever RPO and RTP times are critical. RPO and RTO for each business service are decided in conjunction with the appropriate stakeholders in enterprise Businesses and Technology groups.

The entire network infrastructure is set up in both the new data centers at the start of the migration. For example, Managed Service provider (migration and transformation team) can propose to connect the primary and secondary data centers with a 'dark-fiber', offering high-capacity bandwidth. Secondly, as and when equipment from the existing data centres are migrated, Managed Service provider (migration and transformation team) can use MPLS links with adequate bandwidth to facilitate data replication between the primary data center and the data center(s) that are being migrated. These high bandwidth MPLS links are required primarily for data replication from the existing storage to the new storage. Once the initial data replication is achieved, the bandwidth is reduced and the link is removed when the current data center under migration is decommissioned. Similarly, links are set up and decommissioned for the remaining data centers. The primary and secondary data centers are equipped with internet links of adequate capacity.

13.2.1 Moving to Production in the New Environment

It is important to understand the roles of various stakeholders in the critical process of moving applications from the test/non-production environments into production and the current processes followed by the enterprise. Early engagement with the operations teams will be done so that production norms are met well in advance and the cutover process becomes smooth.

13.2.2 Migration Approach

Business considerations: Managed Service provider (migration and transformation team) should have a deep understanding of enterprise critical business services, which will be leveraged to establish a model to get RTO and RPO for critical services. This model will help in determining affordable downtime during migration and post-migration. To ensure 'near-zero disruption' and 'business continuity' of business services, underlying applications and infrastructure will be grouped for transformation. One of the critical considerations for migration/transformation is DC lease expiry.

13.3 Engagement Approach and Phases

Migration and transformation approach for the engagement involves the following phases of activity:

1. Due diligence: Phase to finalize the assets in scope, asset life, and asset valuation
2. Asses and analyze: Period of detailed information gathering/study, finalization of end-state architecture, identifying RTO and RPO of applications and supporting infrastructure, finalization of move groups and the migration plan
3. Implement and transform: Phase in which assets will be migrated to the new data centers using a mix of lift-shift and parallel cut approaches. Consolidation methods like cloud enablement, storage virtualization, and database consolidation will be used to optimize the infrastructure at the new data centers. In this phase, EOL assets that have been migrated are decommissioned
4. Sustain: Phase in which infrastructure maintenance, technology refresh, and business as usual (BAU) managed services activities will be carried out.
5. Project management office (PMO) and governance: This phase will start in parallel with assess and analyse phase with setting up of project management support services and governance mechanism, which will be practiced through the rest of phases of engagement. The activities performed during this phase will provide high degree of management control and oversight for the inputs, dependencies, and outputs of each task
6. Service delivery: IT service management framework is used for service delivery due diligence

Managed Service provider (migration and transformation team) will conduct a series of structured workshops with the enterprise to validate the current state of IT Infrastructure, which will help us to:

1. Finalize the assets in scope
2. Agree upon the valuation of assets

13.3.1 Finalize the Assets in Scope

Managed Service provider (migration and transformation team) will validate the assets — compute, storage, network, which are in scope. Configuration details of the current assets and the EOL, both on the OS and hardware, will be obtained.

In addition to the asset inventory details, Managed Service provider (migration and transformation team) will obtain the following information for the network:

1. Details of existing network architecture design and setup
2. Remote site connectivity and protocol information

3. Total WAN bandwidth use between data centers and external parties
4. Base network flow process, traffic patterns
5. Identification of network traffic according to Network Layer Protocols and Application Layer Protocols
6. Discussion with network administrative teams regarding current network issues concerning performance, availability, etc.
7. Volumetric of past 6 months to 1 year trouble tickets of the network.
8. Study of roadmaps/upgrade plans

Managed Service provider (migration and transformation team) will obtain the following information for storage:

1. Software used in the current storage environment
2. Details on existing storage architecture, current I/O workload (IOPS), and performance metric
3. Connectivity layout between server, storage, and tape library
4. Existing array configuration pattern and RAID layout, application/database wise storage allocation and estimation of I/O requirement for each of the application
5. Application-wise data retention requirements
6. Number of database/application configured for backup

13.3.2 Assess and Analyze

In this phase, Managed Service provider (migration and transformation team) will do a detailed information gathering/study, finalization of end-state architecture, identifying RTO and RPO of applications and supporting infrastructure through BIA, and finalization of move groups and the migration plan.

Objective: The objective of this phase is to:

1. Perform BIA (Business Impact Analysis) of application and underlying infrastructure
2. Network and security assessment
3. Compute assessment
4. Storage assessment
5. Identify application move groups

13.3.3 Business Impact Analysis

Based on Managed Service provider (migration and transformation team) understanding of enterprise, it is recommended to have a business process-centric view for data center migration vis-a-vis infrastructure centric view. Business process RTOs and RPOs are the critical factors in determining migration strategy.

The business impact analysis (BIA) identifies the urgency of each business activity undertaken by the organization (**Fig. 13.3**):

1. By assessing the time impact on the delivery of products and services due to the interruption of this business activity.

2. This information identifies the timescale of appropriate continuity and resumption strategies for each activity individually and about one another.

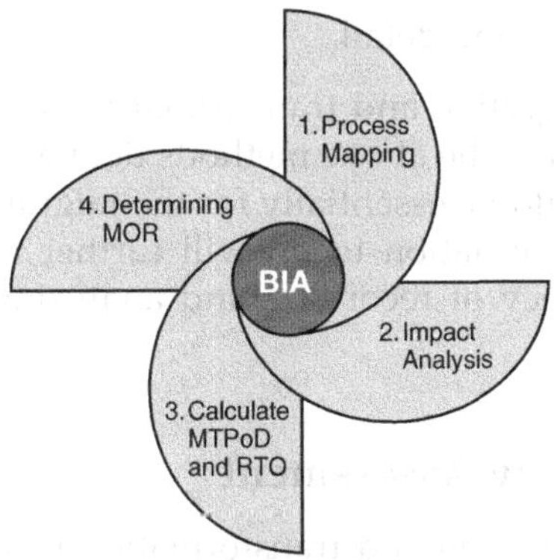

FIGURE 13.3 Business impact analysis.

1. **Process mapping:** The following activities are performed:
   - Identify 'Process to Enabler' mapping (people, vendor, software, and hardware, information)
   - Identify 'Process to Site' mapping (Identify the details of sites from where a particular process is performed.)
   - Classify processes into the following service categories: Customer acquisition, Service Delivery, Revenue continuity, Legal and Regulatory Compliance, Support service, and Support resource
2. **Impact analysis:** Understand the impact of the identified business processes considering impact on following parameters:
   - Financial impact
   - Operational impact
   - Time impact
   - Legal and regulatory impact
3. **Calculate MTPoD and RTO:**
   - Identify maximum tolerable period of disruption (MTPOD) and finalize recovery time objective (RTO) and level of recovery (LOR) through workshops.
   - Obtain approval from functional heads on the identified business processes, impact parameters and calculated RTO and MTPoD values.
4. **Determine MOR:**
   - Document minimum operating requirements (MOR) for the identified critical processes.
   - Obtain a signoff from functional head as an approval to the MOR for process.

The following three methods are widely adopted to perform BIA:

1. **Workshops:** Workshops can provide rapid results and an opportunity for hands-on engagement with the program, provided there is consistent buy-in from all departments and participants.

2. **Questionnaire:** Questionnaires provide large amounts of data, but information quality can be questionable if not completed with consistency.
3. **Interviews:** Interviews can provide excellent information but are time-consuming, and output can vary in format and detail.

Managed Service provider (migration and transformation team) recommends that a hybrid approach, where a combination of the above methods delivers excellent results providing an appropriate level of detail, would be essentially for the migration strategy. Managed Service provider (migration and transformation team) will further use standard reporting format that will assist in the consistency of recording and analyzing information across multiple functions.

13.3.4 Network and Security Assessment

Managed Service provider (migration and transformation team) will study and analyze the network in detail and prepare blueprints of the end-state architecture.

The following are the key activities that will be performed:

1. Detailed architecture and design for current servers, network, and security.
2. Performance analysis of the historical data, current traffic volume, and patterns.
3. Capacity of the existing servers, network, and security elements.
4. Impact of new protocols in the environment.
5. Understanding and impact of passive interface.
6. IP address schema changes.
7. Compatibility and interoperability.
8. Projected demands.
9. Resource utilization and traffic pattern for new data center.
10. Configuration parameters and security implementation (mainly firewalls affecting performance) hardware life cycle (for migration and upgrade roadmap).
11. Current network capacity for volumetric and impact on future volumetric and services.
12. New tools requirement after implementation/upgradation.

13.3.5 Compute Assessment

Managed service provider (migration and transformation team) will study and analyze the compute (server) environment in detail and prepare blueprints of the end-state architecture. The following are the key activities which will be performed:

1. Finalize the application to server mapping which will be used as a parameter to identify move groups.
2. Identify servers which can be re-used.
3. Detailed assessment of server configuration.
4. Deployment architecture will be finalized for production, test, development, pre-production/disaster recovery environments for all the hosts that are going to migrate, including:
   - Hardware sizing

- Operating system licenses
- Tools licenses

13.3.6 Storage Assessment

Managed Service provider (migration and transformation team) will study and analyze the storage environment in detail and prepare blueprints of the end-state architecture. The following are the key activities which will be performed:

1. **Determine the volume of information to be migrated:** Gather the specific information regarding the application, operating system, database and data size.
2. **Size the end-state storage requirement.**
3. **Assess the performance impact:** Determine the performance impact of moving large amounts of data on host, array, network, and SAN fabric.
4. **Publish the storage migration schedule.**
5. **Back out plan:** Managed Service provider (migration and transformation team) will outline the detail back out plan before beginning of migration process.

13.3.7 Identify Application Move Groups

Multiple factors help determine the application move groups. Managed Service provider (migration and transformation team) will identify the following dependencies:

1. Application-to-server/mainframe mapping.
2. Application-to-database/platform mapping.
3. Application dependency mapping.
4. Application security requirements.
5. Applications usage and SLAs.

Detailed list of assets prepared during the due diligence phase identify the application move groups for migrations and also decide on the schedule of the migrations.

The following parameters of the applications are considered for the identifying application move groups:

1. Associated hardware EOL and operating EOS.
2. Business impact.
3. Application complexity.
4. Application criticality.
5. HA requirement.
6. OS compatibility for application.
7. Hardware compatibility.
8. Cluster environment necessity.
9. Number of databases linked.
10. Storage volume linked.
11. Average time required for application integration.
12. Average time required for application testing.
13. Cloud compatibility.

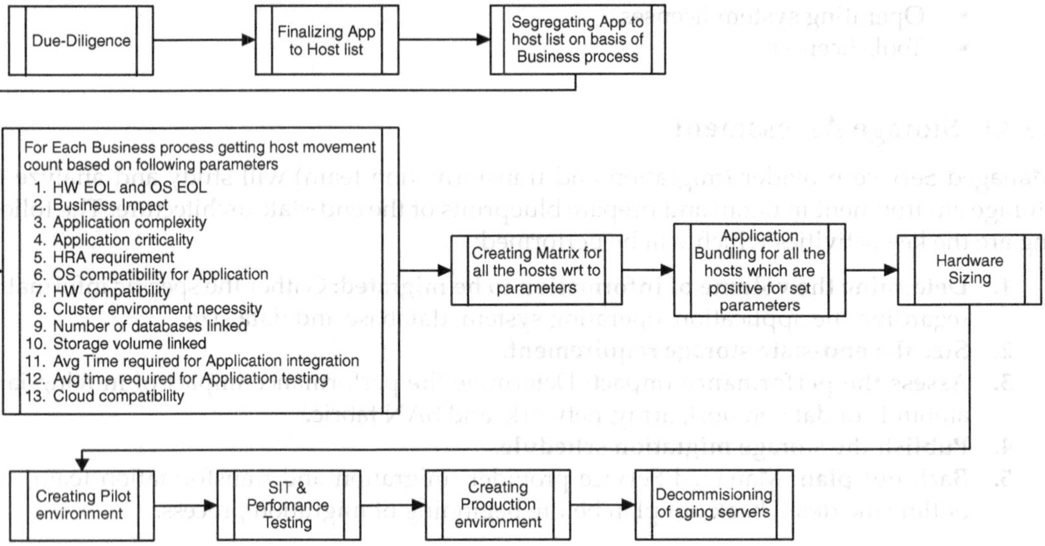

FIGURE 13.4 Process overview of the flow of activities.

All the applications are rated on the above parameters, and the applications that rank similarly on these parameters are bundled to form move groups for migrations. Besides the above parameters, dependent applications are bundled and migrated together to minimize the downtime. The dependent applications are identified by doing a workshop with application owners or by deploying discovery tool.

Fig. 13.4 shows the process overview of the flow of activities carried out to identify application move groups.

13.4 Implement and Transform

Managed Service provider (migration and transformation team) proposes a standard framework for data center migrations, which clearly defines the comprehensive set of services required to successfully plan and execute any data center migration, whether the move is to a new technology stack as in this case private cloud or a physical move to new data center facilities. The framework incorporates best practices, reducing the overall project risk and allowing Managed Service provider (migration and transformation team) to scope the requirements clearly, sequence the many required activities to complete the migration.

In undertaking any data center transformation and relocation project, Managed Service provider (migration and transformation team) focuses on ensuring that all stages of the project (from defining the requirements, through to design, move and management) consider the following key design issues relating to critical data center facilities:

1. Capacity.
2. Reliability and redundancy.
3. Single points of failure.

4. Maintainability.
5. Security.
6. Survivability.
7. Scalability/modularity (optimization of initial investment by incremental modular expansion of support systems as loads increase).
8. Environmental issues (spill containment, noise control, engine exhaust pollution).
9. Cost.

Table 13.1 shows the phases of the engagement followed during transformation and migration.

Table 13.1 | Phases of the engagement followed during transformation and migration.

Track	High-Level Activities
Discovery and design	• DC site and business data capture • Application architecture and server architecture data capture • Analysis of infrastructure, database • HLD and LLD
Wave design	• Business criticality data capture. • Environment to business mapping data capture • Application mapping to environment • Creating Application move groups
Configuration	• HW Installation • OS deployment and virtualization • Storage and backup installation • Database configuration • Software installation and configuration
Execution	• Migrate storage data • LLD validation • Validate contingency plan and process • Capacity, performance and HA validation • Migration move
Managed Services	• Support and transformed infrastructure • Follow existing incident/change/problem management process • Record every activity being performed

13.5 Transformation Migration Methodology

The following section details the transformation and migration methodologies proposed for any project. Enterprise should take a phased migration approach for migrating any organization environment. One of the advantages of a phased migration approach is that various transformation activities can be run in parallel. Such transformation solutions lower the impact of downtimes during the migration activity.

13.5.1 Migration Assessment

The proposed approach is based on a structured framework that takes a balanced view of technology and business requirements and provides a comprehensive analysis of all applications being re-platformed. This helps in making a decision and developing a detailed design on whether the applications have to be retained As-Is, re-engineered (to coexist with the new core platform), or retired (**Fig. 13.5**).

Step-wise breakdown on the migration approach:

Step 1: Data center assessment, plan and design the architecture

Step 2: Data center readiness: This include primarily getting the base infrastructure of the facility in place so that the servers can start

Step 3: Network Build

1. Set-up the LAN according to the finalized architecture plan.
2. Testing of LAN.
3. Readiness of WAN links, Internet link, for the new sites as well.
4. Readiness of WAN link links between the existing and new sites for storage data migration.
5. Acceptance Tests for the links.
6. Setting up a temporary link.

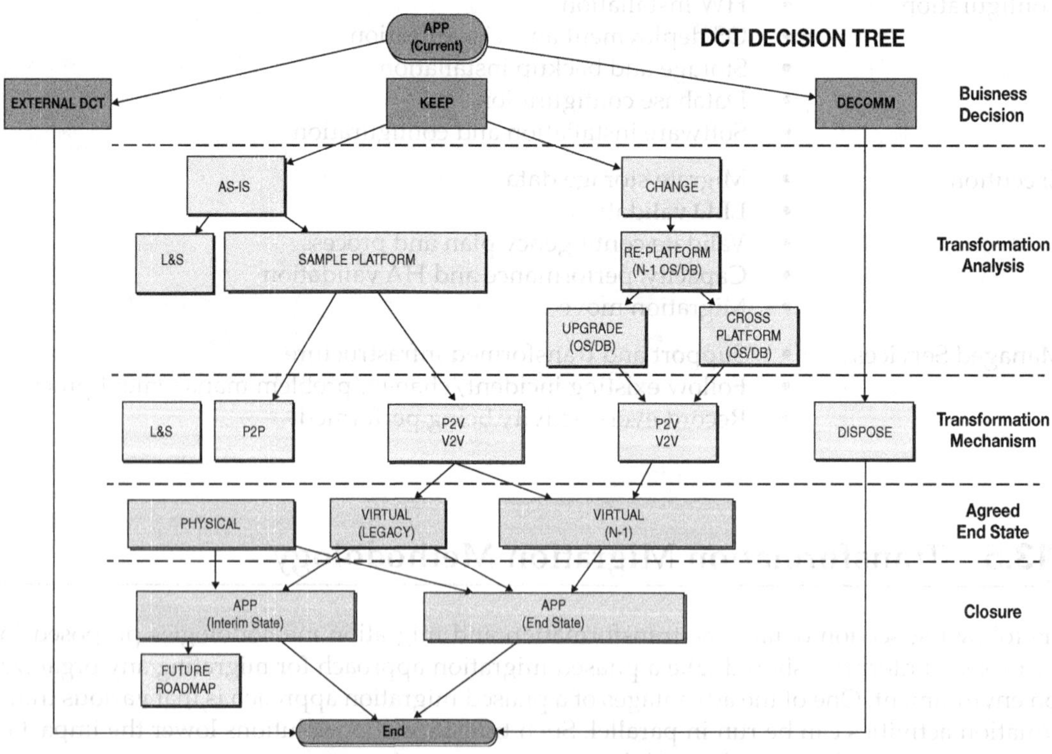

FIGURE 13.5 Migration assessment.

Step 4: Storage and server build

1. New build of storage at the target data centers.
2. Migrate the existing storage environment to the target storage.
3. Server new build/virtualization for migrated application on the new platform.
4. Build the infrastructure at all the sites.
5. Use tools like migration tools to copy the OS images with storage data at the target site.
6. Test and validate the DC and DR environment.
7. Incremental data migration over wire.
8. Cut Over to new DC in a phased manner.
9. Handover to Managed Services team.

Data migration will involve mapping of application to disk group mapping that will enable Managed Service provider (migration and transformation team) to create the move group and sequencing of application in phase manner.

13.5.2 Application Profiling Based on Move Group Approach

Application profiling efficiently implements many data centre initiatives by providing current information about applications, software, servers, network, and SAN. This holistic view reveals dependencies and issues associated with infrastructure and communication flows, thus helps in making better decisions for implementing complex data center and application infrastructure strategies (**Fig. 13.6**).

Information from compute and storage domains is collected through a complete methodology using various discovery tools and a top-down methodology of consultations with domain experts and business process professionals. This combination creates an accurate profile of deployed technology infrastructure and the business processes it supports that is an essential input for data center migration and consolidation.

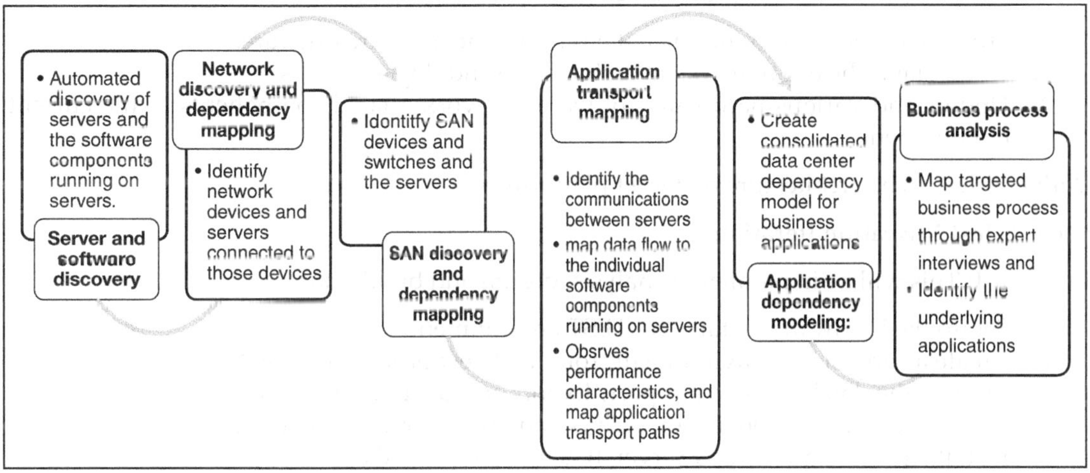

FIGURE 13.6 Application profiling.

The migration is based on application move groups approach. In this case, the entire IT landscape is grouped into logical baskets. These baskets are homogeneous over below-mentioned dimensions:

1. **Application objective:** Interdependencies between applications as defined in the workflow to achieve any business objective.
2. **Data source:** The corresponding database.
3. **Infrastructure interface:** The corresponding interface to networks, security and storage architecture.
4. **Based on Environment:** Prod/Dev/DR.
5. **Based on application functionalities:** Infra, Packaged.

13.5.3 Step-by-Step Detailed Approach for Migration from Existing Environment

Stage 1: Project initiation and kick-off by project management team

The high-level activities carried out during this phase are given as follows:

1. Preparation of kick-off and project initiation document.
2. Prepare project charter.
3. Definition of roles and responsibilities.
4. Nondisclosure agreement sign off if required.
5. Preparation of high-level project plan.
6. Setting up of PMO.
7. Identification of project stakeholders.
8. Preparation of escalation matrix within Managed Service provider (migration and transformation team) and outsourcer **(enterprise)**.

Deliverables: Project charter and project plan

Stage 2: Analysis, design and build by Managed Service provider (migration and transformation team), **database OEM and outsourcer (enterprise)**

1. Study and understand the current environment and infrastructure.
2. Understand the existing system architecture and dependencies.
3. Understand various hardware, software, network related components in the current environment.

Deliverables: To be architecture on target platform

Stage 3: Test Migration Iteration

Iteration 1: This will be in parallel to analysis, design and build phase

1. Set up the hardware, install OS - TEST environment.
2. Create a copy of Test environment from the latest production database.
3. Migrate the database using Import/Export or Transportable Tablespace.
4. Preparation of post-conversion scripts and objects creation on target database.
5. Install and Configure Apps Server, Batch Server, and Web Server.

6. Copy customized file objects on application server, batch server, and Web Server.
7. Sanity check, objects integrity issues and post-conversion checks and fix.
8. Monitor Database performance and optimize/tune the necessary parameters.
9. Identify, fix if any issues, and document all the major migration issues faced.

Iteration 2, 3, and 4:

1. Execute iterations 2, 3, and 4 to optimize production down time.

Deliverables: Migration process, migrated environment, migration issue logs

Stage 4: Testing by Outsourcer (enterprise)

1. **Sanity Testing.**

Managed Service provider (migration and transformation team) will perform high-level sanity check by navigating sample pages on target migrated instance in each iteration.

2. **System Integration Testing.**

In each of the iteration, Managed Service provider (migration and transformation team) team will hand over the application to an outsourcer (enterprise) to conduct system integration testing to ensure that all integrations are working fine. Applications processes will also be tested and compared against the performance benchmark of the source environment.

Deliverables: Instance to an outsourcer (enterprise) for validation and testing. Outsourcer (enterprise) will test and fix if any code-level issues in post-migration.

3. **User Acceptance Testing**

- User acceptance testing (UAT) will be done on the second iteration.
- Test the database and applications in the new migrated environment by outsourcer (enterprise) users for functionality and performance.

Deliverables: Instance to an outsourcer (enterprise) for validation and testing. Instance to outsourcer (enterprise) for validation and testing

Stage 5: Migrate Production environment by Managed Service provider (migration and transformation team), **OEM DBA and** outsourcer (enterprise)

1. Back up the PROD environment.
2. Setup the hardware, OS, and software for Database - PROD environment.
3. Migrate the PROD database.
4. Migrate custom components post-retrofit by an enterprise with the help of service provider (migration and transformation team) OEM DBA for migration.
5. Validate Production database migration.
6. Monitor database performance and optimize/tune the necessary parameters.
7. Check and validate application and database by service provider (migration and transformation team).
8. Go Live.

Deliverables: Updated issue log, production environment

13.6 Data Migration

Managed Service provider (migration and transformation team) will perform data migration in a manner that will achieve an automated migration to reduce human resources from tedious tasks. The planning process involves determining the requirements of the migration, identifying the current and future environment, and creating and documenting the migration plan. These also include migration architecture, specific hardware and software requirements, migration procedures, and deployment and test plans. The below diagram has the approach for data migration (**Fig. 13.7**).

13.6.1 Database Migration

Database transportable tablespace feature allows quickly to move tablespace data across database instances. It is a very efficient method as the data need not be physically imported into the new database. Rather, the metadata alone of the tablespaces is disassociated from one database instance and associated with another, pointing to the appropriate data files (that should be copied over by other means outside of database). Transportable tablespaces can also be used in conjunction with replicated tablespaces to present an exact copy of a tablespace's data to a

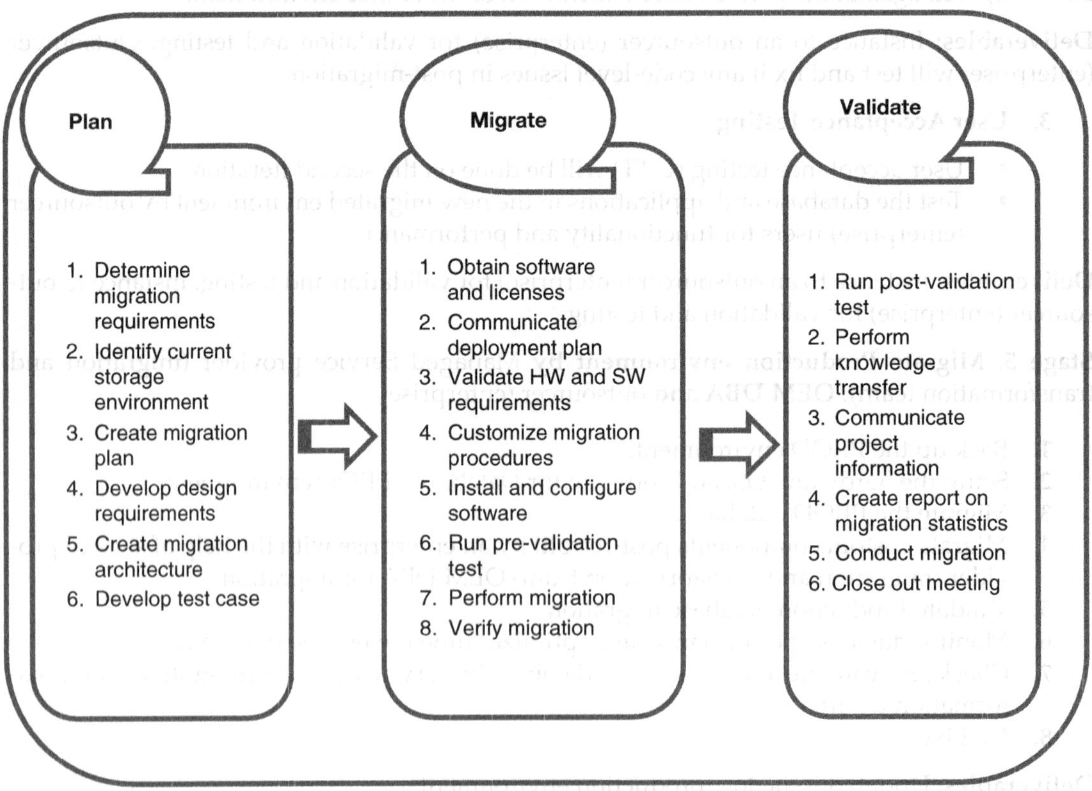

FIGURE 13.7 Data migration.

secondary database instance. The data files of the tablespace are replicated using operating system, volume manager, or storage-based replication techniques. These files are then presented to the same or another host and 'plugged into' a second instance.

13.6.2 Migration

The migration phase consists of migrating equipment and data from existing SOURCE data centre to the new TARGET data centre. Multiple factors contribute towards determining which approach to follow:

1. **Lift and shift:** In this approach, the servers/storage/racks are powered down, de-installed, packed, and then moved to the new site. While this is a lower cost option as compared to Leapfrog or Parallel cut, it involves significant downtime and is not recommended to enterprise applications with high-to-medium RTO and RPO. In a scenario where the hardware assets are new and have a considerable life left, these assets are relocated to the new locations using this approach.
2. **Leapfrog:** In a classical leapfrog model, redundant or backup equipment is used to create a duplicate environment during the relocation of the original workload. In few instances, where redundant equipment exists in the form of a clustering, all the servers are hosted in the same rack thus limiting the use of such setup during physical migration. For equipment that needs to be migrated to the new data center, a hybrid approach of lift and shift and leapfrog will be adopted.
3. **Parallel cut:** Applications with minimum downtime are migrated using this approach. Data is mirrored and synchronized to a duplicate environment. Managed Service provider views this transformation as an opportunity to migrate physical systems to virtual platforms and an opportunity to gain efficiencies, such as those that come from consolidating physical systems. Moves of this type involve setting up platforms to host virtual machines at the target data center performing physical-to-virtual (P2V) migrations at the source site and transferring those virtual instances to the target site over high-speed links. The virtual machines are then started at the target site, and users are pointed to the applications and services running at the target site. Before migration (physical or data) of the assets, passive infrastructure and network readiness will be ensured at the primary and DR data centers.

13.6.3 Passive Infrastructure Setup

Managed Service provider (migration and transformation team) will build Primary Data Centre and Disaster Recovery Data Centre. Data Centre Passive Infrastructure will adhere to best industry standard practice. DC and DR setup will be done in parallel.

Following are the guidelines followed to set up passive infrastructure, which will be done before migration of the IT infrastructure:

1. Rack Placement and Layout

   - Alternate arrangement of cabinet and racks (with the front of racks facing each other) to create hot and cold aisles
   - Perforated tiles will be placed in cold aisles and suction for hot air.

- Provision for installing redundant equipment in separate racks
- Racks will be installed into three different categories, such as
    i. Server racks
    ii. Network racks
    iii. Cabling racks

2. Cabling
    - Implementation will be based on centralized structured cabling standard.
    - Industry standard and future technology will be used for ethernet (Cat 6) and fiber cabling (50 micron)
    - Following colour codes will be implemented:
        i. Primary cable – Blue
        ii. Secondary – Red
        iii. Management – Yellow
3. Power and cooling
    - Two redundant power supplies will be implemented at each Rack. One each from the commercial supply and UPS source.
    - Standard temperature will be maintained between 18 and 22°C

13.6.4 WAN and LAN Setup Overview

After building the Passive Infrastructure, Managed Service provider (migration and transformation team) will implement active network components at primary and disaster recovery data center.

Following hosting environment will be set up:

1. Production environment
2. Test and development environment
3. Pre-production/disaster recovery environment

Connectivity is established between existing DCs and proposed DC. It is recommended to have MPLS cloud solution with variable bandwidth option for connectivity requirement. During storage replication phase additional bandwidth should be considered. Post-migration DC link will be terminated.

13.6.5 Migration – Lift and Shift

Lift and Shift Procedure for Assets which Are Not under EOL and EOS

Infrastructure relocation is a complex activity for any business. The following are the prerequisites before doing the physical movement of equipment at new data center:

1. Environment readiness at new data center.
2. Floor space, power, cooling, and cabling.
3. IP addressing, LAN connectivity, WAN connectivity, and SAN Switch configuration.

Physical Movement Activity

1. Implement relocation based on planned sequencing.

2. Perform safe shutdown procedures.
3. Secure packaging.
4. Transport the equipment to the desired site using air-cushioned transport and perform GPS tracking.
5. Unpack, install, test, and commission as per plan.

13.6.6 Migration – Parallel Cut

Migration – Parallel Cut: Storage

Managed Service provider (migration and transformation team) always proposes to do seamless migration using server automation tool that can do faster, effortless, and risk-free migration.

By server automation suite we can create a golden image of existing OS, application, and database which will avoid time to build new server at proposed DC. Simultaneously, we will create golden image of multiple OSes, application, and database at the same time. These golden images are deployed effortlessly at the proposed data center, and clone of existing environment can be built easily. Storage Data will be moved to the new data center using replication technology.

Table 13.2 enlists the phases and activities of migration steps.

Table 13.2 | Migration steps

Phase	Activity
	Data center environment will be ready at new proposed data center setup
	WAN connectivity between existing DC to new DC
	Agreed and configured IP addresses and VLAN schemas
	Readiness of storage and backup environment for migration
	Security policies and access will be enabled on new setup
	Physical installation of server at new DC
Before Cut Over (Pre-Migration)	Using a server automation tool, take the Configuration image OS, Database and Application Server consider for migration
	Deploy server automation tool Image to newly installed server with unique hostname and IP addresses
	Configure the necessary Network Configuration such as Security policies, Firewall ports open, VLAN configuration, and E2E connectivity
	Assign required storage LUNs to new servers
	Initiate replication between existing and new storage copy required data concerning migration
	Cluster setup and cluster failover testing

(Continued)

Table 13.2 | (Continued)

Phase	Activity
Migration	Update hostiles
	Create file system for application binary, logs keeping same name as existing production
	Update application configuration files with new hostname
	Configure backup for new servers
	Shutdown the existing production application
	Run the incremental sync to have similar data for both storage
	Point new application to production database and sanity test of application
	Update configuration files with new hostname for applications which are communicating with it and keep back of old files as it will be used in case of fallback
	Update host file of other application servers with new hostname details
	Application failover testing
	End to End Testing
	Initiate application server OS and binary backup
Fall back Plan	Shutdown the new production application server
	Revert with backup configuration files for applications communicating with it
	Start old production server, application, and database
After Cut-over (Post-Outage)	Release storage allocated to old production server
	Release servers to reuse
	Close and disable FW policy for old production servers
	Breathing period of two weeks to ensure that application and database is running seamlessly from newly build environment
	Start the decommissioning process for infrastructure and application

13.7 Migration – Parallel Cut: Compute

13.7.1 Compute Resource Migration Using Server Automation

In a significant DC consolidation effort, server automation provides the capability to perform bare-metal provisioning that enables to deploy OS on physical and virtual hosts consistently

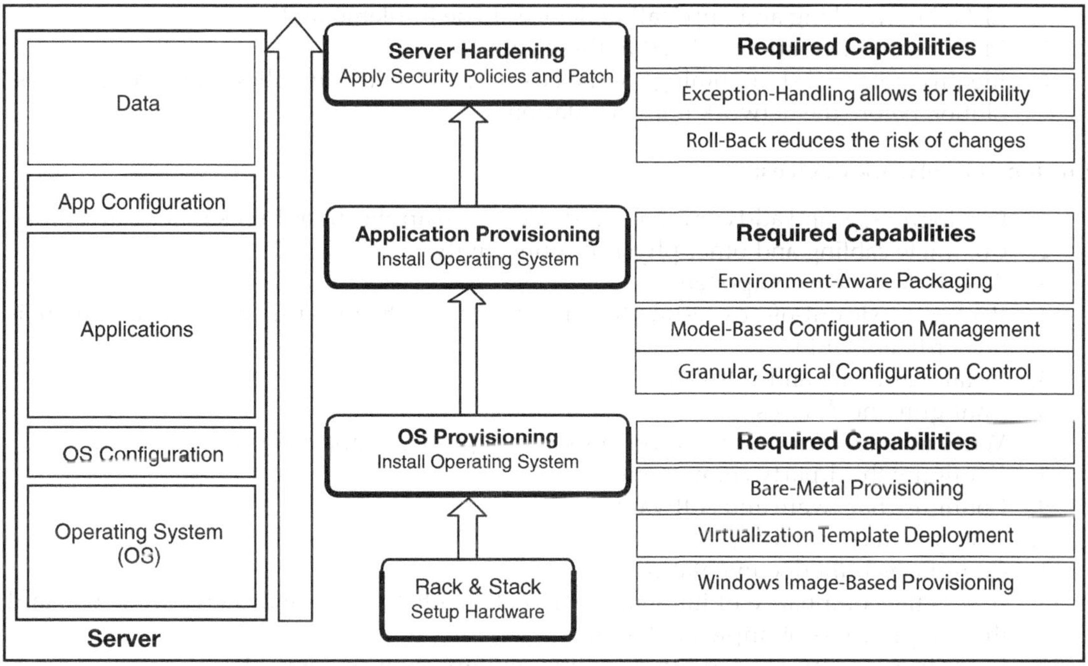

FIGURE 13.8 Resource migration using server automation.

(**Fig. 13.8**). After the required OS is deployed on the virtual or physical hosts, Server Automation allows to create environment-aware packages, and thus enables granular-level configuration control. After the applications are configured on the OS, Server Automation allows you to harden the servers by applying the required security policies, patches, and upgrades.

Migration Network

Managed Service provider (migration and transformation team) will build a new network infrastructure at the new data centers. This phase includes staging, configuration conversion, and cutover. The implementation engineer follows diagrams and instructions in detailed network and project overviews, requirements and task lists, and documented procedures.

Following are some key points:

1. Build base infrastructure.
2. Implement network devices.

Build base infrastructure:

1. Produce site requirements specification, assessing and documenting the physical, electrical, and environmental specifications for each required network element.
2. Determine space requirements for the new equipment.
3. Check power, cooling, airflow, and cabling required for any new equipment being provisioned.

4. List all networking and application devices to be implemented.
5. Make recommendations related to these gaps.
6. Identify potential shortcomings of the customer's facility and allows for proactive resolution before the network implementation.

Implement network devices:

1. Catalogue, tag, and add components, devices, and applications to customer's inventory.
2. Complete cabling and other physical connectivity.
3. Assemble system components.
4. Perform basic out-of-box testing to verify that all units power up correctly and there is no hardware faults.
5. Install hardware and software.
6. Configure the devices.
7. Verify all hardware/software versions and upgrade, as appropriate.
8. Configure third-party components.
9. Configure hardware and software.
10. Test system connectivity.
11. Compile as-built documentation.
12. Assess the compliance of implementation elements to existing design parameters and the completeness of implementation.
13. Describe new features and functionality, configuration changes, etc.
14. Match network parameters (e.g., bandwidth, Hardware resource utilization, throughput, etc.)
15. Keep backup plan ready in case unexpected problem arrive.
16. Keep vendor list and escalation matrix should available.
17. Proper procedures should follow.
18. Present Implementation Report.

Verify and Rollback:

Prepare checklist, check applications are running as anticipated via end-user test, performance management, and other verifications. In case of any issues, roll back changes if needed.

Decommission:

Configure, test, and commission network element management functionality by the Operations Implementation Plan.

Key Consideration in a Migration

1. **IP conflict:** Managed Service provider (migration and transformation team) network team will understand existing IP address schema across all the data centers of the enterprise to avoid IP conflicts during migrations. Plus, the IP dependencies of applications on a network such as Static/hard-coded IP used. To avoid IP address conflict, use different/new IP addressing schema for the new DC as best practices suggest.
2. **Routing Protocol:** Running same routing protocol such as OSPF and using similar area numbers will create routing issues during and post-merger.

3. **Different network gear and configuration:** Using different OEM devices, interoperability and configuration of the devices will be a likely problem. Configuring multi-vendor devices becomes a challenge since each vendor use their command syntax.
4. **Troubleshooting problems:** Troubleshooting on a multi-vendor platform requires expertise on different types of vendor devices. Each vendor will have their configuration syntax, proprietary protocols, and NMS tools and will have various troubleshooting procedures.
5. **Firewall policy and internet routing:** An enterprise can have access to a third-party vendor via the internet, or only one company requires access to the third-party vendor. This situation can result in a security concern. If both companies have connectivity to the same vendor, then the IP addressing, level of access, and internet routing could be a problem.
6. **DNS and DHCP servers:** The DHCP and DNS policies used by the enterprise might not be the same which could result in complex and complicated architecture.

   Managed Service provider (migration and transformation team) will use a complete different IP addressing schema for data center DNS and DHCP. For DNS, it will advertise DNS entries from both locations and wait till published all over the world. Then, it will disconnect the old DNS with the new DNS server.

   For DHCP, different IP pool and IP address lease time use to avoid DHCP issues.
7. **VPN:** Users connecting to the Enterprise/Corporate network via VPN will be accessing different internet gateways to connect to the enterprise network. There are various sets of VPN policy defined based on the user's profiles.

To avoid interruption of services for VPN users, Managed Service provider (migration and transformation team) should understand the VPN policies for users and build similar polices.

13.7.2 Potential Process-Related Problems in a Migration

1. **IP addressing standards:** Each enterprise site will have its IP address assignment scheme designed as per regions and type of site. To re-assign IP addresses to different sites after migration could be a potential issue.

   Managed Service provider (migration and transformation team) will use different IP addressing pool for Primary Data Centre and Disaster Data Centre to have seamless migration and routing issues.
2. **Network architecture standards:** An enterprise has its repository for maintaining network designs, IP and device inventory, naming convention, and LAN cabling standards. Also, depending on the type of site (regarding some ports and types of service), the network design might vary.

   To maintain a particular standard, Managed Service provider (migration and transformation team) will use best suitable guidelines and solution
3. **Security policy:** Security policies may vary with respect to the enterprise. A certain level of access could be allowed in enterprise company but not in Managed Service provider (migration and transformation team) lease data center. For example, a particular internet site browsing could be allowed in one company but not in the other company.

Managed Service provider (migration and transformation team) will understand the requirement from enterprise and in-concurrence with them will define security policies.

4. **SLA:** Two companies might adhere to different SLAs for the same type of service.

13.8 Roles and Responsibilities

Table 13.3 | Roles and Responsibilities

Track	**Project Management**
Discovery and design	Identify various partners and sub cons required
Wave design	Finalize SoWs
Configuration	Vendor management
Execution	Vendor management
Managed Services	Extended support from vendor
Phase	**Server**
Discovery and design	1. Application architecture and Server architecture data capture 2. Analysis of infrastructure 3. HLD and LLD 4. Design standalone systems 5. Design HA systems 6. Design load balanced systems 7. Capacity and growth 8. Performance and fault tolerance
Wave design	1. Business criticality data capture. 2. Environment to business mapping data capture 3. Application mapping to environment, Geo and business data capture 4. Analysis and design of business, Env, Application, and Geo 5. Map application, environment, Geo and Business to Technology, Methodology, Resource and Geo 6. Downtime and Contingency plan
Configuration	1. HW Installation 2. OS Deployment and virtualization 3. Software installation and configuration 4. Application service mapping 5. Network and authentication mapping. 6. Validate capacity, performance, and HA

(Continued)

Table 13.3 | (Continued)

Track	**Project Management**
	7. Tools integration validation 8. Protect initial deployments 9. Documentation 10. Infra test
Execution	1. LLD Validation 2. Validate contingency plan and process 3. Capacity, performance and HA validation 4. Capture evidence of design, performance, capacity, and availability. 5. Ensure Service availability for business-critical application 6. Documentation and handover
Managed Services	1. Support transformed infrastructure 2. Follow existing Incident/change/problem management process 3. Record every activity being performed
Track	**Storage**
Discovery and design	1. Storage and Backup architecture 2. Storage and Backup HLD and LLD 3. Incorporate expected performance and capacity 4. Design HA 5. Design load balanced Storage 6. Performance and Fault tolerance
Wave design	1. Business criticality data capture. 2. Environment to business mapping data capture 3. Application mapping to environment, Geo and business data capture 4. Analysis and design of business, Env, Application, and Geo 5. Map Application, Environment, Geo and Business to Technology, Methodology, Resource and Geo 6. Downtime and Contingency plan
Configuration	1. HW Installation 2. Storage Configuration 3. Additional SW installation and configuration 4. Application service mapping 5. LUN Mapping and replication 6. Validate Capacity, Performance and HA 7. Tools deployment validation 8. Protect initial deployments 9. Documentation 10. Application/DB functionality acceptance test

(Continued)

Table 13.3 | (Continued)

Track	Project Management
Execution	1. LLD Validation 2. Validate contingency plan and process 3. Capacity, performance and HA validation 4. Capture evidence of Design, performance, capacity, and availability. 5. Ensure Service availability for business-critical application 6. Documentation and handover
Track	**Storage**
Managed Services	1. Support transformed infrastructure 2. Follow existing Incident/Change/Problem management process 3. Record every activity being performed
Phase	**Database**
Discovery and design	1. Database and application architecture 2. Database HLD and LLD 3. Incorporate expected performance and capacity 4. Design HA 5. Design HA with DR 6. Design load balanced Storage 7. Performance and fault tolerance
Wave design	1. Business criticality data capture. 2. Environment to business mapping data capture 3. Application mapping to environment, Geo and business data capture 4. Analysis and design of business, Env, Application, and Geo 5. Map Application, Environment, Geo and Business to Technology, Methodology, Resource and Geo 6. Downtime and Contingency plan
Configuration	1. Database installation and configuration 2. Additional SW installation and configuration 3. Database replication configuration 4. Import first database copy 5. Validate capacity, Performance and HA 6. Tools deployment validation 7. Protect initial deployments 8. Documentation 9. Application/DB functionality acceptance test
Execution	1. LLD Validation 2. Validate contingency plan and process 3. Capacity, performance and HA validation 4. Capture evidence of Design, performance, capacity and availability.

(Continued)

Table 13.3 | (Continued)

Track	Project Management
	5. Decommissioning of services and storage reclamation 6. Ensure service availability for business-critical application 7. Documentation and handover
Managed Services	1. Support transformed infrastructure 2. Follow existing incident/change/problem management process 3. Record every activity being performed

13.9 Risk and Mitigation Approach

A snapshot of the risk register along with mitigation prepared by the Managed Service provider (migration and transformation team) is given in **Table 13.4**.

Table 13.4 | Risk and mitigation approach

Risk Type	Risk Description	Mitigation Strategies
Business Risks	Noncooperation by the Incumbent	Strong governance organization/ minute oversight. Extended support by Outsourcer (enterprise) business users to capture business process knowledge. Outsourcer (enterprise) help in identifying critical resources for rehiring
	Process Implementation becomes iterative and takes a lot of time.	Considering transition timelines, it is very important to start with provider standard processes and procedures and sign off with the stated timelines
	New project requirements impact availability of people for DC migration	Plan any rollout of new projects in advance and identify impact areas
	Business resources for user testing or provide planning input or a purchase approval unavailable	Prepare a business resource requirement plan for each phase of the migration process and share with the customer before the start of the project
Technical Risks	Availability of systems delayed because of a move or issues restoring service after the move	Meticulous job stepping, pre-move reviews and compliance checks during the move. Contingency for delay built in plan

(Continued)

Table 13.4 | (Continued)

Risk Type	Risk Description	Mitigation Strategies
	Overnight batch delays caused by complexity of the interfaces and new configurations	Planning for tests and keeping a window for testing all interfaces within the overall Migration plan
	SAN issues, applications may have been carefully tuned in the current environment. Will migrating to the new environment undo some of this leading to performance or availability issues?	No. Configuration change is a crucial principle for migration.
	Performance SLAs for systems not met after move as systems configured differently or not tuned	Configurations and settings being preserved, documented in move day plans
	Damaged equipment	Moves are done by AMC provider who shall be required to carry adequate spares etc.
	Noncooperation by the incumbent	Strong governance organization/ minute oversight. Extended support by customer business users to capture business process knowledge. Outsourcer (enterprise) help in identifying critical resources for rehiring
Operational Risks	Move of scheduled dates	Provide sufficient buffer in project plan to accommodate minor changes in planned dates
	Attrition of SMEs	Special incentives for retention till migration. Backfill operations to create back up.
	Business resources for user testing or provide planning input or a purchase approval unavailable	Advance intimation
People Risks	Retention of incumbent employees who are critical for transition.	Incentive structure for transition completion

(Continued)

Table 13.4 | (Continued)

Risk Type	Risk Description	Mitigation Strategies
	Lack of support from the vendor partner and/or enterprise SME's during the discovery which could jeopardize the timelines and effectiveness of transition	Managed Service provider (migration and transformation team) will come up with a detailed timeline plan and align with required stakeholders. 1. Enterprise will ensure that SME/teams provide the required commitment for discovery phase 2. Outsourcer (enterprise) will track the status of the transition and escalate issues to Outsourcer (enterprise) leadership/transition PMO in a timely manner.

Managed Service provider (migration and transformation team) should have a proven methodology of managing risks during the project that ensures continuity and uninterrupted service to migration and transformation. The methodology is briefly explained as follows (**Fig. 13.9**).

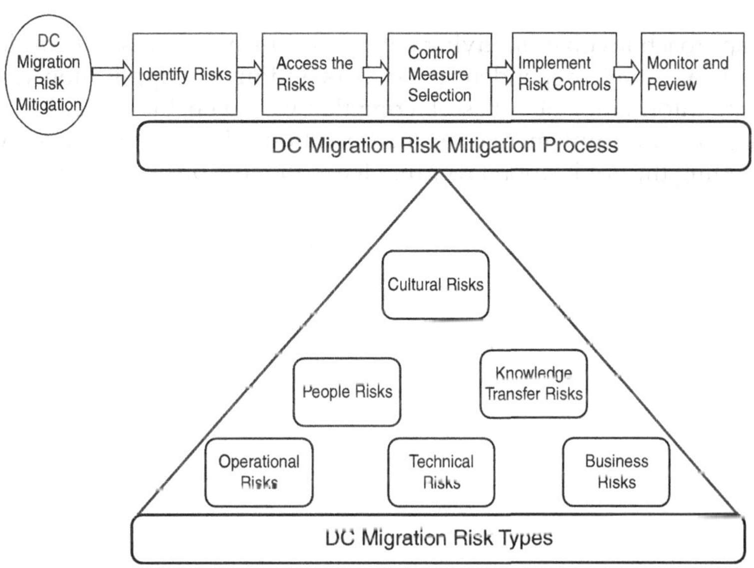

FIGURE 13.9 Data center migration risk mitigation process and migration risk types.

The objectives of risk management are to identify, address, and eliminate risk items before they become threats to success or major sources of rework. Risk involves the likelihood that an undesirable event will occur and the severity of the consequences of the event should it occur. Risk management in Managed Service provider (migration and transformation team) enviornment aims to:

1. Identify potential problems and deal with them when it is easier and cheaper to do so - before they turn into problems or crisis.
2. Focus on the project's objective and consciously look for things that may affect quality throughout the production process.
3. Allow the early identification of potential problems (the proactive approach) and provide input into management decisions regarding resource allocation.
4. Involve personnel at all levels of the project, focus their attention on a shared vision, and provide a mechanism for achieving it.
5. Increase the chances of project success.

To institutionalize the risk management process in the organization, it is made a part of regularly scheduled periodic project monitoring and control activities and reported on a biweekly basis on the PMO meetings. Risks are usually tracked in parallel while new risks are identified and analyzed, and the mitigation plan for one risk may yield another risk.

13.10 Summary

This top-down approach involves studying enterprise business landscape, understanding the application details and their dependencies, understanding the application to infrastructure mappings, gaining information about asset aging that would enable designing an appropriate migration strategy. For the implementation and operations phases, the flow is reversed — with infrastructure feeding the application layer that feeds into the business layer.

APPENDIX

A

Cloud Performance Monitoring Commands

CONTENTS

This appendix discusses several cloud infrastructure performance data collection and performance monitoring commands.

A.1 vmstat Command

`vmstat` command: Account virtual memory information

Syntax

vmstat [-n] [*delay* [*count*]]

vmstat[-V]

Description

The important factors for virtual memory are paging, swap, memory, traps, blocks, IO and CPU. `vmstat` statistics gives the vital information regarding paging, swap, memory, traps, blocks, IO and CPU. It gives information about the system from the time of the reboot as an average. We can add the sampling delay for the `vmstat` as an option.

We will discuss the different parts of the `vmstat` command.

Process Part

- `r` field: Total number of runnable process.
- `b` field: Total number of blocked process.

Memory Part

- `Swpd` field: Used swap space.
- `Free` field: Available free RAM.
- `Buff` field: RAM used for buffers.
- `Cache` field: RAM used for file system cache.

Swap Part

- `Si` field: Amount of memory swapped from disk per second.
- `So` field: Amount of memory swapped to disk per second.

IO Part

- `Bi` field: Blocks received from disk.
- `Bo` field: Blocks sent to disk.

System Part

- `In` field: Number of interrupts per second.
- `Cs` field: Number of context switches per second.

CPU Part

- `Us` field: Time spend running user code (non-kernel code).
- `Sy` field: Time spent running kernel code.
- `Id` field: Idle time.
- `Wa` field: Time spent waiting for the IO.

A.2 iostat command

`iostat` command: Monitors server input/output (I/O) statistics

Syntax

iostat [ ] [ ]

Description

It is important to balance the workload of the system for different physical disk devices to understand the load of the IO devices. The `iostat` command allows administrators to monitor and tune the performance of the system. It gives the flexibility of comparing the average transfer rate of the device.

`iostat` generates report from the time of the first reboot of the system. It gives the information for the CPU usage for all the processors. It gives the CPU information for each device associated with the system.

CPU report requires percentage of the user, priority, IO wait and CPU idle time. It can be defined as

:* `%sys`: System kernel-level processor utilization percentage

Device Information

* `device`: This gives the device name from the `/dev` directory. The given name possess the mapping form the mount points of the file `/etc/fstab`.

* `tps`: This gives the transfers (I/O requests) per second issued to device.

* `blk_read/s`: This gives the number of blocks read per second from the device.

* `blk_wrtn/s`: This gives the number of blocks written per second to the device.

* `blk_read`: This gives the total number of blocks read.

* `blk_wrtn`: This gives the total number of blocks written.

The information that we get from `iostat` as stated above can be used to balance the workload of the devices. This option helps us distribute the workload proportionately to the idle devices.

A.3 `mpstat` command

`mpstat` – Provides account processors information.

Syntax

`mpstat [ ] [ ] [ ]`

Description

The `mpstat` command writes to standard output activities for each available processor, processor 0 being the first one. This can also give the global average statistics of the entire system. This command is also suitable for the symmetric multiple processing-based processors.

The interval option is to specify the time gap between the reports. If we give it as 0, it means we are referring to system boot-up time. We can specify the count parameter also with the `mpstat` command. The command provides the information in the form of multiple reports at different stipulated period of intervals.

Now we will discuss the format of `mpstat` command in brief.
The report generated by the `mpstat` command has the following format:

`%user`	This is the percentage of CPU utilization at the user level.
`%nice`	This is the percentage of CPU utilization at the user level with nice priority.
`%system`	This is the percentage of CPU utilization that occurred at kernel level.
`%iowait`	This is the percentage of time that the CPU or CPUs were idle When the processor got the IO request.
`%irq`	This the percentage of time spent by the CPU or CPUs to service interrupts.
`%soft`	This is the the percentage of time spent by the CPU or CPUs to service softirqs.
`%idle`	This is the percentage of time that the CPU or CPUs were idle when processor did not got the IO request to service.

A.4 `netstat` command

`netstat` – Reports network configuration and activity

Syntax

`netstat [ ] [ ]`

Description

The `netstat` command helps to understand the network configuration and activity. It includes the different functions that we will be discussing in the following sections.

Information about Routing Table

When we use `netstat` command with `-r` option, it gives the information about the kernel routing table.

When we use `netstat` command with `-n` option, it gives the addresses as dotted quad IP numbers. It helps in avoiding address lookups over the network.

If we are looking for the network gateway information for routing entry points, we can look up the second column of `netstat` command output. If we are looking for the network mask for this route, it is given by the third column. The fourth column of the `netstat` command displays the following flags that describe the route:

`G` The route uses a gateway.

`U` The interface to be used is up.

`H` Only a single host can be reached through the route.

`D` This route is dynamically created.

`M` This route is set if the table entry was modified by an ICMP redirect message.

Network Interface Information

Many times we need the network interface information available in the kernel. For this, we can use the `netstat` command with the `-i` and `-a` option. The `-i` option gives the information about the network interfaces and `-a` gives all the network connections and listening ports.

Network Connections Information

To see the status of the network connections, we can use different commands given below. `netstat` supports a set of options to display active or passive sockets.

`-t` This option shows active TCP connections.

`-u` This option shows UDP connections.

`-w` This option shows RAW connections.

`-x` This option shows UNIX socket connections.

A.5 ipcs command

`ipcs` – Provides information about active interprocess communication facilities

Syntax

ipcs [ ] [ ]

Description

There are various interprocess communication (IPC) tools like share memory, message queues and semaphore. We can use the `ipcs` command if we are looking for the information regarding IPC. It gives information regarding the calling process that have the read permission. We can use the `-I` option to get the id to specify the id.

We can use the following ids with `ipcs` command:

`-m`	shared memory segments
`-q`	message queues
`-s`	semaphore arrays
`-a`	all (this is the default)

The output format may be specified as follows:

`-t`	time
`-p`	pid
`-c`	creator
`-l`	limits
`-u`	summary

A.6 ps command

`ps` – Reports process status

Syntax

ps [*options*]

Description

A process is represented by a data structure known as a process control block (PCB) or process in execution. The process image as viewed by the kernel runs in its own user address space that is a protected space, and it cannot be shared by other users. In order to see the details about the status of the process, the `ps` command can be used. To get details about a particular process running on a UNIX system, you can use the `ps` (process status) command.

The following table gives the outcome of a `ps` command. Primarily, it shows four columns that actually depict the status of the process. The column headings have been explained after the table.

PID	TTY	TIME	COMMAND
2330	01	12.09	sh
2340	01	12.09	ps

`PID`: Process Identification Number

`TTY`: Terminal type or input device that the user is using

`TIME`: The time at which the process is being executed

`COMMAND`: Name of the command

The `ps` command has the following options:

- `-f`: In addition to normal ps command, the `-f` option gives the login name, parent PID, amount of CPU time consumed by the process and the command with arguments.

  The `ps` command with the `-f` option is given as

  `$ps -f`

  Given below is the extended information on our process that we get when we use the `ps` command with the `-f` option. This information is given as an eight-column output. Each field is explained after the output.

UID	PID	PPID	C	STIME	TTY	TIME	COMMAND
Kumar	30	1	0	12:09:11	02	2:34	sh
Kumar	89	30	22	12:22:12	02	0.19	Ps -f

  `UID`: User_id

  `PID`: Process_id

  `PPID`: Parent PID

  `C`: Amount of CPU time consumed by the process.

  `STIME`: Time that has been elapsed ever since the birth of the process

  `TTY`: Terminal type or input device that the user is using

  `TIME`: The time at which the process is being executed

  `COMMAND`: Full command with options. So, if you are running the program and forget the exact options, you could use the `-f` option to see the command and argument typed.

- `-u` – Lets you know the activities of the user. This option has to be followed with a user-id.

  Here is another `ps` command.

  `$ps -u kumar`

This command will display what kind of processes the user (`kumar`) is using.

`ps` *Command Options*

The following options available with the `ps` command perform the respective actions:

`-A`	Selects all processes
`-N`	Negates selection
`-a`	Selects all with a `tty` except session leaders
`-d`	Selects all, but omit session leaders
`-e`	Selects all processes
`T`	Selects all processes on this terminal
`a`	Selects all processes on a terminal, including those of other users
`g`	Selects all, even group leaders (does nothing without `sunos` settings)
`r`	Restricts output to running processes
`x`	Selects processes without controlling `ttys`

Process Selection with List

`-C`	Selects by command name
`-G`	Selects by RGID (supports names)
`-U`	Selects by RUID (supports names)
`-g`	Selects by session leader OR by group name
`-p`	Selects by PID
`-s`	Selects processes belonging to the sessions given
`-t`	Select by tty
`-u`	Selects by effective user ID (supports names)
`U`	Selects processes for specified users
`p`	Selects by process ID
`t`	Selects by tty
`--Group`	Selects by real group name or ID
`--User`	Selects by real user name or ID
`--group`	Selects by effective group name or ID
`--pid`	Selects by process ID
`--sid`	Selects by session ID
`--tty`	Selects by terminal
`--user`	Selects by effective user name or ID
`-123`	Implied --sid
`123`	Implied --pid

ps Output Format

`-O`	Is preloaded `-o`
`-c`	Different scheduler info for -l option
`-f`	Does full listing
`-j`	Jobs format
`-l`	Long format
`-o`	User-defined format
`-y`	Do not show flags; show `rss` in place of `addr`
`O`	Is preloaded `o` (overloaded)
`X`	Old Linux i386 register format
`j`	Job control format
`l`	Display long format
`o`	Specify user-defined format
`s`	Display signal format
`u`	Display user-oriented format
`v`	Display virtual memory format

A.7 top command

`top` – Provides information regarding the running processes

Syntax

`top [ ] [ ]`

Description

The `top` command can be used to see the info for the running processes. It also gives other information such as free memory information like physical and swap.

top Command Options

`-d` This specifies the seconds and tenths of seconds of delay. The default is 3 seconds for the two consecutive updates.

`-n` This gives the maximum number of iterations or frames.

`-p` This monitors only processes with specified process IDs.

`-s` This allows you to execute `top` in secure mode and when it is executed from root.

Description of the Fields

`PID`	Process ID of the task.
`PPID`	Parent Process ID, process ID of the parent task.
`RUSER`	Real User Name, the real user name of the task's owner.
`UID`	User ID, the effective user ID of the task's owner.
`USER`	User Name, the effective user name of the task's owner.
`GROUP`	Group Name, the effective group name of the task's owner.
`TTY`	Controlling TTY, the name of the controlling terminal.
`PR`	Priority, the priority of the task.
`NI`	Nice value, the priority of the task. A negative nice value means higher priority, whereas a positive nice value means lower priority.
`%CPU`	CPU Usage, this is expressed as a percentage of total CPU time as the task's share of the elapsed CPU time since the last screen update.
`TIME`	CPU Time, this expressed as the total CPU time the task has used since it started.
`TIME+`	CPU Time, hundredths, The same as 'TIME', but reflecting more granularity through hundredths of a second.
`%MEM`	Memory Usage, a task's currently used share of available physical memory.
`VIRT`	Virtual Image (kb), the total amount of virtual memory used by the task.
`SWAP`	Swapped Size (kb), the swapped-out portion of a task's total virtual memory image.
`RES`	Resident Size (kb), the non-swapped physical memory a task has used.
`CODE`	Code Size (kb), the amount of physical memory devoted to executable code.
`DATA`	Data+Stack Size (kb), the amount of physical memory devoted to other than executable code.
`SHR`	Shared Mem Size (kb), the amount of shared memory used by a task.
`nFLT`	Page Fault Count, the number of major page faults that have occurred for a task.
`nDRT`	Dirty Pages Count, the number of pages that have been modified since they were last written to disk.
`S`	Process Status, the status of the task can be one of the following: `'D'` = uninterruptible sleep `'R'` = running `'S'` = sleeping `'T'` = traced or stopped `'Z'` = zombie
`Command`	Command line or Program name.

A.8 sar Command

`sar`- Informs the CPU activity.

Syntax

```
sar [ ] [ ] ...
```

Description

In order to tune system performance, we need information like CPU utilization, memory paging, utilization, IO transfer rates, process and other information. All these information can be captured with the use of `sar` command. The beauty of this command is that we can collect and save the information captured with the use of the command in the system file itself.

Options

`-a`	Gives information about use of file access system routines.
`-A`	Gives information about all data.
`-b`	Gives information about buffer activity.
`-c`	Gives information about system calls.
`-d`	Gives information about activity for each block device.
`-g`	Gives information about paging activities.
`-k`	Gives information about kernel memory allocation activities.
`-p`	Gives information about paging activities.
`-q`	Gives information about average queue length while occupied and percent of time occupied.
`-v`	Gives information about status of process, i-node, file tables.
`-y`	Gives information about `TTY` device activity.
`-o filename`	Saves samples in file, filename, in binary format.
`-e time`	Selects data up to a set time. Default is 18:00.
`-f filename`	Uses filename as the data source for `sar`.
`-i sec`	Selects data at intervals as close as possible to seconds.

A.9 load command

`load` – Loads machine code and initializes new commands.

Syntax

load fileName

load fileName packageName

load fileName packageName interp

Description

The `load` command is used to load the binary code from a file into the application's address space to the interpreter. We can pass the name of the file that contains the code. We can give the path name of the interpreter into which we are looking the load the package.

A.10 xload command

`xload` – Displays the system load average

Syntax

xload [ ] [ ] ...

Description

This command graphically displays the histogram of the load average of the systems. It is updated periodically.

A.11 tload Command

`tload` – Graphical representation of system load average

Syntax

tload [ ] [ ] [ ] ...

Description

This command prints the graph of the system load average as specified

Options

s	The *scale* option allows a vertical scale to be specified for the display.
d	The *delay* option sets the delay between graph updates in seconds.

A.12 uname Command

`uname` – Prints system information

Syntax

uname [ ] [ ] ...

Description

Prints certain system information.

`-a, --all`	Prints all information, in the following order:
`-s, --kernel-name`	Prints the kernel name
`-n, --nodename`	Prints the network node hostname
`-r, --kernel-release`	Prints the kernel release
`-v, --kernel-version`	Prints the kernel version
`-m, --machine`	Prints the machine hardware name
`-p, --processor`	Prints the processor type
`-i, --hardware-platform`	Prints the hardware platform details
`-o, --operating-system`	Prints the operating system details

A.13 opcontrol Command

`opcontrol` – Controls the profiling session

Syntax

opcontrol [ ] [ ]

Description

The `opcontrol` command helps us to start or end the profiling session. This command is also useful when we want to dump the profile data and set up the profiling parameters.

Options

`--help`	Shows help message.
`--version`	Shows version.
`--list-events`	Loads the `OProfile` module.

`--status`	Shows the configuration information.
`--start-daemon`	Starts the `OProfile` daemon without starting profiling.
`--start`	Starts data collection with either arguments provided.
`--dump`	Forces a flush of the collected profiling data to the daemon.
`--stop`	Stops data collection.
`--shutdown`	Stops data collection and kills the daemon.
`--reset`	Clears out data from current session, but leaves saved sessions.
`--save`	Saves data from current session to `sessionname`.
`--deinit`	Shuts down daemon. Unloads the `OProfile` module and OProfilefs.
`--buffer-size=num`	Sets kernel buffer to num samples.
`--buffer-watershed=num`	Sets kernel buffer watershed to num samples.

A.14 accton Command

`accton` – Enables/disables system accounting

Syntax

accton [ ]

Description

This command helps for getting the system accounting information. This is accounted for each process executed to be placed at the end of the file. No options specifies that account information is not activated.

A.15 Summary

Cloud performance monitoring tools and commands help plan, consolidate, monitor, optimize, and automate server virtualization projects and the virtual infrastructure. This helps you identify potential server virtualization candidates and generate reports quickly. It also helps in growing faster, as corrective workflows automatically avoid recurring problems.

APPENDIX

B Understanding Sizing Lifecycle

CONTENTS

B.1 Introduction

To be competitive in the world, customers are looking for hardware configurations that match the customer requirements. This needs a right size and consistent sizing process. In order to accomplish this needs the understanding of the sizing. So we will discuss the sizing as a process cycle. This section we will discuss with the help of scenario to understand the sizing as a whole. Here is the small case.

B.1.1 Scenario

ABC Bank Inc., big multinational, India-based bank has managed its business successfully for many years since its inception. The bank has now decided to automate its operations to scale up its business. The bank has customers holding savings bank account current account and credit cards. The bank's management board has decided to provide Internet banking feature to the existing savings bank customers. It has three kinds of loan facility also for its Savings Bank customers, which are housing loans, personal loan and vehicle loan. They need a complete banking system for highly consistent, scalable and cost efficient web based banking solution for customers of all sizes around the globe over the cloud services.

In the above situation, the right-sized hardware for banking solutions can make all the difference between successful cloud deployments. It is important to size whenever shopping for a new system or updating a data center for cloud infrastructure. Our sizing solution will require the right processing power, amount of memory, and type and amount of storage for any application-specific job or workloads otherwise it will be difficult the best system(s).

A process sizing should not estimate immediate need but also the growth based solutions to meet the capacity requirements of a particular customer. This needs the combination of hardware and software.

Sizing is a process to estimate system resources that would be required to meet the current and forecasted capacity requirements of a particular customer. Sizing solutions dictate a specific mix of software and hardware, and the right hardware component is critical to meeting customer requirements. This helps the potential customer to estimate the precise solution. It will be big asset to cloud customer if they come to know about hardware configuration and cost.

Now the question is when can we involve the sizing process? This can be initiated when the organization is looking for infrastructure upgrades, consolidation or even totally new installments. It can also be performed when we are estimating the immediate and growth based workload characterization. In order to do so, we need the sizing data. This can be collected from the performance benchmarks, directly from the production or even from the application field data. The type of data that we need as sizing data for the above banking solution can be consumption of key system resources like memory, processor, disk and/or network operations or the factors that impact the solution. It will also require data for calculating the growth based solution as per-user, per transaction like processor utilization per transaction or user, memory required per user, disk storage required per user network operations per transaction, number and size of disk reads/writes per transaction.

This can be in the form of a complex questionnaire based on the banking solution. In order to calculate the CPU and memory requirement sizing solution as well as storage needs, we may require to determine total registered users of the application. We need to compute the number of peak concurrent users necessary from CPU and memory perspective, with total registered users of the application required for determining storage needs. For our banking solution, we can even need peak business transactions per second (tps) required as well as proportional details of transaction types like queries, updates requests, whether the transactions are in online or batch mode, etc. may be required.

The solution looks as an output for supporting operating systems, number of sockets/ physical processors populated, number of cores utilized and projected CPU utilization of the requested workload. At the disk-level, it will look for internal and external storage, number of disks and GB required. Now we are in the green IT age, thus our sizing should also looks into the energy consumption of recommended system for planning cooling requirements as well.

B.2 Sizing Lifecycle

Now we will discuss the banking solution-based sizing lifecycle to recommend a suitable hardware configuration.

B.2.1 Setting the Expectation

As a first step to sizing, we should analyze the actual objective of the sizing the solution. The sizing solution will be more precise if we are fixing the accuracy of our solution as this will be a forecasting. Once we fix our boundaries, it will be easy to collect the significant data for analysis as it will need the complex set of data. It is important to fix all the sizing factors judiciously otherwise it will not be possible to size the actual required mission based solution. This helps in avoiding extra cost and effort for our required solution.

B.2.2 Gearing Up

It is important to be clear about the actual requirements, architecture, application behavior and resources to make our sizing lifecycle smoother. The inputs from the customer may be routed through the sales channel can play the vital role to complete the process. The basic information that is required for the above banking solution can be CPU, memory and disk requirements.

With respect to CPU, we will need the banking transaction volumes. This can be known from the basic question like total number of users. But it cannot be the only question as CPU will need information like load average because it will not be same throughout the day. Another question can be transactions are happening in the web portal based online application.

In order to know the memory requirements based on users, we can ask how much memory is required per account maintenance in the banking solution or how many transactions exist.

These next requirements, disk, looks for the input data in form of the questions like what type of documents are stored and its size. How often does the data need to be archived? Which type of RAID is required?

Here we have discussed some of the basic question that can play the vital role in our scenario. So it is important to come up with most viable and effective set of questions for sizing lifecycle.

B.2.3 Setting Up the Environment

Now we are ready with the questions the next step is to understand the measuring and gauging parameters and finally evaluating them to size the application. In this journey first we will try to know the workload characteristics. If the application is used by many users then the resources needs will be more complex to size. At the same time, when the number of users are there in small sample, it will be simple to size the application.

There can be different set of customers based on the need and application requirements. It is important to know the functionality of the application as per the database volumes as per the transaction details of the customer. We can list the transactional details based on the user groups and their interest.

Now we are ready to execute investigative tests to understand the application tendency at different workloads and it will help us for the behavioral features of application. After this we can go for the functional and load testing scenarios. We can buy some tools to perform the same and play with different simulation for different conditions.

B.2.4 Get Set Go

Now our test bed is ready and this phase will use all the finalized tests for our workload. Here it should meet the test specifications and will actually lead towards the estimated targeted system. This will give us the option that we can see our system running like in the production environment. We can gauge the initial performance of the system and review the initial system requirements and settings. If the performance is not matching, we can fix the issue and make adjustments to deal our situation and start the process once again. It is important to maintain the entire checklists of item that are under consideration to collect the application data required for sizing life cycle.

Now we are on the verge of collecting the final data so we can emphasize on the most essential parameters. We can find the relation between the transaction and CPU required. This may require some formula to estimate. The important parameter that we should emphasize is memory. It can be calculated per web based sessions or depending on the number of user. This can be even at each server level or based on transaction. The next thing that can be collected refers to storage point required by the application. It also refers to read and writes to I/Os as well as I/O request to CPU and vice versa to determine the number of disk drives.

B.2.5 Tapping the Opportunity

We are ready with the data. We have all the relationships for the application behavior for recommending the hardware configuration. Now this is time to generate the sizing results to compare within the family of servers of the same company or competition based hardware that suits the customer requirement. Now, this is the time to validate all the results before going live. At this level, we can take the evaluation suggestion if any to change the sizing solution if required.

B.3 Solution Tier

Now we can discuss the overall environments of the banking solution because it may require the OLTP, Non-OLTP and Web server requirements.

B.3.1 OLTP

In banking solution there is the need of various data archival and retrieval transaction based operation and online transaction processing (OLTP) helps in the requirement to support various SQL transactions required for the above said banking solution.

First of all, we should describe the layer that we were wishing for the solution. We should comment on the DB layers, Application layer and Web layer. The next step is to define the application architecture like all the applications are running on separate servers or it is logically partitioned on the single server. So we can define all the functional layers of the tiers.

The other activity is to understand the different components of the OLTP environment. We can get the answers of the questions like which database and version the banking solution workload is using. Whether the banking solution is requiring High availability option to be configured and what is total storage requirement. The next important aspect is the size of the database and even can now the CPU utilization of the DB tier.

We can also know the interactive part of the OLTP environment based on the applications users groups like total number of users, percentage of active users, transaction per our users and its complexity. The application group can be portal, account holders, bank internal employees and privileged customers.

The next section for the OLTP process requires the inputs on the basis of workload characterization. The inputs can be type of queries, reporting mechanism, batch information and application management requirement. This information can be maintained in the form of complexity like what will be its value during peak and off-peak time and IO rate for all the activities.

B.3.2 Non-OLTP

It is not certain that our banking solution will require on OLTP environment sizing but it can posses the non-OLTP workloads for the application like data warehousing, decision support systems and Business Intelligence systems. Therefore, like our OLTP environment we need to characterize the server tire requirements. First of all we should describe the layer that we are wishing for the solution. We should comment on the DB layers, Application layer and Web layer for the non-OLTP environment.

Like our OLTP environment we need to know that all the application are running on the separate servers or they are working virtual environment. This will give the functionality of each layer with its description. Now we can know the Non-OLTP environment basic activities details like database and its version or whether compression is required or not. We may ask also the application encryption details. It is also important to know about the database segment available to the different groups of the users.

In this environment, we should know the percentage of processed queries. This needs the analysis of the query type. First thing is to analyze whether the query is light, medium or heavy. Then we can know for the specific query how many active users are there or queries per day and even the query mix percentage we can calculate it in the simple, medium and complex bracket.

Our banking solutions require various data extraction process like extracting, transforming, loading and loading the data as different operations require the data from production environment to staging server where transformation happens. In order to accomplish this, we can collect the data like the batch details, time required to run that batches. We can even know that these batch processes should run concurrently with the regular ETL processes or not. It will be good if we know the input size of the data also.

B.3.3 Web Server

In case of the Web tier for the banking solution, the Web server will play the most important role as management requires the banking solution over internet. The functionality for the banking workload will be contributed by many web server configurations factors. This can be sessions are required by the web server at the peak time. At the same time how many licenses are required to match the requirements for web requests. We can take the quote on the session response time that will help us defining many SLAs. We can even collect the data for the complex workflow through the web server.

B.4 Summary

This appendix has given the insights for cloud infrastructure, hardware architecture and sizing. We have seen the sizing practices in OLTP, non-OLTP and Web server environment. This appendix also covers the sizing lifecycles its components and steps required to perform it.

APPENDIX

C Desktop Service: A Vdi Perspective

CONTENTS

C.1 Understanding PC environment

Over the past two decades, PCs have transformed from a single product was shared by a number of users across organization for data computation to an individually owned tool required to perform basic functions.

C.1.1 Lifecycle of PC

As we are trying to calculate the business benefits of VDI solutions, it is important to understand the lifecycle of PC. The PC lifecycle can be split into four stages (Fig. C.1):

1. **Acquisition:** PC hardware and software must first be acquired. Depending on the size of the organization, IT may have very high or very low levels of involvement. Currently, with many options available in the market, most of the organizations have a dedicated procurement cycle.
2. **Deployment:** After acquisition of PC hardware and software, IT department is responsible for maintaining an inventory of the PC's assets, preparing the PC for delivery to the user by installing applications and data, and then physically delivering the device to the user. This phase in the lifecycle of PC is extremely critical as there is a change (management) of user experience involved in this phase.
3. **Maintenance:** After delivery of PC to a user, IT is responsible for maintaining the PC to ensure that it continues in its working state. For this, IT should provide updates, keep track of any hardware/software changes made to the PC, and service the PC in the event of failure. This phase keeps the users satisfied and helps maintain user productivity.
4. **Retirement:** Once a PC has reached the end of its useful life for a given user, IT is responsible for performing the tasks necessary to remove it from the environment or give it to another user. This process can involve various tasks, but typically includes deleting sensitive data, removing installed applications to harvest licenses, and disposing the device.

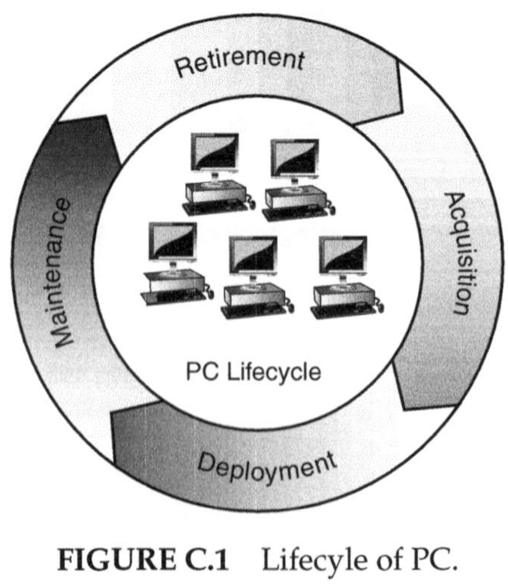

FIGURE C.1 Lifecyle of PC.

To simplify the tasks that make up the PC lifecycle, technology vendors have developed a range of solutions that have been adopted in significant numbers, including configuration management databases (CMDBs), electronic software distribution (ESD) tools, asset management tools, hypervisors, among many others.

C.2 VDI: Cost Factors

The following cost factors need to be considered while calculating the comparison between traditional desktop and Virtual Desktop Infrastructure (VDI) environment:

1. **Hardware cost:** It is important to understand that we need to go through the entire lifecycle after a fixed period, usually three years, for all the PCs as a part of technology refresh cycle. After this duration, the hardware and software available that provides computing capabilities will become redundant and newer technology will be available that will be more efficient and faster than the older technology. Although the upfront investment in building VDI solution is higher, there is a significant increase in the lifespan of hardware. Traditional PCs and their storage typically have useful lives of three years, whereas thin client hardware and data center storage used as a part of the VDI solution have a typical lifespan of six years. Currently, we are assuming the following components as part of the hardware calculations in the VDI solutions:
   - Thin clients
   - Servers
   - Storage
   - Load balancers
2. **Software cost:** To build VDI solutions, a lot of software requirements need to be fulfilled. These include procuring Hypervisor license, VDI license, application virtualization, monitoring software license, remote access (client) software license, server OS license for infrastructure, etc.
3. **Hardware and software maintenance cost and annual operational expense:** This includes the annual maintenance cost that the customer has to pay for hardware and software maintenance to the Original Equipment Manufacturer (OEM) along with the cost of power consumption, data center hosting costs, etc.
4. **Desktop operation cost:** This is the cost of services that the customer has to pay to keep the desktop environment up and running. This includes Level-1, –2 and –3 support provided to end users in the case of desktop-related problems. This also includes cost of desktop management and security.

It is important to note that based on current level of technology maturity, the business benefits of a VDI solution are also dependent on following key factors that have to be taken into consideration before building a VDI solution:

1. User profiles
2. Type of desktop images
3. Environment factors

C.2.1 User Profiles

Profiles of people who use PCs also vary on the basis of the following factors:

1. **Movement – mobility of users and how do they need to move while working:** This can be fixed point, multiple, international, or national location.
2. **Independence – the autonomy users have in defining how they use corporate resources:** Users may or may not have control over data.
3. **Application consumption – what the users need to do and how they need to do:** Users may need forms, Web pages, rich media, etc. and see if the usage is view, listen, respond, etc.
4. **Collaboration – how often the user needs to work with other groups:** This factor determines how the user needs to collaborate and the level of collaboration required. This collaboration may be one-to-one or one-in-a-synchronous or one-in-an-asynchronous mode.

Currently, VDI technology is in a stage of early adoption and hence is lacking in standardization of roles. However, it still helps in visualizing few of them and provides clarity. Following are some broader definitions of the user profiles (Fig. C.2). Please remember that this is an indicative segmentation and we can organize and name them differently based on the customer requirements.

1. **Task Workers:** Factory workers, bank tellers, retail outlet or credit card call center executives, etc. This is a typical scenario for desktop used in BPOs where mobility is less, there is a very limited requirement of independence, defined application consumption is involved; and there is a need for higher collaboration.
2. **Knowledge Workers:** Finance, operations, marketing, administration, etc. In this scenario, the mobility is medium; higher levels of independence and application consumption are needed; and there is medium need for collaboration.
3. **External Contractors:** Offshore workers, outsourcing contractor, branch offices, etc. In this case, the mobility is higher as desktop environment has to be accessed from distant locations; medium level of independence is required; defined application consumption is involved; and there is higher need for collaboration.

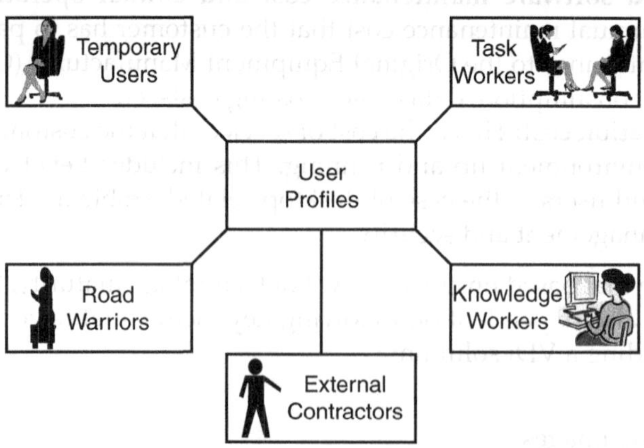

FIGURE C.2 Various user profiles.

4. **Road Warriors:** Sales executives, field services, etc. In this case, mobility is maximum; there is medium level of independence and usage of application consumption, and also medium need for collaboration.
5. **Temporary Users:** University labs, training center, Internet cafe, etc. In this scenario, the mobility is medium; the level of independence is lower; the need for application consumption is medium; and the need for collaboration is limited.

C.2.2 Types of Desktop Images

The different desktop images can be classified into the following two types, shown in Fig. C.3.

1. **On-Request Images:** These are images where a single copy of OS is stored in the data center and serves multiple user images. Images are composed on request when users log on by combining the OS with the appropriate set of applications. This is achieved by using different technologies from different VDI software vendors, but leads to similar results. The main advantage of this implementation scenario over the other two is that it substantially reduces storage requirements and simplifies management of the OS. Different degrees of personalization of the desktop are available for these scenarios today; however, for advanced features, third-party tools are required.
2. **Personalized Images:** These are the images where users are associated with their own unique images. User image is exactly as it was on physical PC, but it is now placed in a VM and runs on a server in the data center. Each image includes a full copy of the OS, applications, and user's personal data. Personalized images are one of the first VDIs deployed. The advantage of this option is that it can accommodate users that require full personalization of the desktop. The disadvantage is that it is typically also the most expensive scenario, as it requires a large infrastructure build out to accommodate personalization of all users.

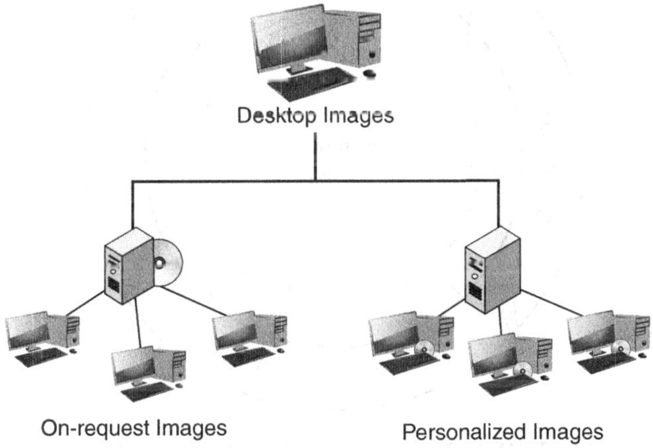

FIGURE C.3 Types of desktop images.

C.2.3 Environment Factors

These factors are based on the environment in which the desktop will be used (Fig. C.4).

1. **Concurrency:** These are the number of users expected to be concurrent at a particular period of time. For example, in an organization there may be typically *x* percent always logged in and using the PC environment. This factor depends on the network usage and design of the VDI solution. In the current scenario, we can imagine that if task workers in a BPO come in shifts and the organization has three shifts, then concurrency will be one-third of the total number of users.
2. **Latency:** Latency is the time difference between when the user provides the input and the time when the VDI environment sends the response. There is expectation from user regarding the latency factor in PC environment. In a traditional PC environment, the computing capacity is closest to user whereas in a VDI solution there is centralized computation from the data center. This factor can be experienced in some of the environments where applications are hosted at a different location and when we access them from the PC environment, there is some difference in the time response. To avoid unacceptable levels of latency, we have to put extra hardware as WAN accelerators in VDI solution.
3. **Software Assurance:** Most PC environments use Microsoft OS. If an organization is a part of Microsoft Software Assurance offer, then it does not have to buy Windows.
4. **OS Migration:** Windows 7 is the latest OS from Microsoft, and most of the organizations are in the planning phase for migrating to this OS. Support for Microsoft XP is going to end in mid-2014. Hence, as part of transitioning to a VDI solution, organizations can go directly to Windows 7 environment and save cost on Windows 7 migration.

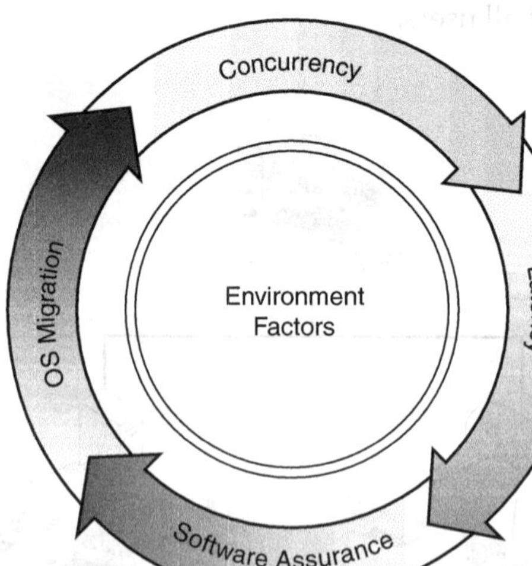

FIGURE C.4 Various environment factors.

C.3 Case Study

Let us assume that we want to compare the traditional desktop to a VDI solution for an organization having 1000 users. Also, let us assume that they have Software Assurance, and hence, do not need to purchase extra Windows VDA license.

C.3.1 Assumptions

The following assumptions have been made:

1. The standard cost of a desktop is USD 900.
2. The standard cost of a laptop is USD 1500. This amounts to 10–15 percent of the user base.
3. The standard cost of the thin-client hardware used in VDI solution is USD 200.
4. Citrix Xen Server is used as Hypervisor.
5. Citrix Xen Desktop is used as the Desktop Virtualization solution.
6. Windows 7 deployment cost is included as part of maintenance and annual cost as this has been the general acceptance.
7. All virtual desktops are standard desktops with 1.5–2 GB of memory.
8. Desktop operating cost includes the entire PC lifecycle management.
9. Calculations are only used for direct cost.
10. Indirect costs like the cost of user training, disruption in training, etc. are not considered as these would vary a lot from organization to organization.
11. Cost savings owing to a longer technical refresh cycle of 5–6 years for thin client vis-à-vis 3–4 years for desktop are not being considered.
12. TCO is compared over a period of three years between both the scenarios.
13. 50 percent task workers and 50 percent knowledge workers are considered for designing of solutions.
14. On-request image has been designed with this solution.
15. Design is for an on-premise cloud implementation.

Figure C.5 shows the breakup of cost for a traditional PC solution across various cost buckets.

From Fig. C.5, it is evident that most part of cost is spent towards desktop operations cost. Next are the hardware cost and annual maintenance cost. We are assuming similar cost spent in traditional desktop scenario as base; hence no additional costs are assigned as spent on the software cost. Above is an optimized scenario where desktop management is an evolved

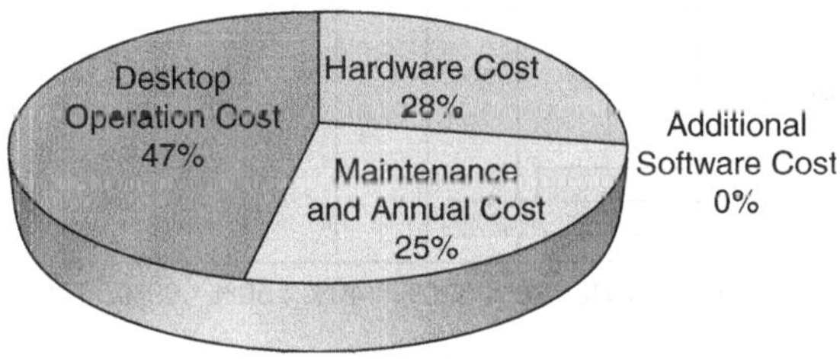

FIGURE C.5 Percentage breakup of different cost factors for traditional PC solution.

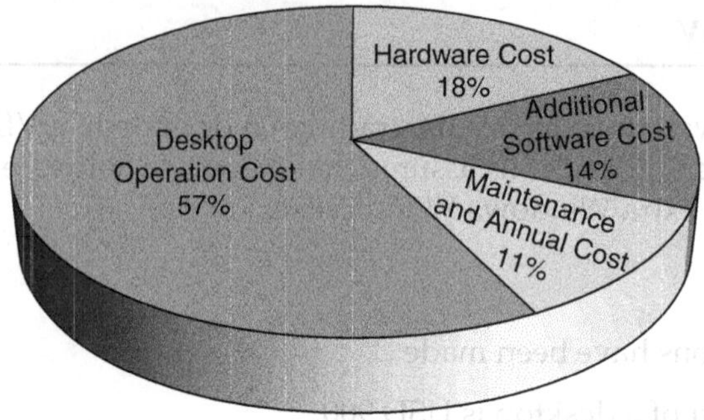

FIGURE C.6 Percentage breakup of different cost factors for VDI solution.

function with proper desktop management function in place. Hence, the number of service requests, incidents, and changes per desktop are controlled. Cost of energy spent per desktop is also included as a part of hardware cost.

Figure C.6 depicts the percentage cost breakup for VDI solutions. This also shows that desktop operation cost remains the largest component. Complexities and number of service request, change request, and incidents reduce for desktop management service in VDI solution but the overall impact on total cost still remains the maximum. Impact of hardware cost on the VDI solution comes the next owing to extra capacity that needs to be built into the data centers for computing, storage, network, load balancing, security, etc. There is an additional component of software that is added on top of the baseline software for traditional PCs. This software includes the software that is used for server virtualization, desktop virtualization, application virtualization, session virtualization, etc. Impact of maintenance and annual cost is the least. Figure C.7 shows the comparison between VDI and traditional desktop services. This provides an idea on the impact of several solutions over the cost function. Hence, desktop operation cost remains a clear winner. Lot of organizations are struggling to keep this in control and are deploying

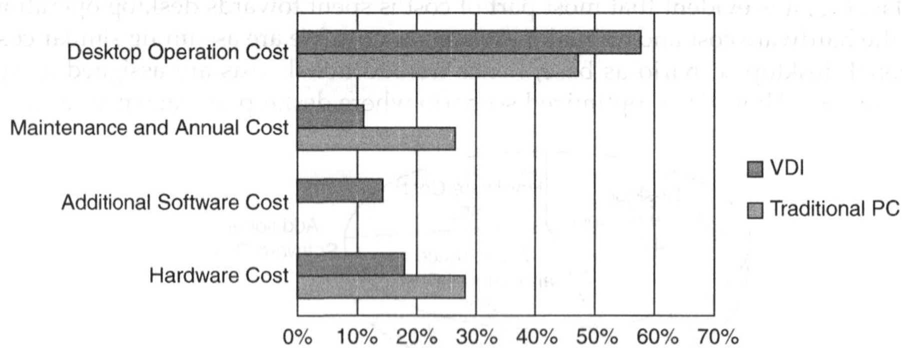

FIGURE C.7 Comparison between different cost factors of traditional PC and VDI solution as percentage of total cost.

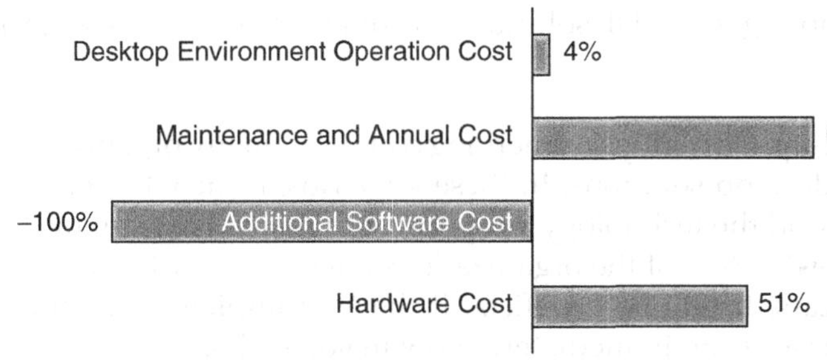

FIGURE C.8 Percent savings across various cost buckets for adopting VDI soltuions.

various methodologies like offshoring, automation of low priority tickets, tool-based desktop management, etc. to keep this cost in control. There is a difference in the impact to maintenance and annual cost, need for additional software and hardware cost owing to the centralization of desktop solution and session, application, and desktop virtualization. Difference in impact would have been more significant if we would have taken this analysis over period of six years; and hence included the two technical refresh cycle of desktop but only one for thin clients. Figure C.8 shows the comparison of percentage savings in both the solutions across various cost buckets.

There are minor savings in the desktop environment operations cost, but again, we have mostly averaged the impact as there are not many data points to substantiate the reduction in incidents and service cost. This savings towards desktop service operations will become more as there are technology advancements with multiple implementations of VDI in complex and multisite locations. There are significant savings in maintenance and annual cost now as the centralized implementation leads to power savings and reduction in the number of devices and components. A traditional desktop solution does not need any additional software; hence, there is a big investment in VDI solutions towards software licenses. We also save on hardware investment on VDI implementation, which is evident owing to the difference in cost between traditional 'thickclient' desktop vis-à-vis 'thinclient' approach for VDI solutions.

C.3.2 Conclusions

On further analysis, overall for a period of three years, there has been a reduction in TCO of 15–20% if we implement a VDI solution over a traditional desktop solution. These savings can be dependent on the factors that are mentioned under user profiles, type of desktop images and environment factors. The current calculation is based on theoretical modeling done and takes industry-wide accepted standards for cost calculations into consideration.

Organizations should adopt VDI solutions not only for TCO reduction but also for functional benefits like better security, manageability, efficient scaling, faster provisioning, and quicker respense during DR and Business Continuity Planning (BCP) scenarios, providing location independence to work force, and so on.

Business case of opting for VDI solutions becomes stronger if we go for the same in following instances:

1. **Greenfield set-up:** Currently, in emerging countries, many organizations are expanding or setting up desktop solutions. In these scenarios, if the CIOs opt for VDI solutions, then they can lead the technology adoption with major TCO savings.
2. **Technical refresh:** Most of the organizations have to go for technical refresh programs every three years. It will be beneficial if the VDI implementation becomes a part of these programs as it can immediately show major savings.
3. **Diverse and distributed work force:** Retail banks' work force is distributed across multiple locations and the need for security and centralization is higher. VDI implementations can provide an immediate relief with significant improvements in security besides centralizing the desktop functions.

C.4 Summary

VDI solution is a revolution in desktop environment. Mostly, organizations have VDI on their radar and will eventually adopt the same. It is only a matter of time before we will think of our own dedicated desktop in the same way as we remember our hand-written postal mails now.

Index

W

Z